Carp Fever

Carp Fever

Kevin Maddocks

Beekay Publishers

CARP FEVER

First published 1981
Second edition 1982
Third edition 1983
Reprinted 1983
Fourth, fully revised edition 1984
Reprinted 1985
Reprinted 1986
Dutch Edition 1987
Dutch Edition reprinted 1988
Special 10th Issue 1988
Reprinted 1988
German Edition 1989
French Edition 1990
Special 10th Issue reprinted 1990

Also by Beekay Publishers:

Coarse

Success with the Pole by Dickie Carr
Pike Fishing in the 80's by Neville Fickling
Basic Carp Fishing by Peter Mohan
Modern Specimen Hunting by Jim Gibbinson
Fishing for Big Chub by Peter Stone
Top Ten edited by Bruce Vaughan
Redmire Pool by Kevin Clifford & Len Arbery
Tactics for Big Pike by Bill Chillingworth
In Pursuit of Carp & Catfish by Kevin Maddocks
Cypry The Carp by Peter Mohan
The Beekay Guide to Carp Waters
Jim Davidson Gets Hooked by Jim Davidson
In Pursuit of Predatory Fish by Neville Fickling
Tiger Bay by Rob Maylin
Understanding Barbel by Fred Crouch
Big-Water Carp by Jim Gibbinson
Mega-Pike edited by Eddie Turner

Sea

Dinghy Fishing at Sea by Phil Williams & Brian Douglas
Long Range Casting & Fishing Techniques by Paul Kerry
Cod Fishing by John Rawle
Uptide & Boatcasting by Bob Cox

Game

The Colour Guide to Fly Tying by Kevin Hyatt
Robson's Guide to Stillwater Trout Flies by Kenneth Robson
Dressed to Kill by Bob Carnill & Kenneth Robson

(send for free catalogue)

© BEEKAY PUBLISHERS
WITHY POOL
BEDFORD ROAD
HENLOW CAMP
BEDS SG16 6EA

Printed and bound by Castle Cary Press

ISBN 0 947674 12 8 (hardback)
0 947674 13 6 (softback)

CONTENTS

Cover photographs: The two sides of carp fishing today; on the front, the author with a 44¼ pounder from Lake Cassien, France and on the back, not so impressive but a far greater achievement, the author with a near-30 pound common from a very difficult Cambridgeshire water.

"Clad in polished plates of bronze they feed 'neath trailing willow fronds"

J.B.

Foreword

Into this book I have put my total knowledge of all aspects of carp fishing; I have kept no secrets. I have tried to write for the novice and experienced carp angler alike, but I have made a point of only including material which is of practical use to the angler. I can see no place for the inclusion of theoretical and 'scientific' material, such as information on scale reading and other technical matters, in a book on carp fishing. My interest is in information which will help others to put carp on the bank, and therefore any omissions in connection with this type of material which may have been included by other writers on carp fishing is intentional. Unlike many authors who say that it is impossible to acknowledge all those who have helped them, I intend to thank the many people without whose sincere friendship and assistance I would never have continued carp fishing long enough to make this book possible; they are more than worthy of this space and I truly value their friendship.

Special thanks for direct help with the book goes to two people who are both angling companions and personal friends. I would like to thank Peter Mohan for accepting my application for BCSG membership back in 1976, for joining the group has been one of the best things I have done in my carp fishing career. Secondly, my thanks to Peter for his general help and advice with the whole book, on which he has spent many hours in Bristol, Enfield, and many other places correcting my terrible English, reading every word of the manuscript and proofs at least three times, and making many helpful suggestions.

The same thanks are also due to John Baker, who accepted my request to combine our knowledge in writing the bait section, and I am also most grateful for his encouragement at a time when the whole thing nearly ended up in the dustbin. I also wish to thank John for all his excellent photographic work. A quarter of all the shots were taken by him especially for the book, and his printing of all my negatives involved much hard work.

My wife Brenda has typed an incredible quarter of a million words in her lunch breaks and evenings for the past year. Words cannot describe the problems she has so willingly accepted; the phone calls, the flying visits to Bristol, the undeserved lack of attention, the hundreds of evenings writing until three in the morning and the awkward moods I got into when the going was difficult.

I am also most grateful to Alan Whibley, a carp angler whose hobby is drawing, for the original line drawings which appear throughout the book. Thanks also to Len Gurd for providing the many new drawings in this Special 10th Issue.

I would like to finish by mentioning the many good friends I have made through carp fishing, without whom the sport would not be worthwhile. Firstly, thanks to Duncan Kay, whose many years of friendship I truly value. Duncan has shown the carp world how to develop and run an excellent fishery, and we could do with a few more like him.

Along the way I have made other good friends, some of whom have shared many enjoyable hours with me at the lakeside, and all of whose company I would welcome at any time: Keith Gillings, John Barton, Bob Davies, Ron Middleton, John Dunn, Paul Regent, Bill Phillips, Texaco Joe, Banger, Dave Albone, Geoff Booth, Dave Campbell, Vic Hull, Geoff Kemp, Roger Emmet, Vic Gillings, Jack Simpson, Roger Hurst, Len Middleton, Peter Springate, Paul Nash, Leo Westdorp, Luc de Baets, Bob Baldock, Dave Thorpe, Des John, John Eggett, Len Gurd, Kevin Nash and my brother David.

Everyone mentioned in this foreword has had some influence on my carp fishing and has, therefore, contributed directly or indirectly to the material in this book, and I hope that they, and everyone else, will find it enjoyable to read.

1 The Big Carp Scene

It has been said that the author of this section of the book has had more influence on carp fishing in this country than anyone else in history, except perhaps Richard Walker. Since Peter Mohan founded the first large national carp fishing organisation, the British Carp Study Group, in 1969, and the Carp Anglers Association six years later, he has spent over 2,000 hours a year working for members of these organisations.

In the past 12 years, Peter has written nearly 50,000 letters, many articles and five books on carp fishing including 'Cypry, the Story of a Carp', which is regarded as a classic, and he now receives over 8,000 letters and 3,000 telephone calls a year. He also started the first ever specialist carp fishing magazines, and has now edited 60 of these BCSG and CAA magazines, as well as four BCSG Books. Peter has organised many national carp meetings of different kinds, and the BCSG and CAA Conferences, the last of which, in 1987, was attended by nearly 2,000 people, making it the largest angling conference ever held anywhere in the world. This conference and tackle show took place at Wembley Conference Centre – the first ever angling event to be held at Wembley. He runs six carp fisheries, most of which are small waters where the owners will only allow fishing for a syndicate, and on these he provides good, peaceful carp fishing for more than a hundred BCSG and CAA members.

Peter has been a carp angler for over 30 years, and although some people seem to think of him solely as an angling administrator, it is worth remembering that he still does 700 hours carp fishing each season, including at least two trips a week throughout the winter, usually after dark and regardless of the weather, and he still catches over a hundred carp a year – mostly small ones, he says, as he has never regarded himself as a 'top' carp angler.

The BCSG and CAA are social organisations, and neither get involved in angling politics. They now have more than 3,000 members between then, and both are run without any rules or regulations, so that carp anglers, who tend to be very individualistic, can join them without fear of being told what to do. Most of the leading carp anglers in the country – including all those who have written in this book! – are BCSG members, and the BCSG, which is a national one-species organisation, and not a 'group', is for experienced and successful carp anglers, although many BCSG members belong to the CAA also. The CAA, which is open to all, is affiliated to the BCSG, and would never have come into existence without the support and encouragement of BCSG members. There is no doubt whatever that carp anglers who don't belong to one of these carp fishing organisations are missing a lot. Dozens of local meetings are held throughout the country every year by the BCSG and CAA, some jointly, and some separately. Between them, the two organisations publish several magazines about carp annually, including 'The Carp Catcher', the colour magazine of the CAA, and also the BCSG Book, which is a colour hardback on sale to the general public from time to time. Those outside the organisations, who are so often heard to complain about the lack of reading material in connection with carp fishing, only have to join and they can take advantage of this enormous amount of carp fishing literature, and of the many lively social events where carp anglers can discuss with others as keen as themselves the topic that interests them most. Peter Mohan is Secretary of both organisations, and if you write to him he will tell you how to join.

All of this carp fishing organisation – the meetings, Conferences, social events and the mass of reading material published by the BCSG and CAA for its members – has come about almost solely through Peter's enthusiasm and hard work, so with his enormous involvement in every aspect of carp fishing, who better to introduce us to . . . The Big Carp Scene.

Kevin Maddocks

Carp fever – those I am going to write about in this chapter have the 'disease' all right; they are so seriously infected that their lives are totally ruled by carp fishing and the thought of carp fishing, often to the extent that work, friendships, and every other normal aspect of life takes second place. Here, I am referring not to the average carp angler, like myself, but to the superstars of carp fishing, whose catches are so remarkable as to be almost beyond the understanding of most of us who go carp fishing. Thirty 20s in a season; ten 30s; 250 doubles; two upper 30s in a day; three 20s in one hour's fishing; a forty, a thirty and a 20 in one session; a fifty-one pounder – all genuine catches made by top carp men.

What must these anglers do to achieve such success?

First of all, they have to keep fishing; two to three thousand hours a year is not unusual. There are now many full-time carp anglers who do no work and just go fishing. Some of the top carp anglers leave their homes for up to a month at a time, and stay by the waterside, day and night, for the whole of this time. Others have been known to have spent up to 70 days and nights at the lake without leaving, except for a quick trip to the pub, the supermarket for more food and bait, or to the fish and chip shop. Still others arrive at a popular water ten days BEFORE the season starts, camping in their chosen pitch until midnight on June 15th, to ensure being able to fish their favourite spot. Add to this hundreds of hours making baits, carrying out pre-baiting schemes, observing carp on the waters, building rods, planning and talking about their plans, and you will see just how much time is involved.

The cost, too, is phenomenal by average standards. Membership fees alone may cost £500 a year; his outlay on every aspect of his fishing is likely to be at least £2,500 a season.

Then, there is the dedication. His family will be neglected; his work will be done just sufficiently to earn him enough money to live and fish. Almost every minute of his spare time will be spent fishing, discussing fishing, planning for fishing and reading about fishing. He goes to almost any lengths to 'get into' any water he hears about which contains big carp – and they must be big. Little time will be wasted on small fish waters; as soon as a new big carp water appears – he will be there, even if it is 300 miles from his home, asking, begging, pleading and intriguing, until he gains membership or permission to fish. He will do almost anything to 'get into' that water, once he is convinced that it really holds the big fish he is after. His obsession is such that he must fish that lake, and his means of doing so are not always ethical, to say the least! Once 'in', the lake becomes to him a world of its own, with every inch of the bank as familiar as his own front room and probably more familiar than his neglected garden. His only satisfaction, at the end of the many long, dark, cold hours is that big twenty or thirty at last on the bank, the long period of enforced inaction ending finally in the few short hectic minutes of the battle with a great fish, and the final photographic proof.

Given the choice of losing his wife, his family, or his job, rather than his carp fishing, he will, if he has to, choose carp fishing every time, for his obsession must come first, or he will not achieve his aims. This is no exaggeration, for I have known carp anglers who have given up everything, including all these aspects of life mentioned above, for their fishing.

Of course, as he gets older his sense of proportion will reassert itself, and he will compromise; his wife, his family, his friends, even other spare time interests will get some attention, if he is at all a reasonable person; and if not, he will go too far, and make himself ill. But then, he will not be one of the superstars of carp fishing if this happens, because they are sensible, intelligent, well-balanced people who know when the obsession is becoming too great, in time to ease off, and to relax. Indeed, it is because they are intelligent anglers of this kind that they have reached the top.

Throughout carp fishing history, writers have tried to analyse what it is that makes top carp anglers so obsessive about their branch of angling; all have failed, and I am not likely to be any more successful than those who have written on the subject before me; it is, as far as I can see, a combination of the sheer size and power of a big hooked carp, and the challenge of super-specialisation; not simply just catching carp only, even in mixed fisheries, but of catching very big carp only. I am told that the competitive element must also be considered; the top carp angler wants better results – more doubles, more twenties, bigger 30s – than all the others he hears about who catch big carp, so he sets himself targets, as Kevin does, for each season; twenty 20s this season, two or more thirties the next, and so on. There is no doubt that this is correct. The average carp angler doesn't take much notice of the catches of others, but the leading carp catchers undoubtedly do, and they are not satisfied unless their results are at least as good as their rivals'. The successes of others is one of the incentives for them to fish longer and harder to get better results themselves. Without the incentive of the knowledge that others are also doing well, they would fish less hard, and probably catch less. Some anglers who read this will dislike the idea of carp fishing being competitive in any way, but I am not concerned with whether this is the 'right' attitude for carp anglers, or not; who, after all, can say what is right? I am only trying to explain to the reader what it is which motivates the leading carp anglers of today, and competition from others is clearly an important factor which affects the way they fish.

He is a person of very special temperament, the big carp man; he must be able to bear with equanimity the long, sometimes tedious hours whilst the indicators remain immobile, yet be able to support without panic the enormous excitement and frantic action which puts an end to the long wait. The surging power of the hooked fish, the great swirls on the surface, and the huge shining bulk at last in the net are rewards enough. All his planning, all his ingenuity, has gone into presenting his bait in such a way, in such a place, and at the right time so that the great fish, whatever its experience and cunning, will at last have been deceived into taking the bait as a food. As the sweeping strike connects, the rod bends, and the clutch screams; the scales register the great weight and the camera records yet another huge carp, he feels a satisfaction that is impossible to analyse. Perhaps it is little more than the realisation of the basic hunting instinct; he has planned, prepared, travelled and fished – and, finally, succeeded, which is what matters most. He is the best at his chosen sport. He enjoys the planning, the bait preparation, his own skill in casting correctly to the right place, his bankside isolation – for even on a busy water he is apart from others in his way and, eventually the complete satisfaction of yet another big fish landed. It is no more possible to define the exact reasons for his obsession with catching big carp than it is to explain why a great athlete will obtain satisfaction through running a mile in four minutes, or in scoring a century at cricket.

The secretiveness of the water itself, promoting endless discussions amongst the anglers as to how the fish are acting beneath it; the placidity of the surroundings; the sense of isolation from the 'normal' world; the realisation that he is one of the very few who succeed in catching such immense fish regularly; the pride in his mastery of the many different skills necessary for success; the bulk and solidity of the big carp itself; the inexplicable sense of satisfaction as it swims slowly away, unharmed; all these contribute to his carp fever, and even the achievement of the biggest carp he is ever likely to catch is not going to abate that fever.

I have done my best to explain why the big carp man is obsessed; if I have not succeeded, it is because nothing I or anyone else can write will ever convey to those who do not have it what it all really does mean to a top carp man – a man such as Kevin Maddocks, the author of this book. Let us escape from the purple prose for a bit, and examine some statistics of Kevin's own fishing. He used to do about 2,000 hours actually carp fishing in a season, with another 500 hours mixing baits, tank testing, and travelling to other waters. He did about 7,000 miles a year for his carp fishing and spent around £2,000 a year on it, and he also travelled all over the country to BCSG and CAA meetings. As he was self-employed, most of his fishing was done during weekdays, and he usually went for a three day, two night session of around 50 hours, during which time he did not leave the waterside. No trips to the pub for Kevin; he deplores the trend introduced by some anglers to mix their fishing with drinking, even to the extent, in some cases, of actually leaving the baits out whilst visiting the pub. He normally spent 70 full nights a year fishing, and did just as much

Peter Mohan with a magnificent brace of commons, weighing 19 and 15 pounds.

during the winter. On his average session he took about two pounds of bait – about 300 balls, although very little of it was used on pre-baiting. Since his average session involved at least two nights at the water, even in winter and arctic conditions, he carried with him a good deal of gear, including equipment for cooking.

Over the past few years, Kevin's circumstances have changed, and he has done much less fishing of this kind. He got married and now has a young child, and he also moved from a terraced house in Enfield to his present property, Withy Pool in Bedfordshire, where he has his own 2½ acre lake containing carp to over 30lbs, and big catfish. Much of his time previously spent on fishing has gone into working for 16 hours a day on the grounds, which were in a bad state, and converting the old transport cafe into a house. He has also been building up his publishing and wholesale and retail angling book distribution business, BK Publishers, which he and his wife Brenda started at the time this book was published, and which is now the biggest company of its kind in the country. There is a syndicate on the lake and also three caravans, and you can book a caravan and fishing holiday at Withy Pool.

In addition, Kevin took up fishing for catfish a few years ago when he helped to form the Catfish Conservation Group, and he edits the CCG magazine, 'Whiskers'. For two summers he spent his time fishing for catfish with considerable success, and his carp fishing was confined mainly to the winter months. Because of these other activities he has done very little carp fishing over the past four years, and obviously his 'results' have suffered compared with some of the other carp superstars. I imagine, though, that very few of his 'competitors' have moved from a small ex-council house to a 6 acre country property with lake, saved many thousands of pounds by working on repairing the property, built up a successful business with a turnover of £250,000 a year, caught catfish to over 30lbs, and written yet another book in this time!

Some years ago, Kevin ran his own business and also played in and managed a well known pop group, but he gave all this up for carp fishing, realising that application and single-mindedness were essential if he was going to be a top carp angler. He then built a huge tank along the whole of one wall of a room in his house which he stocked with carp up to four pounds, and where he has spent hundreds of hours testing out baits, methods, and rigs on the captive fish. Many of his ideas and theories evolved from his observations of the behaviour of the fish in this tank, and he then went to extraordinary lengths to prove the ideas correct. Regardless of conditions and results, he experimented with the methods and tactics until they succeeded, as most of them did. How many anglers would stay up all night, not while fishing, but to observe the fish in a tank in his living room, and to record the results of his experiments, as Kevin has so often done? How many would have the confidence to fish for hundreds of hours with the ideas which evolved, with no proof that these methods would succeed under actual fishing conditions?

It is impossible to say how much better one carp angler is than another, except by the results of his catches, and Kevin's catches have been consistently better than most other anglers on the waters he fished. That his approach, which, you will notice, depends far more on methods and tactics, and pure angling ability, than on exotic and elaborate baits, is the right one, is proved conclusively by those results: in the past 10 seasons he has caught 800 double figure carp, which includes nearly 200 twenties. Twenty-one of his fish of over 20lbs were 30lbs, with the best of 38¼lbs. All of these fish were caught in England and many from day ticket waters in different parts of the country, and Kevin spends as much of his time fishing club and day ticket waters and he does syndicate waters. In three winters from November 1st until the end of the season, he caught 143 winter doubles, and in 1979-80 he had 84 winter doubles: incredibly, 10 of these carp were twenties – in the winter!

His fishing in the past few years has included a number of notable 'firsts' and records, although it must be remembered that these are all unofficial, as no official records of this kind are kept. As far as I can ascertain, Kevin was the first carp angler to catch more than twenty 20s in a season, and he was certainly the first – and possibly the only person – ever to catch four thirties from four different waters in a season, an achievement about which I shall write in more detail later in this chapter. In 1979-80 he caught 165 doubles in the season, which was a record, and in 1980-81, besides his four thirties, he had twenty 20s for the second time. These catches came from a number of very different waters in different parts of the country, some of which were syndicate waters, and others day ticket or club lakes. In 1982 Kevin joined the famous Redmire syndicate and went on to catch 23 twenties, including two thirties, from the pool, which also set a new record.

One of the factors which has most affected the big carp scene recently has been the 'discovery' of Lake Cassien, in France, and again Kevin was involved, as he has been with most of the developments in modern carp fishing. Kevin's friend Paul Regent, of Regent Coaches, was looking for a carp water where he could take coach parties of English anglers, and he was told about Lake Cassien by an English CAA member who lives in

France. The lake – correct name Lac de Cassien – is near Nice and Cannes in the south of France, and is more than 14 miles round and 180 feet deep in places. Kevin went with Paul on a reconnaissance trip there, and also on the first ever coach trip, when they caught carp to 35 lbs, and heard of much bigger fish. Paul started to run coach trips there and many huge fish were caught. English anglers have now taken carp up to 77 lbs from Lake Cassien, and even bigger fish are reported. Kevin considers it quite possible in the next few years to catch a carp of 100 lbs from this lake.

The trickle of English carp anglers going to Lake Cassien became a flood, and many leading carp anglers went there and recorded enormous catches. As usual, some people went too far, and rules were broken – especially the 'no night fishing' rules, and English anglers ended up in trouble with the police. Some became unpopular with locals for their success and for putting the fish back – the French kill and eat them – and cars were vandalised and tackle damaged. The angling papers gave enormous coverage to catches from Lake Cassien – and still do – and anglers who had caught very little in this country made names for themselves by catching one or two big Cassien fish. Some got over-fanatical, and went out and almost lived at the water; indeed, Kevin tells of one angler who actually sold his house and went out to France to live on the banks of Cassien for a year!

Beginners caught 30s, 40s and 50s from the lake, and were then spoken of by the angling papers as 'ace carp anglers'; Cassien fever in place of carp fever gripped many English carp anglers, some of whom just wanted to beat their personal best, while others saw fame and fortune beckoning with the help of a few Cassien monsters.

This fishing is quite unlike anything in this country. The huge lake with its rocky, tree-lined shore and innumerable snags which include hundreds of 18 inch high tree stumps left when the valley was flooded to make the lake, needed a totally different approach from English waters. Anglers used 10-20,000 baits for pre-baiting, fished with lines up to 30 lbs breaking strain, caught carp in 60 feet of water – or so they say – and followed the hooked fish up and down the lake in boats and pedalos, sometimes actually being towed for long distances. The English carp angler not only had to cope with hostile locals, armed police and Rangers, and unfamiliar laws, but with 95 degree heat and with the thousands of French and German holidaymakers who sail, swim, wind-surf and troll baits through their swims. Add to this a 1,500 mile round trip and you have some idea of the expense and problems of a trip to Lake Cassien.

Obviously, the effect on the big carp scene has been enormous, and in Kevin's opinion has much devalued English carp fishing. A few years back the capture of a 30 or two made you really someone in this country, but now, however experienced and successful you are here, you will meet someone soon, possibly much less experienced as a carp angler than you are, who will tell you quite casually that he had a 40, a 50 and a 60 last season – at Cassien; match that if you can!

Kevin's approach is methodical and systematic. He takes a book with him and records on the bank EVERY CARP BITE of more than four inches on the indicator, and he keeps painstakingly accurate notes of every observed carp activity, which he has done for the past ten years. His fishing diary is packed with these records, with the tactics used by himself and others, water temperatures, weather details, the type of runs experienced, the exact dimensions of terminal rigs used, exactly where and how each fish was hooked, and his written thoughts on how to fish the water on his next visit. As his whole life revolves round carp fishing, the information in this record book is endlessly analysed when he is not actually fishing. He will travel any distance to visit a new water and to plan his future fishing there, and may make several visits before starting to fish. When he does start to fish a water, he seems to delight in fishing in unpleasant weather conditions, and in proving his theories against all the odds.

The Maddocks tackle and set-up are fairly standard and he neither worries about the appearance of his tackle nor follows carp fishing fashions. He particularly dislikes excessive secrecy, is always ready to be pleasant and helpful to other carp anglers, and will even tell them exactly what bait he is using, and how it is prepared. With all this, he still finds time to attend meetings all over the country, sit on 'panels' to give advice to others and to do much other work for the BCSG and CAA, for both of which he is a committee member. In the 1987 BCSG and CAA Conference at Wembley he took complete charge of the organisation of the huge Conference Tackle Show, which featured 40 stands and where £100,000 changed hands in the day. His films 'Ashlea Record', and 'Mid-Northants Carp Fishery', which he has shown in many parts of the country, have inspired most of those who have seen them with new enthusiasm for their carp fishing. Although a friend tells me that 'serious' carp fishing must be a selfish pursuit, Kevin is one of those carp anglers who finds time to help others and to put much back into the sport out of which he gets so much pleasure and personal satisfaction.

Whereas catches of numbers of huge fish in a session are remarkable enough, it is a fact that if you are doing everything correctly, and the carp are feeding, you should catch more than one of them, whether they are forties or four pounders, but what skill and angling ability must be needed to catch four thirties from four different waters in one season, which is Kevin's outstanding achievement? Each water was chosen with one purpose in mind – to catch a thirty from it, so it had to be a water where there were known to be carp of this size, which had been caught. Kevin chose Ashlea Pool in Gloucestershire, one of the most difficult carp waters there is, where more than half of those who fish it never even catch a carp. In this one and a quarter acre, crystal clear and totally weed-choked pool he caught a 38¼ pounder, after dark, at ten yards range; a new Ashlea record. He then fished a five acre pit in Northants, where he had a 30 pounds 10 ounce fish, again at night, fishing at 50 yards this time, and in the most terrible thunderstorm ever seen – I know, because I was there, and I sat under Kevin's umbrella while he netted the fish; the rain was too hard for me to go out in, even to net a thirty! The lake rose three feet that night. The third thirty was caught in daylight, at a 70 acre lake in the Home Counties, and at 100 yards range; it weighed 30 pounds 12 ounces. The fourth fish came from a 20 acre 'town' lake in Kent. It weighed 35 pounds, and again was taken in daylight and at a hundred yards. Both of the last two fish came from day ticket waters, showing that as good carp can be caught from waters of this kind as from private syndicates.

Just look back over that last paragraph, and note the extraordinary differences in the size and type of the waters where each of those four thirties was caught by Kevin, and try to imagine the variety of tactics and methods which he had to use to succeed.

I haven't gone into details of the many long hours of fishing, planning and preparation which went into the capture of these fish, of course; he didn't just shoot from water to water catching thirties, but had to spend an immense amount of time and planning to effect the capture of each of those fish. In my opinion, Kevin's four thirties in a season is one of the greatest catches in carp fishing history, if not the greatest.

In this chapter it has been my task, and indeed my pleasure, to introduce the reader of this book both to the big carp scene and to the author. I have tried to add to your enjoyment of the book by giving some insight into Kevin Maddocks' carp fishing and his unique skills and achievements. In the final analysis, it is not just time, money and persistence which marks out the top carp anglers; each has that indefinable extra quality which we all know about but which we cannot describe, which sets him apart from the rest, and which causes him to catch when others fail; Kevin has this quality.

And now read on, as they say; if you do not already have it, I am certain that you will catch carp fever from this, the most outstanding and remarkable of all the books ever written on carp fishing.

Peter Mohan, 1988

2 Tackle

It is my intention throughout this section to cover the basic aspects of carp tackle, and only go into long technical explanations where I think it necessary. The reason for this is that most people have a good idea about modern carp tackle because so much has been previously written on this subject and I would only be repeating others. However, the reader might be interested in the tackle I use, so in the following pages I have described this, along with some of my own opinions. In most cases I have tried to compare my tackle with that likely to be used by the majority of carp anglers.

RODS

The choice of rod really depends on the type of carp fishing you are likely to encounter. A rod that is suitable for fishing multiple baits in the margins will be completely unsuitable for fishing a boiled special at long range, and vice-versa. Because of this wide range of demands, there is no rod perfectly suited to all types of carp fishing.

Basically, there are two main types of carp rods: the all-through action compound tapers, which are suitable for close range and medium range fishing (up to 50 yards or so) and the stiffer fast-taper rods which are best for fishing at greater distances. To be able to fish successfully at all distances, from the margins and up to 140 yards away, you will need rods of both types. You could catch carp on compound taper rods at long range, but you would find as the distance fished increases that these rods become less efficient at pulling hooks into the fish's mouth. There comes a point when far more fish will be properly hooked using a fast taper rod. A study of the test results contained in the long range fishing section clearly shows why this is so.

If the angler only fishes at close range then obviously he need only possess soft compound tapered rods. When it becomes necessary to fish a bit further out, then the angler should change both his tackle and his methods. If he doesn't then he is a poor angler, for no matter how skilful he may be, he cannot do the job properly without the right tools. He would be rather like an engineer using pliers instead of a spanner.

I mention this because I know of anglers who only own compound rods of one to one and a quarter pound test curve and think it is best to margin fish at all times and this is bound to limit their catches. The better equipped the carp angler the more easily he will be able to adapt to any condition. Ideally the complete carp angler needs to own two types of rods if he is to fish a variety of waters efficiently. If I was for some reason limited to owning one type of carp rod then I would choose a fast taper rod of medium strength, but not because I prefer them or think they are good for playing fish. Indeed, a compound rod is not only more pleasant to play fish on, it is most certainly better. I would choose this rod because I could fish efficiently at long range, and 'get away' with using it at close range by exercising a little more care when playing the fish.

As far as reverse taper carp rods are concerned, I cannot see the necessity for these rods. I believe there is nothing they are capable of that a given equivalent in the normal tapers cannot do equally effectively.

The power of a rod is often expressed in 'test curves'. This is the amount of force required to pull the tip of the rod to a ninety degree angle with the butt. The blank is usually given its test curve rating after manufacture and for this reason the figure must be regarded as only approximate, because mass production inevitably produces variations in rod dimensions. Test curves do not indicate the action of the rod but will give a better guide to a rod's overall strength than any amount of testing and checking in the tackle shop. Pulling down the tip of a blank shows a completely different action from that experienced by the line going through a set of rings. I have learnt from experience that pulling down on the tip, waggling or false striking will not indicate the actual performance of the rod. The only way is to go out and use it. This is especially so with the carbon rods as their lighter weight is not sufficient to flex the rod when it is waved about as with fibre glass. In fact, they feel stiffer than they actually are.

For the newcomer, the right choice of rod becomes even more perplexing when considering the semi-fast and ultra-fast tapers available. Because both compound and fast taper rods are available in such a wide range of test curves there is an overlap, with rods of different tapers being suitable for the same type of fishing.

Compound taper rods suitable for carp fishing normally have test curves of between one and two and a half pounds and are ten to eleven feet in length. I only use rods shorter than eleven feet when stalking in confined conditions or when fishing at extremely close range in a restricted swim, and for most close range work I find that a one and a half pound test curve rod of eleven feet is ideal. This type also seems to be the favourite among carp anglers. For fishing at 30 to 60 yards, a slightly stepped up version of about two pounds test curve is best in my opinion. This is especially so when using stiff textured baits that have to be struck through before the hook can penetrate into the fish's tough mouth.

For very long range fishing of from 70 yards plus, a soft compound taper rod is completely useless, being far more suited to beating down stinging nettles. For this type of fishing the choice of rod is extremely important if maximum efficiency is to be attained. Casting over 70 yards requires a lead of around one and a half ounces, and often even heavier. The rod also has two other tasks to perform efficiently. These are: 1) to be positive enough both to strike through a bait and set the hook at this range and, 2) to be 'gentle' enough to play a fish without fear of tearing the hook out when the carp lunges at close range on a short line. Fast taper rods were developed in an attempt to provide rods which would fulfill these three functions. This type of rod was given a soft tip to improve casting and to give some action for playing fish. It was necessary, however, for the rod to have little or no action in its lower section, so, rather than a gradual tapering of the glass fibre, the rod became a very fast taper. This design however, was, in reality, only suitable as a casting stick.

Fast taper rods made from glass fibre tend to be rather heavy and unbalanced. This has the effect of slowing down their passage through the air during striking. They are, in fact, too large in diameter to allow the sort of fast, effective strike so vital in long range work.

The use and versatility of phenolic and polyester resins in the bonding of glass is unquestioned but, like all materials, there are limitations. Rod designers could not produce a suitable compromise between a casting tool and an actual fishing rod for long range carping. Fast taper rods must still be used with care for playing fish on ashort line. They have very little shock absorbing quality and will often cause light lines to be broken or hooks to tear from their holds when a fish is plunging under the rod tip.

Fortunately, modern technology has provided us with what appears to be the ultimate in rod-making materials: carbon fibre. This material offers the same versatility as its glass fibre cousin but is far stronger. Its actual strength for comparable diameter and weight is many times greater even than steel. Already used in the aviation industry and other specialist fields, carbon fibre began to find its way into the subtle complexities of the sports world, and is used for bicycle racing frames, golf club shafts and, of course, for fishing rods.

A powerful compound taper rod finally subdues a big fully scaled mirror
after a ten minute fight.

The search for lighter rods has been historical, so it was natural that fly rods were the first to be tested with carbon fibre. It was not until about 1975 that its use for long range carp rods was researched. A famous tackle dealer, Jack Simpson of Simpsons of Turnford in Hertfordshire, and myself were able to persuade a rod manufacturer to produce a blank which might fit the bill. Until this time we had obtained several types of carbon fibre rods from America, Germany, Japan and England, only to find that after testing they were either completely unsuitable for carp, or only suitable for close range fishing. The problem was finding a replacement for the fast taper glass rods, not so much for the slow and compound tapers. Most of the blanks we tested were not unlike the carbon carp rods already on the market, which were derived from trout and salmon, fly or spinning rods, and were not better and not worth the extra cost.

The long wait for the right blank to be produced was well worth it for, after considerable tests, it became obvious that these rods were as near perfect as possible for long range fishing. After slight modifications by Simpsons, it was decided in 1977 to promote the rods as the KMCF1 and KMCF2. The KMCF1 was rated at two and a quarter pounds test curve. A model of around three pounds test curve was also made available for those preferring 'stepped up' rods. Since production, my findings have been more than endorsed. The rods have been praised as excellent by all who have purchased them. Because of their lightness and thin diameter, they are exceptionally positive, even when used for striking from a sitting position using one hand. They are also completely safe for playing fish on short lines, because of their 'semi-soft' action, and have no tendency whatsoever to tear out hooks. Besides top quality rings, we decided to fit a handle that would hold the reel in a permanently fixed position. Reel movement has always been a problem with cork handles when continually casting long distances. Initially a special sea trolling rod handle was cut down and honed out to fit the blanks, but soon these became available as separate handles. The rod was perfect and the KMCF1 quickly became my favourite model for all types of carp fishing. Because of its unique action it could even be used for marginal work and I also found it suitable for hauling out the bigger fish in really weedy conditions.

At places like Ashlea Pool, I found that the rod allowed more direct control of the fish so the angler could therefore actually keep the fish on top, away from the masses of underwater lilies and weeds. In the first three seasons of using this rod as Ashlea, I hooked a total of eight carp over 20 pounds (not including several doubles) which resulted in seven fish up to a weight of 38¼ pounds being landed. These were exception-

Ron Middleton with a 25.8 caught at very long range using a 12 foot KM2 'Dual' taper carbon rod.

ally high landing rates for Ashlea and I am convinced I owe a great deal to this rod.

Today, you will find several models in the Kevin Maddocks range of carbon rods and this is for two reasons: firstly, there is no single rod on the market that is perfectly suited to all types of fishing and secondly, many specialist anglers demand certain specifications. Whatever your choice or demands you will find the rod you need within the high quality KM range manufactured by Simpson's of Turnford, Britain's finest rod builders.

You will notice from the list of rods that the KM rods are divided into three ranges: the standard carbons, dual-taper and the Trident MPR range.

The 'standard' carbon carp rods are based on the original, highly successful 1976 range although the blanks used now are different from the originals. The advances made by new technology have made it necessary to change the blanks but it should be appreciated that these have been especially designed to be an improvement on the old ones and not simply to 'fill' another gap. Many thousands of these rods have been made and there is no doubt that they are the most successful top quality carp rods in use today.

For multi-range fishing from 40 yards to 100 yards the 11ft KM1CF (2¼lb TC) is ideal and is undoubtedly my No. 1 choice for this type of fishing. If, however, you require a rod that will cast up to about 120 yards and still remain effective at middle range (50 yards) then the 12ft KM3DT with a TC of 2¼lb would be ideal.

For close margin fishing up to 60 yards the 11ft KM3CF (1½lb TC) is perfect. The 11ft KM4CF (2lb TC) with its reserve of power makes it a first class margin to middle range rod. Both rods have very pleasant through action compound tapers. I am very fond of these two rods and use them whenever I can; they are, however, best suited to small carp lakes and would not be a suitable choice should your fishing dictate that you would be casting 90 yards or more.

The dual-taper range with their unique jointing system are among the most versatile rods in the KM range. Their carefully calculated compound tapers make them suitable for rod tip margin fishing to middle and long range fishing. The 12ft KM1DT (2lb TC) is a very pleasant through-action rod, excellent for margin and up to 100 yard fishing. The 12ft KM3DT (1¾lb TC) with a more progressive tip to middle action is my favourite and if I was forced to use only one carp rod for the rest of my life this would be the one. I am happy to use it for under the rod tip or at up to 100 yards; a truly superb margin to middle range carp rod. If, however,

A KMCF1 carbon in full action – attached to the other end is a 30 plus mirror.

the lakes you fish are heavily overgrown with trees making casting difficult with a 12ft rod, then the perfect choice would be the 11ft KM5DT (1¾lb TC), a well proven margin to middle range carp rod.

The Trident MPR range is a very modern development and our intensive research and efforts on the production of this range has proved itself beyond any doubt. These are for very long range fishing only and I would not recommend them to be used for fishing at less than 70 yards. With these rods many anglers cast 150 yards using ordinary overhead techniques. My favourite one of the three is the 12½ft version and all three will handle leads from 2 to 4 ounces. These rods are lighter than Boron and are easily the best available for fishing big pits – need I say more?

Application Guide

Margin up to 50 yds
11' 2 piece KM3CF 1½lb TC
12' 2 piece KM1DT 2lb TC

Margin to middle range up to 80 yds
11' 2 piece KM5DT 1¾lb TC
12' 2 piece KM2DT 1¾lb TC
11' 2 piece KM4CF 2lb TC

Multi-range – up to 100 yds plus
11' 2 piece KM1CF 2¼lb TC
12' 2 piece KM3DT 2¼lb TC

Long to extreme range – up to 140yds plus
1½' 2 piece KM Trident MPR 2½lb TC
12½' 2 piece KM Trident MPR 2¾lb TC
13½' 2 piece KM Trident MPR 3lb TC

Please note that Simpson's of Turnford in England are the sole manu-facturers of the Kevin Maddocks range of carp rods; they are not produced anywhere else in the world. In Belgium the official distributor of genuine KM rods is Watersportcentrale, Grote Straat 58-60, 3600 Gent, Limburg, Belgium, and in Holland the official distributor is Hengelsportuis Bruins Boxmeer, Steenstraat 111-113, 5831 JD Box-meer, Holland.

REELS

For all types of carp fishing a reel of the fixed spool variety is best. Although at one time there was only one manufacturer who produced a fixed spool reel of good enough quality to satisfy carp anglers' needs, today we have a large choice. Recent advances in technology and production made by modern companies have undoubtedly given us the best fixed spool reels yet to be seen. The three most commonly used for carp fishing are the Mitchell (various models), the ABU Cardinal 55 and the Shimano Baitrunner. I use the Cardinal 55 and have done so since 1978. I could find no faults with this superb reel although they do need to be packed with grease when first purchased to pre-load them slightly. The most impressive feature of this reel is the clutch operation which is totally reliable, smooth, easily controlled and is also unaffected by temperature variations. I play all my fish on the clutch and for handling big carp, especially at close range, an efficient clutch operation is vital. Besides high quality engineering, another good point is the twin bail arm springs, which are definitely needed at times. Unfortunately, the 55 is no longer made but it is well worth obtaining second-hand ones as they will give many years of good service.

When choosing a fixed spool reel suitable for most types of carp fishing, I look for several qualifying features. Firstly, I would not consider

A Cardinal 55 clamped to the exclusive 'Simlock' handle.

a reel which has a spool width of less than ⅝ of an inch. Anything narrower than this will be a disadvantage for long distance casting for the line becomes rapidly lower on the spool during the cast, thereby creating more resistance to line departure. A retrieve ratio of between 4:1 and 6:1 is suitable, about 5:1 being ideal. This is fast enough to recover line at a carp's maximum speed if it is swimming towards you. It also helps to alleviate the job of reeling in from 80 or so yards, several times a day. Another essential feature is a roller line guide in the bail arm. This takes much more care of your line and is especially important when using the less durable pre-stretched lines, or even when bullying fish at close range. It also gives the angler a better 'feel' for the fish, whether using clutch or back-wind methods. Other features, such as reliable, controllable clutch operation and good bail arm design are obviously important. It is also worth noting that many of the smaller fixed spool reels, besides having small diameter spools, are of poorer quality and will not withstand many years of carp fishing use. My advice would be to buy second hand full size reels with larger spools than to settle for cheaper, smaller ones, if the initial outlay cannot be afforded. Several spools are obviously required, the amount depending entirely on circumstances. I find a need for about fifteen!

Although the centre pin reel is completely unsuitable for most carp fishing, great excitement can be had when it is used in capable hands. If you fish for fun, which I presume most of us do, then you can use a centrepin when circumstances permit. I must say, that it really puts the angler into closer touch with the hooked fish, and makes him appreciate what playing a carp was like before our more sophisticated reels were invented.

LINES

Numerous manufacturers produce lines suitable for carp fishing and because of this wide choice, each angler is able to choose his own favourite brand. A line which suits one angler may well not be suitable for another. Choice of the type of line depends on many factors but choice of manufacturer is usually more of a personal one. When choosing a line, tests should be done before use with relation to: the true wet knotted strength, the most suitable knot for that line, and the line's resistance to fraying when in moving contact with snags such as underwater tree branches. It is best not to take too much notice of the manufacturers' quoted breaking strains. I compare the true knotted wet strength against the thickness stated by the manufacturers, which is quite often the only figure given that can be relied upon.

For carp fishing three main types of line are used. They are the standard nylon monofilament, pre-stretched nylon lines and braided terylene lines.

1) Standard monofilament lines are the cheapest of the three and are the most commonly used. It is worth investigating the cheaper ones as they are quite often the most reliable. Of these lines the two most popular are Maxima and Sylcast (regular). I prefer Sylcast for most situations because not only is it totally reliable but it is very resistant to damage when in contact with underwater objects. It is especially suitable for snag-ridden waters as well as being very cheap, so one does not hesitate to replace slightly suspect line, which is made even easier by the availability of bulk spools. With Sylcast I find no need to use a strength of more than 15 pounds BS, even for bullying really big fish in problem waters. For most of my fishing in snag-free conditions I use the eight pound BS Sylcast and it is available in several colours. I prefer the brown, although on most occasions it seems that the line colour is irrelevant and that similar results can be achieved on all colours. It is believed, however, that carp can see the colours on the red side of the spectrum better than on the blue/violet side. Other factors such as light reflection and background do occasionally make a difference. Brown Sylcast must not be confused with Sylcast Bronze which is a completely different type of line. Maxima is only available in one colour at present and is a dark greyish-green. Many anglers tend to use a line which is fashionable among carp anglers despite there being better ones available. A test of several brands of line of this type, besides the two mentioned, will not be time wasted.

2) Of the pre-stretched varieties, Platil Strong, Sylcast Bronze and Stren are the most popularly used for carp fishing, and in that order. Which one is best I do not know as I have only used Platil Strong, which incidentally is reliable when used with care. These types of lines have two main advantages. They are generally much thinner in diameter at the same BS and in some cases are more supple; the suppleness being the more important factor of the two. They are low stretch lines, and are therefore an advantage when used for long range fishing as a more positive strike is transmitted to the business end of the tackle. Unfortunately, a considerable disadvantage is their high cost, which is greatly exaggerated by the shorter life normally associated with continual long range use. Greater care must always be taken when using these lines as the slightest damage will result in probable failure. I would not advise a novice to try

Returning an immaculate upper twenty; part of an eight fish catch.

these lines. To ensure reliable, long life, a roller bearing line guide in the bail arm is essential. Rod rings of the low frictional type, such as Seymo or Fuji hard-wearing aluminium oxide and silicone nitrate centres (fitted as standard on all KM rods) are helpful too. Pre-stretched lines generally require much greater care, and regular inspections should be made for any visual damage, especially the last few feet. Really, they should only be used in snag-free conditions, except perhaps in the case of soft weeds. Another possible advantage of this thinner line is when used for fishing floating baits. I have found them slightly better on these occasions.

3) The third type of line used by a fair proportion of carp anglers is the various braided terylene types. Those most commonly used are Gudebrod Dacron, Cortland Micron, Milwards 'Black Spider' and flyline backings, and others such as terylene kite strings. On some waters, severe problems with regard to line shyness are encountered. These are generally waters which are fairly rich in natural food and sometimes only contain a small head of good fish. After several years of angling pressure the carp may be seen, or are known to feed on free samples of bait, but are hard to tempt on the hook baits. Sometimes they simply avoid the area one is fishing. Although the sight of line can be a problem in clear water, one of the main

problems is that the fish either feels the line across or against its lips when mouthing the bait, or actual contact with other parts of the body frighten it. In either of these cases a more supple line, such as the braided type, is quite often the answer. This can increase the amount of fish caught, especially if the carp have only been used to encountering stiff, heavy nylon lines in the past. The thickness of the line is immaterial in these circumstances, unless of course the fish can actually see it. Although most braided lines are 10-15 times more supple than their equivalents in nylon, there is a variation between different brands. A simple, quick test for suppleness is to hold a short piece upright between thumb and forefinger and see how much it droops when comparing different brands and breaking strains. Another interesting variation between these lines seems to be their resistance to abrasion when pulled across objects, such as gravel bars or underwater branches, when playing a fish.

While discussing suppleness variations with carp enthusiast Alan Downie, it came to light that very little was actually known of the comparisons of different braided lines on the market today. At that time I was becoming increasingly interested in suppleness in lines, and not wanting to leave any stones unturned I asked Alan if he would like to assist me in having a closer look at these lines. Indeed, Alan was already convinced that braided terylene lines were better than nylon and had been using them exclusively for a considerable time. A subjective test followed which was designed to quantify characteristics of braided lines together with a comparison of the more popular monofilaments. It was decided to include one pre-stretched nylon line and one popular monofilament that we knew to be on the 'stretchy' side. Listed below are the test results.

To determine the true breaking strains of the lines, various 'favourite' knots were tried and the KM type blood knot was found to be best. (This knot is described in detail elsewhere in this section.) Tests were carried out by means of lifting a dead weight with a hook tied to the line using a wet knot. Once the BS was found an average of four readings was recorded.

Using a micrometer to measure the diameters initially proved to be somewhat inaccurate because the pre-set pressure determined by the micrometer's ratchet was squashing the line. As two of the lines were not compressible and two were coated, it was decided to use light finger pressure with the micrometer to obtain more accurate results.

To determine suppleness, one end of the line was taped to a knitting needle and then passed around the needle and attached to a miniature weighing sling. The same sling was used for each line and the same length

BRAIDED LINES COMPARISON CHART

Sample Tested		True Breaking Strain (knotted)	Diameter	Suppleness Number of split shot (see text)	Abrasive Resistance Number of 24" strokes with one pound weight (see text)
Gudebrod G.6	6lb	4lb 7oz	.007"	10.5	18
Platil Strong (Nylon Monofilament)	11.5lb	9lb 4oz	.011"	202.	68
Gudebrod G.6	12lb	8lb	.0115"	16.	60
Sylcast (Nylon Monofilament)	9lb	10lb 12oz	.012"	212.	300
Milwards Fly Line Backing (light)	12lb	10lb 12oz	.012"	19.	71
Cortland Micron	15 & 20lbs	11lb 14oz	.014"	27.7	161
Eze Caster*	12lb	8lb 3oz	.014"	18.	137
Gudebrod G.6	20lb	13lb	.015"	27.5	264
Gudebrod GT†	20lb	12lb 12oz	.016"	51.5	185
Milwards 'Black Spider'	11lb	12lb 6oz	.0175"	20.5	246
Milwards Fly Line Backing (medium)	20lb	17lb 14oz	.020"	30.5	384

* Wax coated   † Teflon coated

Gudebrod G6 and GT is no longer available as this company was taken over by Ryobi Masterline and they now produce Masterbraid instead.

of line was added to the sling to tension the line until it formed a perpendicular from the needle. The shots were counted and each line was tested twice. A mean of the two results was recorded for each line. The figure given in the table (column 4) is the number of split shot, so the lower the figure, the more supple the line. It must be accepted that these figures are only a rough guide as a completely accurate test was impracticable. Obviously, human error was present to a small degree and other factors such as varying temperature probably has an effect on the lines, especially the coated ones. However, all lines were subject to exactly the same tests as far as possible and we believe the figures have considerable value.

The abrasive resistance results must only be taken as a rough guide. A one pound weight was attached to the line and was passed over a piece of angle iron. The number of upward strokes of 24 inches was recorded until the line fractured, and this is the figure quoted in the table (column 5). Although each line was tested in exactly the same way, various factors causing inaccuracy emerged throughout the tests. The most notable were the following three factors: as the tests progressed it was observed that the piece of angle iron was becoming smoother thereby subjecting earlier tests of lines to a rougher surface. Some allowances were made for this by reversing the order of the tests after each complete set of lines had been tested. An average of four tests was recorded. The second noticeable factor was that the coated lines were depositing a smooth coat on the angle iron during their test. To help counteract this, the line was occasionally moved to a new area. And thirdly, on each test it was observed that the main wear on the line was at the start of the upward stroke. This point of abrasion moved throughout tests with lines that contained a fair amount of stretch. The most noticeable were Eze Caster, Gudebrod GT (Teflon coated) and Sylcast nylon. It was thought that the abrasive resistance tests were slightly biased towards these types of lines.

All lines were freshly purchased for the tests, except for one. This was Cortland Micron of 15 pounds breaking strain. Being unobtainable at the time, a spool believed to be about one year old was used. Surprisingly, it appeared to be exactly the same line as the freshly purchased 20 pound BS Micron for all four readings were identical. This, together with the fact that the BS figure given on the 'Black Spider' label was hand-written in biro, made us wonder how sure one could be of obtaining an identical replacement of a line that the angler has already found desirable. Because of this, and the fact that manufacturers' breaking strains cannot be relied upon, obviously the only way to be sure is to check the line with a micrometer.

Usually it is only necessary to use the braided line for the hook length, unless the fish are avoiding the area completely when nylon lines are present. When attaching the hook link to the nylon main line, a swivel or non-split ring can be used and this also serves as a ledger stop. Alternatively, the two different lines can be attached using a four turn water knot. If required, a small bead can be used on the line and will serve as a ledger stop against the knot. For margin and close range fishing this line can be used direct to the spool but casting problems will be encountered if any reasonable distance is required. Braided lines do not flow through the rod rings freely like monofilament. For tying the hook it is advisable to experiment with various knots. As mentioned earlier, I have found my own type of blood knot very good for these types of lines. If the line is an undesirable colour it can be dyed using a leather dye such as 'Meltonian' or Dylon, as used for dyeing various nylon garments. Dylon is available in a wide range of greens and browns and it is advisable to choose a shade a little lighter than is required as the colour tends to be darker when in water. Short lengths can also be dyed using a Panatone felt tip pen, which is waterproof and obtainable from most art shops. Dylon is undoubtedly the best for dyeing nylon lines. When hot Dylon is used, this treatment makes the line slightly more supple yet gives no real measurable reduction in line strength.

Care must always be taken when filling spools with line. For long range fishing I have found it best to fill the spools just a little higher than the level of the front lip. Anything much higher than this will result in 'bird's nesting' immediately after release, causing a possible 'cracking off' of the terminal tackle. Just as important though, if one is expecting to margin fish, the line should be kept no higher than about ⅛ inch below the level of the front lip, otherwise overspilling of the line could be experienced during a run. This is especially true of new line.

Generally it is best not to purchase line until it is needed, and to check that it has not been exposed to sunlight or even artificial light as nylon monofil can deteriorate in such conditions. This is rarely a problem nowadays as the majority of tackle shops are run by discerning anglers. It

Dyeing braided lines.

CORRECT FILLING OF SPOOLS

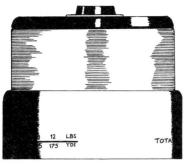

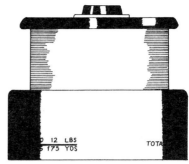

LONG RANGE USE   MARGIN FISHING

is worth watching out for at the less specialist type of shop or super-markets. Immediately after filling spools, using tiny self adhesive labels from stationers, I label the back of each spool noting the type, the breaking strain and date filled.

Generally, a lot of attention must be directed to the care and maintenance of lines. Breakages of any kind should not be accepted under any circumstances; they are nearly always the fault of the angler. This may sound a bit harsh but you must be strict with yourself over this. I expect the two main arguments against my statement would be: that the line might be 'under par' when purchased or secondly, that breakages are acceptable on waters full of snags. First, once the line has been purchased the breaking strain should be checked at home before filling the spools. This only takes about a minute using a spring balance. Who would argue the fact that it is better to spend that minute checking at home than to sit at a lake for perhaps several hours only to break on a fish because of weak line, yet how many anglers do this, I wonder? I have always checked new line ever since I started fishing but I know of many anglers who never bother! I accept the fact that you cannot check 100 metres of new line and that there may be a weak spot somewhere, but in general most faulty line is similar throughout its whole length. Once you are satisfied with the line, all that remains is occasionally to check the bail arm line guide and the rod rings for any wear which may cause damage. This is especially so with chromium types as the line can eventually wear grooves in the rings which will then cause fraying.

Regular breakages such as the line continually being cut by a resident snag while playing fish is yet another example of what some anglers seem happy to accept, despite the fact that they are continually leaving tackle in fish. This is not acceptable to me. If you cannot find a cure then stop fishing that swim until you do. There are ways around this, such as using long, heavier breaking strain shock leaders which will be much more resistant to underwater objects. If this heavier nylon is still being broken then one can use a stainless steel wire as the shock leader, such as Pike Strand. This is thinner than nylon in the same BS, yet will not break on any snags and unlike most wires can be cast as a shock leader with comparative ease. Snag fishing of this nature is explained in greater detail in the Methods and Tactics section.

I hope that some of the points I have mentioned help put over the fact that breakages must not be accepted under any circumstances. A close eye should be kept on all lines for any visual signs of wear. Even in darkness, it is possible to run the line through your fingers if damage is suspected. Perhaps surprisingly, most line damage can easily be felt in this way. Obviously, if a line is slightly suspect it must be renewed at once. Finally, whether worn or not, it is good practice to renew all lines at least twice a season.

HOOKS

As in the case of lines I believe that any failure with hooks are the fault of the angler. I say this because, if the angler chooses a particular make and model of hook suitable for the job and he checks each hook before use, then no failures should occur. This is perhaps more easily explained if we look at the most common faults. First, as soon as hooks are purchased they should be examined carefully to see if any are sub-standard. It is not uncommon to find ten per cent or more in a batch to be faulty in some way. Sorting out the bad ones could well save you from losing fish.

The two most common failures with hooks are either partial straightening or actual fracture, either in the barb area or on the bottom of the bend. If partial straightening is experienced then the angler has chosen the wrong hook for the job in hand, or he has subjected the hook to more strain than he intended to. These both amount to the same thing and are really the angler's fault. Fracturing of the hook at the barb does not necessarily mean it is a poor hook. Many failures at this point are due to poor presentation: I had an instance of this back in 1975 when a size two Au Lion d'Or (1534 pattern) broke at the barb, despite it being a perfectly good and strong hook. This incidentally is the only hook failure I have ever experienced since I became seriously involved in carp fishing.

I was fishing a 1½ acre lake at Northaw in Hertfordshire. Two factors accounted for the failure. Because of the numerous small fish present I was fishing with a very hard boiled special that was almost impossible to strike off despite using a two pound test curve compound rod at a range of about 30 yards. This obviously impeded hook penetration as the bait had really to be pushed off the hook once the point started to penetrate. In this case the hook hadn't penetrated past the barb. At the start of the fight I had to put immediate and extreme pressure on the fish in order to stop it reaching a mass of lilies that were only inches from the baited spot. Unlike a normal situation, the hook did not have a chance to work in during the course of the fight. This resulted in the hook breaking at the barb. As all the force was subjected to the point only, the fault was mine and not the hook's. In this case the remedy was to alter the bait mounting on the hook so that it would come off easily on the strike. I wonder how many times a similar thing has happened to other anglers and the hook has been blamed when in fact the mounting of the bait has caused the problem? (The mounting of baits is discussed in detail in the Methods and Tactics section.) Obviously, this is not always the reason for a good hook fracturing at the barb. Other reasons for only partial penetration can be put down to incorrect rod choice, weak striking or more often a blunt point.

As in the case of fracture on the bend of the hook, partial straightening or opening, is again the fault of the angler for not choosing a suitable hook, and then checking each one before use.

When I started carp fishing I experimented with several different makes and types of hooks but many of them were simply not strong enough. In 1974 I began to use Au Lion d'Or hooks, pattern number 1534. With these I have caught hundreds of carp in many different situations and have had no problems with the hooks. This is a mass produced hook, so each should be inspected carefully before use. Poor quality is apparent in many hooks and has always annoyed me although I am afraid it is something we are going to have to put up with for ever. I prefer larger hooks when side-hooking baits, usually sizes 1/0's and 2's, as these are the strongest. Even when using small baits the carp do not seem to be put off. It is debatable whether carp are suspicious of hooks anyway. Generally with paste type baits I use the 1/0's and for the larger multiple baits I use 2's, which are equivalent to the English patterns sizes 2 and 4. For the smaller seed type baits it is necessary to use a smaller hook as the thick, heavy wire of the larger hooks makes mounting and presentation difficult. Au Lion d'Ors are not necessarily the best hooks; it just depends on what type of fishing you are doing, or even the way you play your fish.

For hair rig fishing a completely different type of hook is necessary; the bait and hook are often sucked in and blown out by the carp. In this case the hook needs to be small, light in weight, very sharp and with a straight or out-turned point. When I first invented the hair rig in 1978 there was no hook available that had all these qualities and yet was strong enough to land a big carp. For a long time I was not completely satisfied with the hooks I was using with the hair rig, so I approached Alan Bramley of Partridge of Redditch with a view to producing a hook especially for the job. Several prototypes were extensively tested and two years later, in 1986, we launched the range of Kevin Maddocks Hair Rig Hooks, code numbered Z11. The hook is thin in the wire but very strong for its diameter, has an out-turned chemically sharpened point, an up-eye and a small shallow cut barb. These hooks are not really suitable for 'hooking and heaving' tactics when fishing in snag-ridden waters but they are very suitable for open water fishing when the fish do not need to be played hard. The hook's lightness ensures that it is easily sucked in with the bait and the out-turned chemically sharpened point, together with the up-eye, encourages self-hooking – the point often catches hold as the hook is ejected, thereby giving the angler more runs than when using a conventional hook.

KEVIN MADDOCKS OUT-BARB HOOKS

(actual size)

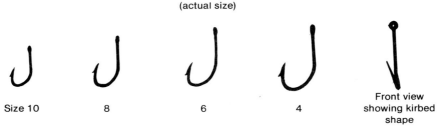

Size 10   8   6   4   Front view
showing kirbed
shape

In 1987, following much field research and testing, Partridge Hooks and I developed the new Out-barb carp hook. This is a very strong hook made from the finest Sheffield steel and chemically sharpened. Its main feature is the unconventional position of the barb and it appears that this is the first production hook to be made like this anywhere in the world. The Out-barb hook has several advantages; it has far better penetration and hook-holding qualities. As soon as the point of any hook touches the fish's flesh it pivots on initial resistance and remains pivoted while the pull on the line is maintained. The two drawings top left on the next page show this; on initial contact the normal barb causes the flesh to 'bunch up' and, as

HOOK WITH CONVENTIONAL BARB

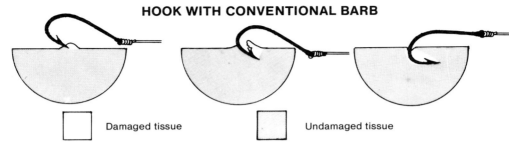

Damaged tissue   Undamaged tissue

shown, the barb pushes against the flesh all the time the hook is entering thereby impeding penetration. Once the hook is 'home' and the pressure is lessened, or released, the conventional barb is in a damaged area of tissue (as shown on the right), and its hold is obviously limited. However, the situation is quite different with the Out-barb hook as shown in the drawings below. When it penetrates, the barb 'trails' behind and easily enters the hole already being made by the point thereby offering much better penetration than a conventional barb. When the pressure is lessened, or released, the Out-Barb is in completely undamaged tissue and therefore offers a much better hold. This can be a terrific advantage when fishing among snags or in weed because as the pressure between angler and fish varied the Out-barb will 'bite' new flesh. These hooks are available from all good angling shops and are code numbered Z12.

HOOK WITH OUT-BARB

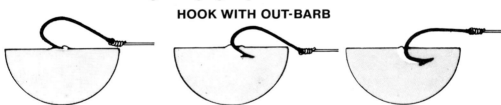

Generally, if the hooks you use are satisfactory, then I advise you to continue with them. If, however, you want to change, then comparing several well known makes would be advisable. I do this by testing samples from each batch, usually recording with a set of scales the amount of strain which the hook will stand before starting to distort on both the point and on the bend. Try attaching a heavy piece of nylon to the hook and fixing it in a rigid position, on something like a steel bar of about an eighth of an inch in diameter. Attach the other end of the line to the hook of a spring balance and watch the scales while you pull. By the trial and error method find out the strain at which the hook starts to become permanently distorted. To test the point, push it into something solid (such as a block of

The Kevin Maddocks Hair Rig Hooks, shown here in sizes 6, 8 and 10 (actual size), are manufactured by Partridge of Redditch and are code named Z11. An extra strong version is also now available.

hardwood, not the dining room table), and test it in the same way. When you have compared the results, you will know the strength of the hook, especially between the point and the bend, which is the area subject to the greatest strain. No single test will show which is the best hook. You also have to consider the hook design, position and size of the barb, the dimension of the gape, length of shank, and so on.

It must be stressed that the perfect hook does not exist, for hook choice is again a personal matter – two anglers with the same quarry in mind will often use two entirely different models. It is for this reason that I think it unnecessary to write about hook design etc in great detail.

One point that few people would argue against is that really strong hooks are needed at certain times. I have occasionally used the Au Lion d'Or pattern number 1545. This hook is incredibly strong and is suitable for hauling out big fish in tricky conditions. It is probably impossible to break this hook using any carp tackle. Unfortunately, being somewhat heavy and thick in the wire they are limited to the more specialised types of close range fishing. Another very strong hook used by some carp anglers is the Partridge Z2.

Most new hooks which are not chemically sharpened are blunt when bought, but once correctly sharpened they are improved no end. A fine carborundum stone is best. For most of my fishing, especially long range fishing, I am careful to have my hooks very sharp. At close range I find it far less important. Care must be taken not to remove too much metal when sharpening, as the point will soon become short and after several 'touch ups' will be too close to the barb. I sharpen my hooks from two sides only (as shown in photo). This may not be the 'correct' way according to the experts, but it is the method I have used for many years. I find it totally reliable and it removes very little of the metal. Once sharpened, check your work by pulling the hook across the top of your nail, a good method to indicate whether it is really sharp or not. If nail is removed, hook is sharp!

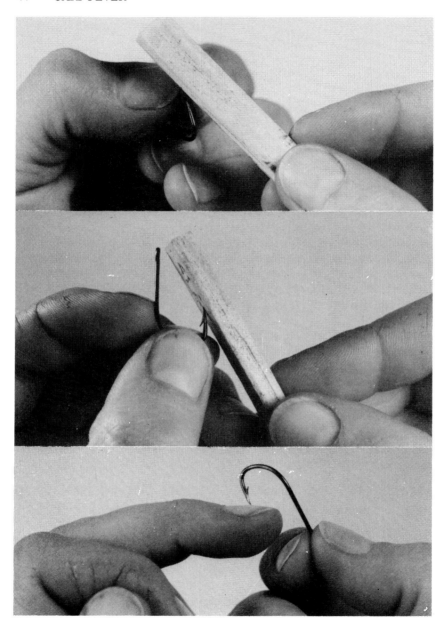

Hook sharpening method.

Barbless hooks are an anomaly, in my opinion, for surely the barb has a purpose; undoubtedly a barbless hook will penetrate better, but I am convinced this small advantage is far outweighed by the disadvantage of there being a less secure hold. I have lost so few fish on barbed hooks that I find it impossible to accept the fact that barbless hooks would have improved my catches in the past. Indeed, for the short period I did use barbless hooks, the evidence definitely showed no improvement in the catch rate. As previously mentioned, the loss of a fish is often wrongly blamed on the hook, which is made worse when removing barbs. I will say little more, other than that any problems with hook penetration can be solved far more easily than by removing the barb; methods such as correct bait mounting, correct rod choice and of course a sharp point in the first place will improve penetration. Finally, one advantage of using barbless hooks is that they do cause far less damage to the fish's mouth when being removed. This may be worth considering on hard fished waters where the same fish are caught regularly.

KNOTS

For all my carp fishing I use eyed hooks which I tie using a special version of the untucked blood knot, incorporating five turns. Instead of tucking the end I put the line twice through the eye of the hook and I find this to be far better than the normal blood knot, especially for heavier lines. Once pulled tight it will never slip and is over 95% efficient.

If spade end hooks are used the best knots are the multi-turned whipped variety.

When tying two ends of nylon together I use a three or four turn water knot. There was a time when I used the double blood knot, but I found this weakened the line considerably and I would not advise its use where the line would be subject to any real strain, such as on a snaggy water where one may have to resort to hand lining fish or tackle out of snags.

K.M. TYPE BLOOD KNOT

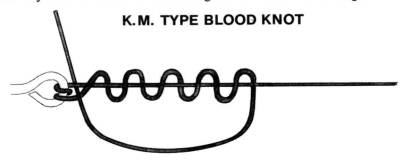

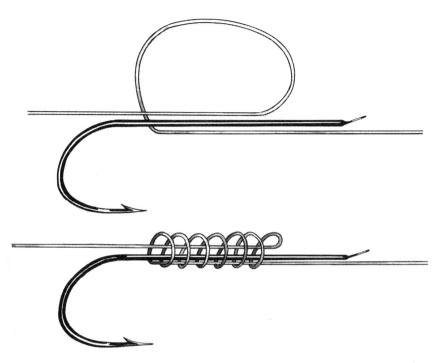

MULTI-TURNED WHIPPING KNOT

There are many other good knots, although I prefer to use my type of blood knot, as described previously. It is perhaps worth mentioning one other which I know is very good. This is the Palomar knot, and is again a knot which is far more efficient than most in common use.

All knots in nylon monofilament should be tied when the line is wet. Dry knotting substantially reduces the breaking strain. Knots should be tied carefully and then inspected to see that the loops of line are correctly aligned. I test all knots to about three-quarters of the line breaking strain before use.

BITE INDICATORS

Most carp anglers of today use a double bite indication system – an electric or electronic bite alarm combined with some type of indicator on the line.

For many years I used modified Heron heads fitted with GPO contacts and in place of the jack plugs I had longer leads which were

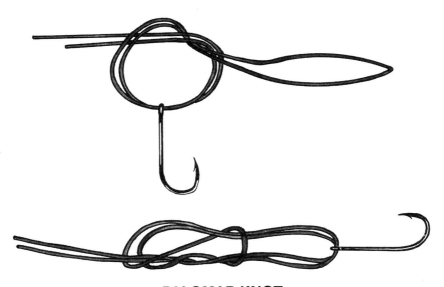

PALOMAR KNOT

1. Double about 4 line and pass through eye of hook.
2. Let hook hang loose and tie overhand knot in double line—avoid twisting the lines and do not tighten the knot.
3. Pull loop of line far enough to pass it over the hook, making sure loop passes completely over.
4. Pull both tag ends and standing line to tighten.

FOUR TURN WATER KNOT
(FOR ATTACHING SHOCK AND SNAG LEADERS)

passed through the existing holes and soldered directly to the contact terminals. A 'granny' knot tied in the cable made it impossible to strain the connections. The heads were painted white on the side which faces the angler for easier location at night and were a dull green on the back and sides. The original antenna was used but reshaped with a sharp upward bend so that any water droplets fell off the V shape and then left the head via the lower holes, thereby avoiding the possibility of water running down onto the contacts.

However, in 1980 I used an AJS bite alarm system (no longer made), which consisted of a MK IV electronic buzzer box and three antenna type heads. Until this time I had been very reluctant to use anything other than my old trusty Herons which had given me incredible service. They had had no maintenance whatsoever and were quite often dragged around the lake as I decided to fish yet another swim. They sometimes ended up in the lake and were kicked and trodden on, besides being subjected to 50 hour weekly sessions in summer and winter conditions, yet they still remained totally reliable. However, after using the AJS set for the whole summer and part of the winter I decided to rewire my old Heron heads, fitting LEDs and using them in conjunction with the MK IV box. My only

Despite the manufacturers, Dellareed, introducing improved models, the Delkim conversion still remains the best in my opinion.

complaint was that the AJS heads were a little too sensitive and would on occasions sound when there was no bite. They appeared to be slightly affected by changes in humidity and temperature.

Words cannot describe how important I regard perfect bite indication. I am absolutely meticulous about it and have yet to see any other buzzer head that doesn't give false buzzes in rough weather conditions, even when correctly adjusted. Nowadays, like most carp anglers, I use the Optonic bite alarms and I find the Delkim conversions are excellent and virtually trouble-free.

As with buzzers, it is very important to have totally reliable visual indicators, or 'bobbins' as they are called. They must be tangle-free no matter what type of bites are experienced, whether they are twitches or runs, fast or slow, and must also be unaffected by weather conditions, such as strong, gusty winds or heavy frosts. Looking back I would say I have tried at least twenty different types of indicators, most of them home-made. I laugh when I think of some of the designs; one or two were so weird that people would stop and look at them, pull all sorts of funny faces and then walk off without saying anything. Despite this, I can honestly say that I know of only one indicator that is perfect in every way. There are one or two others that are quite good but I would rather describe this one only as it is undoubtedly the best I have used. Most carp anglers use nothing else once they have tried them. I have used them exclusively since 1977.

The indicator is made from plastic and is mounted on a 'needle' which can be made from old umbrella ribs. These are placed into the ground at any angle, from 45 degrees to an upright position (the upright position being favourite). Normally the needle is long enough just to reach the rod, as the indicator will automatically fall off the line once it leaves the needle. With the needle any longer than this the 'bobbin' will tend to fly through the air on the strike, instead of gently falling onto the ground below the rod. Obviously the indicator can be set to fall off before a strike, by simply shortening the length of the needle. Because of the varied heights I set my rods at, I find it best to carry two sets of needles, one about 16 inches long and the other set about 24 inches in length. Obviously if you prefer a high rod set up, longer needles will be required.

My normal indicators are made from the soft plastic wine bottle tops which are available from most good wine merchants. I also carry a heavy set for fishing when the sub-surface drag is bad, which is usually on the larger water and when long range fishing. This version is made from the plastic containers in which some food manufacturers sell spices and curry powders. 'Boots' also sell them as wine bottle tops. Once the desired length is cut, the plastic is then held flat between the fingers and the groove is cut using a pair of scissors. Several shapes and weights can be made as shown below. If you do not wish to make your own, then ones which work on the same principle are available, complete with needle, from most specialist angling shops and are manufactured by Gardner Tackle and other companies.

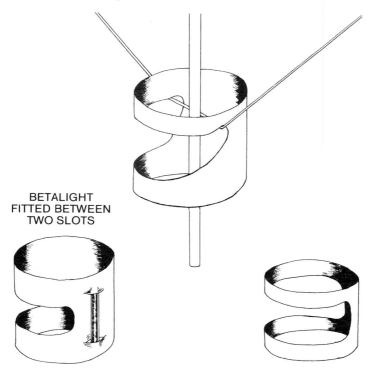

BETALIGHT
FITTED BETWEEN
TWO SLOTS

The needle can be placed either between the butt and second ring, or immediately in front of the reel and can be fished with either open or closed bail arm. If placed between the butt and second ring, which is the position I prefer, then one needs a line clip above the reel if an open bail arm is to be used. When used close to the reel, no line clip is necessary. The following diagram shows exactly how I set up my alarm and indicator system, with the buzzer head positioned between the second and third rod rings so that the line runs horizontally across the antenna.

TYPICAL ROD SET UP

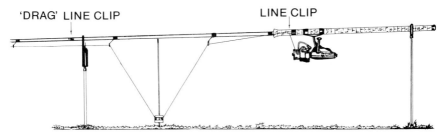

'DRAG' LINE CLIP   LINE CLIP

All my rods have the line clips as shown. These are a necessary part of the 'perfect' indication system and are used to stop line spillage from the spool when an open bail arm is used. Resting a stone on top of the spool is unreliable. These line clips are plastic and are made from shirt collar stiffeners – the type which are about two inches in length and a little less than a quarter of an inch wide. The stiffener is cut in two, a little off centre, so that one part is an eighth to a quarter of an inch longer than the other. These are then taped to the side of the rod handle just in front of the reel, with the longer part outermost. This enables you to separate the two plastic strips more easily in the dark. It is best to have about three-quarters of an inch of clip protruding out in front of the tape as shown on the following page. Several companies now make line clips and they are available from all good specialist angling shops.

Line clips hold the line securely, even in gale force conditions, yet cause minimal resistance to a taking fish. I have never known them to cause enough resistance to put a fish off.

All my rods are fitted with additional line clips, which are taped onto the rods in such a position that they are a little in front of the buzzer head once the rod is in the rests. These are used when excessive drag is experienced, ie when the heaviest of indicators continually creep upwards or for use with advanced rigs.

I don't use betalights on my white indicators because I find that I can see them easily at night, but this is a personal preference and they can easily be fitted to the indicators by wedging them between two small slits cut into the plastic (as shown in line diagram).

Silver paper cylinders can be used successfully, as they make a rustling noise when they move, which is obviously an advantage if you are not using a buzzer.

There are many other types of electric and electronic bite alarms on the market including those with self-contained head units, but most need

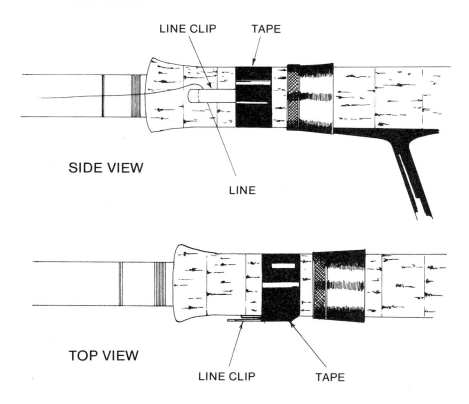

LINE CLIP   TAPE

SIDE VIEW

LINE

TOP VIEW

LINE CLIP   TAPE

some adapting before use. The problem with most types is that they are too sensitive and continually sound in windy conditions, although sometimes this is the angler's fault for not adjusting them properly. Anglers who put up with false buzzes tend to get into a carefree mood and as a result quite often ignore the first sound, which is often the one that matters. This leads to inefficiency, besides annoying other anglers. Alarms that require regular maintenance also have no place in my tackle box, even if it is simply regular battery replacement.

I would never fish seriously for carp without using an alarm, no matter how short the session. Firstly, I do not believe the resistance caused by antenna type alarms puts fish off; indeed, I believe a certain amount of steady, unchanging resistance is of definite benefit on many occasions. More important though, I have lost count of the carp I have caught as a result of observation while I am fishing. Scores of carp have fallen to my rods either by casting to jumping fish or by moving swim. I would definitely not have caught these fish had I not been using buzzers. Some anglers think it is clever to be able to carp fish without buzzers – I do not think so, as they are missing out on this continued and vital observation. I suppose it is fair enough if they genuinely prefer not to use them, but no matter how strictly you watch the indicators there will be times when you have to take your eyes away and then 'Sod's Law' will inevitably play its part.

ACCESSORIES

Apart from the usual carp anglers accessories, such as waterproof, warm clothing and numerous items of tackle, I use a Kevin Maddocks Mobile Adjustable Bedchair system. This represents the very latest in bedchair design and is the only bedchair which carries the KM name. Unlike other bedchairs, leg adjustment is easy even with gloves on and in cold weather, and the metal feet are welded onto the legs and cannot fall off (unlike other bedchairs!). The legs fold away completely flat, and if required are detachable in seconds; the whole emphasis is on a reliable, durable product which may never need to be replaced. There is also a KM Trolley Conversion kit for the bedchair which contains four separate wheel assemblies which instantly clip onto the legs and convert the bedchair into a trolley which will carry all your tackle.

For long sessions (over 24 hours) I use two sleeping bags in order to be really warm and comfortable during the night. The inner bag is of top quality duck down and the other, a cheap Terylene one. These work extremely well as a combination and are very warm even on the coldest winter nights. Over the top of both sleeping bags I have a waterproof sleeping bag cover called an Aqua-Shroud which was manufactured by Dave Barnes. The Aqua-Shroud is made from Dartex material and has a roomy base pocket on its underside which fits around the base end of the bedchair. There are four 'D' rings fitted along the outer edge of each side so that the side from which you do not intend to depart can be pegged down to the ground. It is then a simple matter of throwing back the Dartex cover with one hand should you wish to leave the bedchair in a hurry. The Aqua-Shroud is no longer made but similar ones manufactured by Kevin Nash Tackle are quite suitable.

I never use a bivouac, and prefer just an umbrella throughout the summer and most of the winter. The umbrella is simply positioned to cover the top of the body while remaining right next to the rods. At night the sleeping bag cover protects the lower half of the bedchair. I have long been of the opinion that using a bivouac makes the angler far less efficient and fortunately these are now being superseded by products such as the

These photographs show a prototype of the new KM Mobile adjustable Bedchair; *above:* set up level on a very steep sloping bank in chair position, *below:* a trolley conversion kit instantly converts the Bedchair into a trolley, shown here carrying all the tackle needed for a long session.

Dave Barnes Aqua-Shed (sadly no longer made) and the Kevin Nash Brolli-Wrap. These are far better than bivouacs because the tilted brolly can be set up right next to the rods in such a position that the water can be observed for signs of fish while an instant strike is also possible without leaving the bedchair. However, I would not use one in the summer as they hinder movement to other swims which is often necessary on many lakes throughout the summer months.

For many seasons now I have carried two landing nets; one has a five foot handle and 32 inch glass arms for stalking, and the other is a 42 inch model for general use. This has a six foot glass handle. The nets themselves are shallow – about two feet deep and the mesh on the larger one is nylon knotless micromesh for the bottom nine inches and the remainder is large, knotless mesh. This makes it easier to move the net through the water in the netting process, yet the fish will be undamaged in the finer mesh when lifted.

As I tend to fish for longer than 24 hours at a time I carry a double burner stove for hot meals and regular cups of liquid gold (tea). I'm a great believer in comfort – staying warm, dry and well fed. To power the double

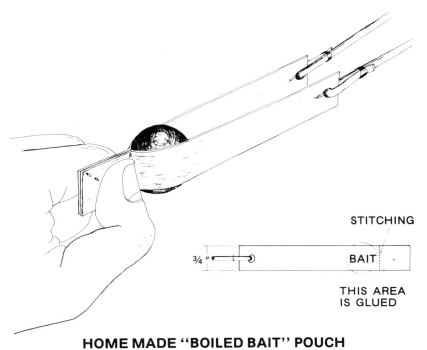

STITCHING

3/4 "   BAIT

THIS AREA
IS GLUED

HOME MADE "BOILED BAIT" POUCH

The above photographs show just two of the many ways a Brolli-Wrap can be
set up close to the rods.

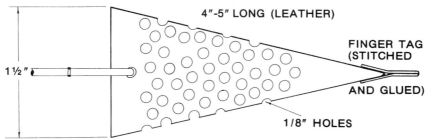

4"-5" LONG (LEATHER)

FINGER TAG
(STITCHED

AND GLUED)

1 ½ "

1/8" HOLES

HOME MADE "MULTIPLE BAIT" POUCH

burner I use a 13 pound Calor gas bottle which only needs changing twice in a season. The only problem is the weight of it and the wages ghillies now demand!

A more unusual item of tackle which I found useful at times is a walkie talkie set. When fishing very large waters with a friend it can make location of fish a lot easier. If you split up, the sighting or movements of fish can be monitored at will.

Besides the very obvious items of tackle, the serious carp angler should carry such things as a small recording book or diary, artery forceps, Salter 44 pound scales, a reasonably good camera, PVA string, plasticine, polystyrene, etc. I always carry a float tube containing five or six very basic floats and 'controllers' for floater fishing, although I only float fish when it is absolutely necessary. Another item which I now carry, although for years I disagreed with the idea, is a small, dull, pocket torch. I have always believed that any angler who fishes at night should be able to perform all tasks, such as tying a hook, without the aid of a torch. On mentioning this to Peter Mohan one day, he pointed out the fact that although he agreed with me, he thought that a torch should be carried in case of an accident. After he had given me a couple of examples I agreed, and although I have not needed the torch to date, I now carry one.

I use two types of catapults; one for multiple and paste baits and the other for boiled baits. The pouches are very important. For multiple baits the pouch should be conical in shape and with several holes, of about ⅛ inch, punched in it. These two features allow a reduction in air resistance and also tend to keep the bait in a tight area. The best pouch I have found for boiled baits is a home-made one. Mine is made from a strip of leather about eight inches long and three-quarters of an inch deep (the depth varies slightly, depending on the size of the boiled baits you favour). This is then folded in half and the folded end is glued and stitched over the last three-quarters of an inch, this being the finger tag. Because of the

Bob Baldock with a lovely winter common from Withy Pool in Bedfordshire.

dramatic reduction in wind resistance, it is possible with this type of pouch to catapult boiled baits to virtually any fishable distance. For catapulting boiled or paste baits up to medium distances, a conventional pouch is adequate. Anglers not wishing to make their own pouches can purchase 'wrist rocket' type catapults from most good angling shops but unfortunately they are not very reliable when pushed to their limit.

On many waters, the sacking of fish is totally banned. While in principle I agree with restrictions, I think total banning is wrong and that anglers should be allowed to retain what they regard as a good fish from the hours of darkness until first light. To return a good fish during darkness for me removes much of the pleasure from the capture. With modern carp sacks and careful handling, very little damage is done to the fish. Undoubtedly the best type of carp sack is the KM Safety Sack which, apart from the very soft material with a zip along the top, has the bottom corners cut off and these are replaced by a small area of soft mesh to enable the fish to breathe outside water more easily. The bottom of the Safety Sack is weighted to nsure that it is always the right way up and this product represents a major breakthrough in fish safety and care. I don't think it's worth discussing the merits of other makes as these are arguable, but what is worth mentioning is the following 'Code of Practice' that I think all carp anglers should follow. Firstly, carp should not be sacked at all, except in the case of an emergency. By this, I mean perhaps a good fish caught at night that you really want to photograph, but you haven't a flash gun or conditions make it practically impossible. Another possible reason might be that you have to go back to the car for something or to walk round the lake to get somebody. Whatever the reason, the length of time should be kept to a minimum. The absolute maximum time, I think, should be eight hours. A sack must be wet before the fish is put into it, as a dry one will remove much of the fish's protective slime. Not more than one fish should be put in any one sack, for two or more will cause unrest, resulting in continued struggling and possible damage. The use of several sacks for a number of fish is outrageous, for all the angler is trying to achieve is multi-fish photographs. This is totally wrong and shows no respect for the fish. When I think of some of the photographs I could have had, such as two thirties and eight doubles, one thirty and five twenties, four twenties and five doubles, three twenties and thirteen doubles, and so on, yet only four times I've photographed more than one. On the rare occasions that I have photographed two fish together, it has simply been because the action has continued while photographic equipment was being prepared. Finally, the location of the sack should be carefully considered in the summer months.

In shallow, hot water, the oxygen content can be so low that an exhausted carp would soon die. I have buried a 15 pound mirror that drowned in such conditions within an hour, so please be very careful.

Not as controversial as carp sacks, yet still a topic which is looked at closely nowadays, is the use of weighing slings. I use the KM Safety Sling which no fish can ever fall out of. A continuous zip runs along two sides so that the fish is weighed in a completely enclosed bag. The Safety Sling is made from the same excellent material as used for the Safety Sack and the cord is carefully measured so that the scales can be read with the fish only a few inches off the ground. As with carp sacks, the sling must be wetted before use. In fact, ideally anything that touches the carp should be wet, and anglers would do well to moisten their hands before handling fish, although this is easily overlooked during the excitement of the capture.

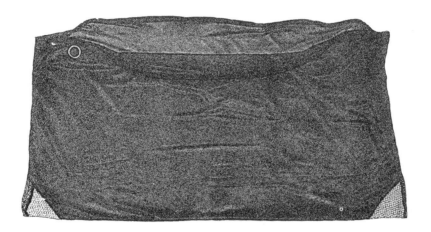

The revolutionary KM Safety Sack.

3 Methods and Tactics

Choice of Water

There is no doubt that choice of water for a carp angler is very important and however good a carp angler you are, the wrong choice could easily spoil your fishing. As a beginner, it is best to find yourself a heavily stocked water where the carp are easy to catch. You can only learn when catching carp, however small, and not by sitting fishing a hard carp water and catching nothing. You need to be successful from the start, and this will give you the confidence you need when you move on to lakes with bigger fish. Once you start catching regularly on this easy water, use it for experimentation with rigs, baits and methods. This will teach you much about carp fishing, and you can also practice bite indication systems, striking and playing methods, and every facet of carp fishing. This experience will be most useful when you move onto a harder water. Even when you are more successful and experienced, it is often worth while to return to this easy place to try out new baits or methods. Experimenting of this kind is much more valuable where the carp are caught easily and frequently, than on difficult lakes where the fish are wary. I find that the best type of water to return to for experimentation is not the very easy water, where anything will be accepted, but the heavily stocked, heavily fished water, where you know your bait will be among the fish, but also that they will be cautious, and not too easy to catch.

If you are already an experienced carp angler, it is necessary to choose the water to suit your own requirements. The lake should not be chosen because it is nearest to your home, but because it contains the type and size of fish that you wish to catch, or because it is a quiet and peaceful place, if that is the sort of water you like. If this doesn't worry you and you are quite happy with a crowded water where there are many other carp anglers, then the local club or day ticket water, if it contains good fish, may be the sort of place you want. If it's big fish you require, then ensure that they are in your chosen water, and you can only be certain about this if you have seen them caught. Never spend a lot of time fishing a water where you are only told that there are big carp, or you may be wasting your time on an untrue rumour. The best way to find new waters is to buy the Ordnance Survey maps for the area, and to go and look at the local lakes in the close season. Tackle shops may also be able to tell you of waters you can fish or clubs you can join. Buy all the fishing papers and note catch reports, fishery locations, and advertisements of waters to fish. Rumours of big fish being caught should be investigated carefully, and should not be believed unless you can prove them to be true. Reports of catches are often exaggerated, and some are simply not genuine. Even in cases where the numbers and weights of fish caught are correct, remember that it may often be the same 20 or 30 which is being caught a number of times, so that the water concerned may not contain as many big fish as it appears to from reports.

Many carp anglers seem to think it is necessary to get into syndicate waters to catch big fish. This simply is not true. Far more big carp are taken from club and day ticket waters. The main reason for paying more to join a syndicate is to obtain fishing of a different sort. Syndicate waters are normally less heavily fished, less crowded, and more strictly controlled. One of the best reasons for joining a syndicate is that you will normally be able to fish the swim you want, as the lake will never be crowded. Also, it will often be run for carp anglers, without the unnecessary rules and restrictions found on so many club waters. However, many first class carp anglers have achieved considerable success without ever having been in a syndicate, so it is certainly not essential. It is easier to get into many syndicates than some people think, although you will need patience, persistence, and a lot of tact at times. I know of no syndicate water where the waiting list is rigidly adhered to; those who control the waters tend to make their own choice, so don't be put off by long waiting lists. For some reason, many carp anglers who fish only club and day ticket waters think that syndicate waters are easy. This is rarely so; most are hard. In fact, there is no difference between a day ticket and a syndicate lake as far as the water and the fish are concerned. The main difference is in the way the fishing is organised, and in the quality of the anglers who fish. A carp syndicate is much more likely to have all its members who are good carp anglers and who have joined solely to fish for the carp. There is, therefore, more skilled angling pressure than on many open waters, and fish can be harder to catch.

Syndicate waters are not necessarily better stocked waters, nor are they often better carp waters; they are different, and they cater for different tastes.

Don't be over-ambitious, especially at first. Before looking for that magical 20s lake, get plenty of experience of catching small carp, followed by some doubles, both of which you should achieve if you pick the right places to fish, before looking for the 20s and 30s. Be warned that many well known club and day ticket lakes are very heavily fished, and this may cause friction between anglers, making the fishing less pleasant. If you are prepared to put up with this for the sake of the large number of good fish to be caught, then it is worth choosing this type of water. If you only like secluded, scenically beautiful, little fished waters, then it would be better to choose one of this type – if you can find one. Your requirements for enjoying your carp fishing must, to a certain extent, dictate the type of water you choose to fish.

Obviously, your choice will be affected by the amount of time you have available for fishing and travelling and the cost involved. However, if you want big fish, and there are none in your area, you must be prepared to give up the time to travel, and also to bear the cost. If you are not prepared to do this, then you will have to fish your local waters, whatever they contain. Anyone can find the time and the money for their carp fishing if they really want to do so. Lack of time and money is no excuse and nor is lack of transport; if you are not prepared to provide both, you are not likely to be successful, unless you are one of the very few who has a good, easy big fish water just down the road. Even if you do have a water of this kind, you will eventually become bored with fishing it year after year, catching the same fish each season, and your fishing will stagnate. You will only regain your enthusiasm and improve your angling skill and knowledge, by moving on to other waters, even if this involves you in spending more time and money over your fishing.

With regard to my own choice of waters, I start planning the following season throughout the winter and finally make decisions in the early part of the close season. My usual course of action is to fish two completely 'new' waters every season. I usually fish three or four waters on a regular basis and study my results to sort out the waters on which I have been most successful. I then consider moving away from some of these. Factors which govern my choice of new waters are either that they are of a type I have never fished before or that they contain particular fish I would like to catch. I do not let bankside pressure or distance from my home influence my decision. I plan my fishing in this way because I strongly believe that you can only become a really good carp angler if you fish a variety of waters. Of course, you must also be successful on each type of water and I have never moved off a lake unless I am completely satisfied with my results.

Location of Fish

Over the years I have learnt that the location of fish is the most important part of carp fishing. Excluding grossly overstocked waters, the location of fish on most fishing trips will certainly influence you degree of success. Because it is time consuming, the majority of carp anglers spend very little time, if any, on locating fish. This sorts out the really good carp anglers, for undoubtedly all successful carp anglers are good at locating fish. Who can deny that it is better to fish one hour in the right spot than it is to spend eight hours in the wrong one, yet how many anglers seriously attempt to locate fish before starting? The answer is very few. Only about one carp angler in twenty will leave his gear in the car and patiently observe the water, searching for signs of carp, taking weather conditions and angling pressure into consideration.. He will put this, and many other factors, together with his experience gained from scores of previous trips. He is the consistently successful carp angler of today. The majority of other anglers pick their favourite or fancied pitch regardless of whether the fish are there or not and for this reason they fail on many of their trips.

Generally, the larger the water or the few fish it contains, the more important location becomes. Having said that, it can still be vitally important on small waters. Take Ashlea Pool in Gloucestershire, which is only a little over one acre in size, where unless you accurately pinpoint the fish you are completely wasting your time. Here it is pointless waiting for the fish to come to you as they may not visit that area for many days, especially if they think an angler is present.

Once a water is chosen, you must learn as much as possible about it, and after collecting and piecing together as much information as possible the next step is to learn the movements of the fish throughout different times of the day, the type of food they feed on and where, and the effect that weather conditions have.

When attempting to locate fish there are two ways in which you go about it – by sight and by sense. Visual signs are obviously the most reliable although it must be accepted that where you see the fish is not necessarily the spot where they will feed. While carp may visit practically all the places in a lake, the actual areas where feeding occurs will only be a small part of the lake and this will vary from time to time depending on many factors. Carp do not feed all day and therefore they will at times be seen simply 'resting up'.

One of the most influential occurrences affecting the feeding and movements of carp, especially on the larger waters, is undoubtedly the wind. There are probably several reasons why this is so. I think the two

Paul Nicholls with a 31-6.

main reasons are that the carp tend to feel more secure in shallow water when the water is rough, the movement and noise of the water instilling a feeling of safety in the fish, and secondly that the coloured water caused by turbulence attracts them and encourages a feeding reaction. The higher oxygen content caused by the water movement can obviously be an attraction. The old belief that the food is 'blown' to the windward side is, I think, not usually the reason why carp are drawn to these areas. Surely, in most cases the only food being blown would be the fly life on, or immediately below, the surface, as the sub-surface current would be moving in the opposite direction. This type of food either leaves the water before it reaches the banks or shortly after coming to rest and I believe very little of this finds its way back into the lake away from the margins. This is confirmed by the fact that carp are not usually seen to be surface feeding in these conditions, unlike trout which quite often are. One thing that is certain is that the underwater current can be strong enough to stir up the bottom causing items to lift, which in turn colours the water. Besides this suspended food being itself an attraction, the coloured water, whether holding food or not, is apparently something which the inquisitive carp finds hard to ignore. There is little doubt in my mind that purposely dragging swims on some waters is definitely a way of attracting carp.

In windy conditions, the first place I would investigate would be the roughest area of the lake and the most common signs in these conditions are jumping or rolling fish. Sometimes it can be very obvious; carp crashing out frequently, or pushing their heads and shoulders up out of the water and then quietly dropping back down again. On other occasions only a very keen eye will spot the fish for they may just show the top of their dorsal fins followed by the upper sections of the tails. When the carp are showing in this less obvious way, they can easily be confused with large bream. This is most noticeable on large open gravel pits where shoals of large bream frequently adopt this activity. With the wind in your face you are more likely to hear any splashes, which can be very helpful when the water is choppy, as single fish can easily be missed unless you are looking directly at them. For this reason, it is best to position yourself somewhere on the windward side but in such a way that the light appears to be reflecting off the water. The sight of any part of a fish is then very noticeable against this light background. The old tell-tale sign of a sudden calm patch appearing in the ripples is very reliable and especially helpful when you've only heard the fish. Carp rolling just under the surface will show similar signs. It is sometimes possible to tell from these calm patches which way the carp had faced when breaking the surface. If the fish breaks surface and dives in a downwind direction the calm patch appears semi-circular, for the carp has re-entered the water it has already broken. If the fish is facing upwind, however, then the calm patch will be more circular or even oval in shape, Observing these signs can sometimes give you an idea of which way the fish are travelling. On large gravel pits or reservoirs, if the fish are travelling, it is best to keep watching until you have some idea of where they have settled. Where travelling carp cease to jump can quite often be the area where they are feeding, especially if the odd fish shows itself. It must be appreciated that carp leaping and rolling are not necessarily always feeding. I believe carp are sometimes highly active simply because they are happy and contented, which is even more noticeable when the carp shoal up. Rather like human behaviour perhaps, for we too often act differently when in a crowd. If carp show themselves in any numbers and are not feeding, it is probably due to high oxygen levels, non-interference from anglers and general contentment encouraged by warm water and the like. There are other incidences, especially on waters with considerable depth when the fish are active on the surface yet have no intention of feeding near the bottom. This can be very frustrating, for the baits receive no attention yet one feels very confident of catching. On one water I fish, an 85 acre reservoir, unless the carp are rolling over a depth of 15 feet or less, it is quite often a waste of time using a bottom bait. A surface or suspended bait is treated with such suspicion in this clear water that one doesn't know what to do next, and it is simply a matter of waiting for a change in weather conditions, or for the carp to change their mood. This is most noticeable in calm conditions, when the carp are either enjoying the warm upper layer of water or are feeding on emerging fly life. The use of a fly fishing outfit has also failed to tempt them. However, on most waters, more often than not the sight of rolling fish, especially in windy conditions, is a good indication that they are or will be feeding on the bottom.

The procedure for locating carp in calm conditions is a little different and the angler should basically be looking for two signs. Again visual sightings, which are either fish slowly cruising or basking, and the tell-tale signs caused by the movement or feeding of fish, such as coloured water or bubbling.

On warm, calm days, carp will spend many hours just lazing around in the warmer water. The areas chosen by the carp will only be where they feel safe. This will either be near the surface, in which case they will be well away from anglers and their tackle, the warm marginal areas around islands, weed beds or some banks where perhaps the path moves away from the water's edge and a few dense bushes grow. To spot these fish it will be necessary to spend considerable time creeping about slowly and quietly. Polaroid sunglasses are extremely helpful, even in cloudy conditions when there is apparently only a little reflection on the water. Big carp tend to have favourite 'lies' and until they are frightened off a couple of times it is always worth remembering specific haunts. Wherever possible, climb trees and get as high above the water as you can. This removes all reflection and your chances of spotting fish are much greater. It can also change your whole outlook on the water for besides spotting fish, gravel bars, weed beds, sunken branches, etc. often become visible and this can be useful. Whatever your chosen viewpoint, whether it is up a tree, perched on a high bank or hanging onto a telegraph pole, it is worth getting comfortable as more than just a couple of minute's observation is necessary from these points. It's surprising that sometimes you can be looking directly at a fish and not realise it for a while.

On some lakes the water is coloured or so deep that it is impossible on most occasions to see fish below the surface. Then you have to identify the signs made by the carp while they feed or move around. When the water is calm, the most noticeable signs will probably be bubbling fish, and this is most likely to occur during the first part of the morning and to a lesser extent in the late evening. It is worth stating at this stage that while bubbling is a common sight on some waters, on others it can be quite rare. This is not because the carp don't grub around on the bottom in some lakes, it is simply due to the type of bottom. Some types of lake beds such as hard, clean gravel do not harbour many gas bubbles while the more silty type of bottom does. The size and quantity present will depend on the exact make-up of the silt layers and this will vary in different areas of the lake and also throughout the year, depending on the stages of decomposition. The amount and size of bubbles seen on the surface will not indicate the size of the fish. A three pounder could send up a mass of bubbles, perhaps trapped under a hard thin crust over the silt and on another occasion a 20 pounder rooting with abandon may only send up the occasional bubble.

Waters that are long established will, in most areas, excluding gravel bars, have a layer of very soft silt covering a firmer layer. The thickness of the layers obviously varies greatly from lake to lake and is variable in different parts of a lake. Prevailing winds, bankside vegetation and the geography of the lake's bed will dictate where the silt accumulates. In some places there might be half an inch while in others considerably more. Alongside gravel bars, islands and margins are typical areas where silt collects. A study of the lake, by plumbing depths and feeling the make-up of the bottom by slowly dragging tackle across it, will help locate these areas. The use of a boat in the close season is probably one of the best ways, as the bottom can be prodded using a long pole. Stream-fed lakes, especially those which have received no maintenance for a number of years, are generally very silted. One such lake not far from my home has a minimum of two feet of soft silt covering 90% of the bottom. On this water, correct presentation of bait is essential if any real success is to be achieved. This top layer of silt is generally very soft and light in weight and is therefore very susceptible to disturbance by fish. I always remember inspecting the lake bed of a Cambridgeshire clay pit I used to fish. Using aqualung equipment I very slowly made my way down to the bottom and on approaching it I noticed the silt starting to lift and stir up. So soft was this silt, that the slow waving action of my hand two feet above the silt would lift several inches of it off the bottom. What immediately entered my mind was that a lead would drag a standard terminal tackle and bait well and truly out of sight, which would often be a disadvantage unless of course the fish were actually feeding in the mud. Besides the silt layers harbouring these gas bubbles, weed beds contain them at certain times.

In some lakes the silt appears to be so foul that the carp do not feed in it. I have noticed this on two waters where, when the bait is retrieved, it is black in colour and smells evil. In the areas holding this type of silt I have never had a take from a carp unless the bait is presented on top of it.

As far as I can see, there are two problems to overcome when considering or trying to catch bubblers. Firstly one has to differentiate between gas bubbles leaking naturally from the bottom and fish causing the bubbles to be released by their digging activities for natural food living in the mud. The second problem is that correct presentation and position-ing of hook bait is absolutely essential. So, the first step is to decide whether the bubbles are caused by feeding carp or not, and the only positive way is to study the bubbles carefully for a considerable time. You must look for movement, which sometimes can be very obvious, but on many occasions the carp is moving very slowly along the bottom and it is often necessary to align the bubbles between yourself and some landmark on the opposite bank and then patiently watch. If the bubbler is some distance away then the use of binoculars is very helpful. On one Middlesex water I fish, a 66 acre gravel pit, natural gas bubbles are continually breaking surface all over the lake and this causes a problem because the carp send up similar size bubbles when feeding but in addition

A 26½ pound leather taken on Yestamin special.

they move very slowly. It can be a painstaking job studying one set of bubbles after another and I would be very reluctant to cast to a set of bubbles that were not showing movement along the surface.

Sometimes large, sudden patches of bubbles hit the surface in one go. These patches, when caused by carp are usually between one and three feet in diameter. I get very excited over this type of bubbler because what has usually caused this is a fish rolling on the bottom apparent not pre-occupied, yet in a feeding mood. I first became aware of the nature of this sudden mass of bubbles while observing a 30 pound plus mirror at Ashlea Pool. From the top of a willow tree I watched the fish, which was very active in a confined area and at no stage was it pre-occupied by a certain food. On two occasions it rolled against the bottom, sending up a massive patch of bubbles each time. I had already suspected this cause from earlier observations at a Cambridgeshire gravel pit. This type of bubbler is well worth casting a bait to as they may be in a feeding mood, yet are not onto anything in particular. The positioning of the hook bait in these circumstances need not be very accurate for the carp will be moving about in that area.

Another observation I have made on two pits recently is fish sending up a narrow stream of bubbles in a circular pattern in a matter of a few seconds. The fish causing this on both waters were large bream, as in such cases they were seen rolling while this bubbling occurred and during one such occasion a big bream was foul hooked. I assume the bream were violently digging up the bottom as if loosening or turning it over and then getting in to feed. There are obviously many variations in the way feeding carp bubble and their style of bubbling is quite often peculiar to a particular water. Therefore, experience on a water will help you to make the correct assumptions there.

When presenting the bait to a bubbler one can either float fish or ledger. I personally feel that ledgering is better for a number of reasons. Firstly, it is normally necessary to present the bait in the actual sediment in which the carp is feeding, for a bait lying on top is usually ignored. This is more easily achieved using a ledger rig. Secondly, a bubbling fish will be feeding confidently and therefore when the bait is taken the fish will move very little. In this case the fish will either pass the bait back to its throat teeth and chew through the line or will have the bait in its mouth long enough (giving no indication to the angler using a standard rig) to detect the line and subsequently eject it unless a sensitive set-up is used. To overcome this problem it is necessary to scare the fish before it gets a chance to pass the bait back into its throat teeth. In this case a sensitive float set-up is not what is required. It will show the bite perfectly but it might also indicate line bites. A ledger set-up can be presented in such a way that line bites do not occur and as the take from the fish will not be delicate, a ledgering style is adequate providing positive indication is induced. I have therefore found the use of a 'bolt-rig' (described in detail later in this chapter) ideal for catching bubblers. Freelining for bubblers is normally bad practice and although bite-offs can be avoided by using a 'frightener' on the line, it is impossible to get the bait down to the level in the silt that the bubbler is feeding at. With the running lead stopped close to the hook and being of at least one ounce in weight, the bait will be pulled into any soft silt that is present. Knowledge of the silt layer on the bottom (and how deep the carp dig into it when feeding) will help dictate what length of tail between hook and stop is best to use. If this is not known then one has to guess. Unless I had reason to believe an excessive amount of soft silt was present I would use a tail of between three inches and six inches. I have taken several bubblers using this type of rig, the largest of which was a mirror of 33 pounds two ounces. Even if you have made the mistake of assuming the silt to be very soft when in fact the carp are bubbling on a hardish bottom, this rig is still very suitable. The procedure for fishing a bolt rig to a bubbler should be similar to that of fishing multiple baits at close range (as described later) except that it is best to position yourself a few feet in front of the fish to help to ensure that the fish comes across your bait before the line. I usually slightly overcast and then, keeping the rod very low in the water, I try to drag the terminal tackle into the silt just in front of the fish. This will help position the line tightly to the bottom which is necessary in the vicinity of feeding fish. In the case of close range fishing, the rod should be positioned very low and a little slack line pulled off from the rod tip. A tight line is not necessary as the bolt rig will serve its purpose and a run will occur. This set-up will then ensure no line bites. It should be appreciated that you are dropping your tackle right in the path of a very active fish and therefore when fishing with a tight line you can expect line bites and possible foul hooking. In the case of accidentally foul hooked fish I believe that in most circumstances, except for one, it is up to the angler to decide whether he is happy or not that he deceived the fish into taking his bait. Personally I only count fish that are hooked inside or immediately outside the lips. Any hooking that is more than approximately two inches away from the lips I do not count, unless there is evidence that the hook has freshly torn out of the mouth. Most of my friends are of the same opinion as I am, and that is that there is always a good chance that a foul hooked fish had given you a line bite and was not interested in taking the bait. The one circumstance when I think no angler should count a foul hooked fish, no matter what his policy, is in the case of a bubbler, for the chances of foul hooking in these circumstances are higher than normal. If bubbling ceases after the carp has reached the bait then it is probable that the fish has felt the line against its body and has stopped feeding. In these circumstances a more supple line can be an advantage. The choice of bait is always a difficult one for bubblers and I have not found a bait which is consistently successful. Worms have probably accounted for more bubblers than any other bait but I would expect this is because more bubblers have been presented with worms. I have caught random bubblers on lobworms, brandlings, redworms, bread, sweetcorn, a wide variety of pastes and boiled baits, a mushroom, luncheon meat and various bean and seed baits.

Although I have only taken one bubbler on a liquid bait (as described under Unusual Baits) I would think these could be very successful and I shall be using them more often in the future. The easiest way I have found to catch regular, resident bubblers is to bait heavily the known area, before bubbling usually commences, with small boiled specials or a smallish multiple bait. I then only propose to fish that area if the bubbling occurs.

As mentioned earlier when referring to windy conditions, carp find cloudy, disturbed water attractive. However, the colouring up of the water in calm conditions means feeding fish have caused it. The main problem is that on many occasions it is impossible to know what species of fish is responsible and so one simply has to give it a try or ignore it. One type of colouring which the carp are usually responsible for is known as smoke-screening. I call them 'Puffertrains'. This is when the fish leaves a long trail of coloured water caused by the disturbance of mud and silt. Sometimes this is associated with bubbling, although more often than not only a light dimpling of tiny bubbles hits the surface and this is not always noticeable. 'Puffertrains', like bubblers, are fish feeding in the bottom mud, although I sometimes have reservations when I see 'Express Puffertrains' which are travelling at such a speed that I find it difficult to accept that the carp is actually feeding.

There are obviously many other signs which can help locate the fish. The knocking and rustling of reed stems, the disturbance or lifting of surface weeds and lily pads which is known as tenting, tiny vortices or underwater boils disturbing the surface, or small sticks and other debris breaking surface, are all signs that indicate the presence of fish. The angler himself has to decide which are carp and which are not and this becomes easy after a few years' experience.

All the factors mentioned so far are actual sightings. On many occasions the angler is presented with the problem that the carp cannot be located in this way in which case his water-craft instinctively takes over and a calculated assumption must be made. To anglers who have an instinctive ability the 'guess' can be correct virtually every time. Some anglers appear to have this ability naturally as they seem to draw the correct conclusion effortlessly. For others, like myself, it can take several years of hard work and even then considerable effort is still required on most occasions.

All waters have holding areas for fish, such as fallen trees, islands, overhanging branches, patches of weed and places where there is a good supply of natural food. Also, areas of the lake which are inaccessible and

John Baker with a nice brace caught from a densely weeded swim in late autumn. The mirror weighed 22½ pounds and the common 17 pounds.

where few anglers go, are holding areas as the fish tend to congregate in these safe places, where they feel secure. A survey was carried out in a Kent water and it was found that the areas where fish were rarely caught contained very little natural food; conversely, well-known 'hot spots' are often places where there is plenty of natural food, or even where anglers are constantly throwing in baits. It is often impossible, however, in a water where there is plenty of natural food, to lure fish into another area where they don't wish to go, however much bait you may put in that area. At some times of the year it is best to avoid parts of the lake where there is a heavy concentration of dead leaves on the bottom, as these give off gas when decomposing, and the fish sometimes do not feed in the area. This is most likely to occur in the autumn, but at other times of the year these may be good feeding places.

If you are unable to see the fish, or you can't find them feeding, you are most likely to find them in the holding areas. It is worth fishing in weed and snaggy places as long as you use adequate tackle. Don't forget to look very close to the margins, as the fish often lie up right under the banks when there is no-one about, although to catch them you have to approach the water with great caution. If most of the anglers are fishing in one area, it is often an advantage to be different and fish elsewhere; if they are all casting long distance, try close in, and vice versa. Plumbing the depths will show where the bottom is irregular, so there may be gravel bars or ridges with troughs in between. Food often collects in the troughs and although the bars or ridges are clear, opportunist fish may spot baits placed on them and pick them up, while a bait in the troughs may also attract feeding fish.

When the water temperatures are high, many fish will be found in the upper layers of the water, or on top of any bars that exist, but they may not be feeding. Although extremes of water temperature may affect feeding, I have found that the temperature of the water doesn't usually influence where the fish feed; whatever that temperature, they will do their feeding where the food is.

Undoubtely, in some waters, fish feed in different places during the night and in the day time. If you know that there is a long period when you get no activity in your chosen swim, you will often locate the fish by moving to another area, or by fishing where you hear or see fish leaping. On some waters there are definite preferred travelling routes which are taken by carp on most occasions. If you learn by observation where these routes are, you may be able to intercept travelling fish and to present a bait to them.

It is worth taking note of other anglers' captures, but not just what they've caught; other details such as times of captures, the spots fished and weather conditions will all help. Knowing the angler's style and how good an angler he is may also be of help; in this way other people may indirectly help you to locate fish. Friends may help too, either in discussion or by arranging for them to let you know what is happening at the water when you cannot be there.

Attitude and Approach

The angler's mental attitude towards the fish (and other anglers) plays an important role in being successful and therefore some thought regarding the 'intelligence' of carp is necessary if one is to have the right frame of mind. Many people are convinced that carp are highly intelligent just because they've heard that they have a large brain compared with most other fish The carp's larger brain doesn't necessarily make it more 'intelligent' and I think that some other fish, such as large bream, for example, are harder to catch than big carp. Whereas it is almost certain that fish of any kind are not capable of a rational thought process in the same way that human beings are – and for this reason we should not really use the term 'intelligence' in connection with carp – carp can gain knowledge from experience, in a similar way to that by which humans learn from education. Repetition will teach them to avoid baits with hooks in, not because they are able to work out that a bait may contain a hook, as we could, but simply because they have learnt from experience after being hooked a number of times, that a bait of a particular kind has unpleasant associations, and they may therefore treat it with caution.

What is more, as with humans, some carp have a greater capacity for learning than others, and all carp, except perhaps those in exceptionally hungry waters, will appear to become more 'intelligent' the more they are fished for, and the more often they are caught.

Many anglers seem to think that big carp are the most difficult to catch. This is not true; in my opinion, it is simply because big carp are usually heavily outnumbered by the smaller ones that they are caught less. All lakes contain some small carp which are as difficult, if not more so, to catch than the largest fish. It should be appreciated that some carp become knowledgeable with age, but that the age of a carp must not be associated with its size. A fish under ten pounds could be over 20 years old while a twenty pounder might be less than half that age. Some carp are naturally difficult to catch while others are easy regardless of their age or size and I believe this is caused by a variation in their individual abilities to learn as already mentioned. Again, we can compare this to humans – some will never learn and continue to make the same mistakes throughout their whole lives while others will only need to be told once and they never make the same mistake again. However, I sometimes wonder which fish is the cleverer: the one that feeds on easily available anglers' baits and get caught regularly and is then returned apparently unharmed, or the carp that struggles at times to find enough natural food and is constantly suspecting everything it comes across! My friend Keith Gillings caught a large carp five times in a weekend and in fact virtually everyone who visited the water caught the fish, especially if they made plenty of noise! Once this carp knew of baits in the vicinity it would gobble then all up and even if it got caught before all the baits were gone it would continue immediately it was returned. This carp obviously retained its weight almost solely by feeding on anglers' baits. Was the carp stupid or was it clever enough to realise that in the end it was always returned safely?

Regardless of whether carp are 'stupid' or 'clever', one thing for certain is that anglers who have a defeatist attitude are not very successful at catching carp. You must, therefore, have confidence and tell yourself that you can and will catch carp. The right attitude of mind is important. Obviously you cannot expect to catch all the carp in a lake easily; it will take time and hard work but you will catch them. Your approach must be flexible – do not be afraid to try something different. Your fishing should be taken seriously but don't forget you have gone fishing for enjoyment so don't take yourself too seriously. Many carp anglers of today forget how to smile when they meet somebody and it sometimes makes me wonder why they've gone fishing in the first place. You should be friendly with people and be willing to share many of your findings. You will obviously need to keep one or two things to yourself but not everything. I have found from experience that you learn as much from other people as you are willing to tell them. It is worth stating here that newcomers to carp fishing should appreciate that it is annoying for an angler to have somebody standing in his pitch for a considerable time continually pumping him for information. By all means say 'hello' to somebody but don't immediately ask them if they've caught anything. Talk to them only for a short while and avoid outright questions; try to discuss things and describe your own findings. On no account stay with an angler while he is getting action or even casting out unless of course he is a close friend. It is good manners to walk away when a carp angler wants to bait up and cast out, for there is nothing worse than someone chatting continuously while you are trying to think of bait presentation or the exact spot to which to cast. Do not envy the successful angler; remember it is not his fault that you are not catching, and don't bombard his area from the next swim along, for the chances are that neither of you will succeed if you do this. The experienced carp angler will respect you if you do this and will no doubt soon become a friend.

I am often told by people I meet that they could not afford to fish or pay as much for their carp fishing as I do, and that they have to fish only their poor local waters for this reason. This simply is not so. It is a question of priorities, and if you want to catch big carp enough, you will find a way of doing so. Do you spend several hundred pounds a year on cigarettes and beer? If you do, then you could use this money to pay for travelling to better carp waters. If you are not prepared to do so, then catching better carp is not your first priority. My money, and that of other successful carp anglers I know, is not used for these things, or even for buying clothes, for example, but is used for carp fishing.

One thing in carp fishing that has always surprised me is how willing anglers are to accept fishless sessions simply because they have witnessed an unusual act of nature. This may sound ruthless, but I can't understand how some people can enjoy blank sessions just because a kingfisher landed on their rods, or something similar. Before all you nature lovers attack me it may be best to point out that I too have a love for the countryside and all its wild animals. I have many books on wild life, birds, etc, and have lost count of the bird watching trips I have been on, yet if I was looking for a rare bird and a Concorde flew overhead I might be interested, but the sight of this unusual aeroplane would be no substitute for the rare bird I had hoped to see. The same applies to my fishing; I go fishing to catch fish and while I may be enthralled by the sight of something unusual, this does not compensate for a fishless session. You should not, however, be so confident of your own ability that you are sure your approach is always right; the good carp angler is always willing to learn.

Assuming you have chosen your water, located the fish and are confident of catching them, the next step is to consider your approach and this must be a cautious one otherwise all efforts will be wasted. By this I do not just mean the initial approach to stalking or to the start of a session; your behaviour throughout the whole length of stay must be included. While for medium to long range fishing the physical approach can be very casual, care and attention will be necessary for all other types of fishing.

To determine the correct approach some understanding of the carp's senses is vital. Its eyes, inner ears, nasal sacs, lateral line and various nerve endings in the skin are all sense organs which are connected to the brain and spinal cord via the nervous system. The angler therefore needs to know what movements and noises are likely to be detected by the carp. Although knowledge of this will be learnt from experience, one must accept that many carp will be frightened off without the angler ever knowing that they were there, no matter how careful he may be.

In the past I have always found it difficult to determine what a carp can and can't see. Despite spending hundreds of hours stalking fish I am still surprised on many occasions. I have noisily stumbled across a fish in the margins only one or two feet away from me yet the fish has been totally unaware although I was in full view. On some of these occasions I have stayed in full view for fear that more movement would alarm the fish and have gently lowered a bait to the fish and caught it. I sometimes wonder on these occasions whether the carp has been in a totally relaxed state – what we would term as asleep. Yet on other occasions you can be almost completely hidden, making no noise, yet the carp detects you and skedaddles. Some knowledge of what the carp is likely to be able to see is obviously useful to the angler. Although the fish's visual system is similar to ours, it functions differently because of the properties of water and of light when it enters the water. If the surface is disturbed, it is probable that the fish can see very little; if the water is opaque the fish obviously cannot see well either, although a carp can almost certainly see us better in murky water than we can see it, so the angler should be careful even when the water is opaque.

Since a carp's eyeballs are moveable, it can direct them either upwards or downwards. When it is looking upwards it can see objects outside the water, but only if these objects are in a certain position. Because of what is called light refraction, that is, a bending of the rays of light as it enters the water – a carp appears to be able to see objects on the bank which are higher than the level of the bank. For this reason, when the water is clear the carp can probably see the top half of an angler's body when he is standing, so that if he crouches down he may not be seen at all. It has been said that because of refraction you are not likely to be visible to the carp at an angle of less than about 20 degrees from the surface of the water. Even biologists are not positive about the exact extent of a fish's vision, so anglers would be wise to assume that they are likely to be easily seen in clear water at all times except when they are near ground level.

Hearing in carp is reported to be particularly good and they are reputed to be able to detect sounds of between 60 and 6000 cycles per second. Normal human speech easily falls within this category. The carp's ear is not visible and does not detect direction easily. It does pick up sound vibrations as they travel through water, and these are thought to be amplified by some tiny bones called ossicles, which are particularly well developed in carp. In addition to using its ears, the carp can detect sound vibrations by means of its sensors, or nerve cells which lie along the lateral line. The sensor can locate the sound more accurately, and is especially good at picking up water disturbances or vibrations such as heavy footsteps on the bank which cause the sound to be transmitted through the water. These sensors are activated by electrical activity in the nerve fibres, and are able to pick up very slight low frequency vibrations in the water, and can also register water pressure changes. According to biologists the human voice does come within range of a carp's 'hearing', so quietness may be more important than some people believe, especially when fishing for carp which are near you.

To sum up this section, then, I would say that a good carp angler's mental approach should be positive and confident, although not over-confident, and his physical approach to the water should be cautious, quiet and unobtrusive at all times. Even if he is intending to fish at long range, he may find that this will not succeed, in which case the fish might be found closer in – but not if he has leaping around on the bank, shouting across the lake, listening to a loud transistor radio, or hammering umbrella poles or bivvy pegs into the ground!

Choice of Swim

Once the fish have been located, usually through observation, then the right choice of swim will come naturally to the experienced angler. What he will consider is his line of 'attack'; the best position to present a bait from but also the best to the land fish. Many factors will need to be considered. It is impossible to explain to others exactly how to do this, so I will explain my own way of doing things. Once I have located the fish I initially decide which swims are within casting range. Sometimes this may only be one swim but on many occasions there will be several to choose from. When the situation allows a choice of swim, besides obviously considering the positions of snags, various weedbeds, any steep gravel bars between me and the fish, etc, I consider other factors. What are the limitations of the swim – if the fish move will I be able to cover other areas? A swim which is in a correct position to get to the fish and also to areas either side of them is obviously the best choice. But is that swim limited in other ways? For instance, is the majority of the session at a time when the fish avoid this area even if they are there on arrival? Many lakes have areas which will produce fish only at certain times of the day so this needs to be considered. Is the swim a good vantage point? I always try to pick a swim where I can see a good proportion of the lake so that I can carry out observation for any signs of fish while fishing and this is especially so if the fish have not been located or if the session is likely to be a long one. Other factors which govern the choice of a place to fish depend on the type of fishing intended. If the area is full of underwater snags, for instance, it is an advantage to be able to move about once the fish is hooked. This will help control the movements of the fish in relation to known snags. If long range fishing is needed then obviously the swim needs to be roomy with no overhanging trees; if the intention is to margin fish then bankside vegetation and cover is usually necessary and needs to be considered. Most of these points are obvious.

Fishing Styles

Because of the wide variations in the types and make-up of lakes and the differing habits of the carp that reside in them, particular styles of fishing are necessary on some waters if any real success is to be achieved. The three styles I practise are static, opportunist and stalking.

a) *Static.* Approximately 50% of my carp fishing is carried out in this way. This is where I arrive at the water, spend some time looking for fish and then after deciding where they are I prepare to spend the whole session in one pitch. This usually requires two journeys to the swim, the first to carry my tackle and the second to carry my stove and enough provisions to last over the whole session, which in my case is usually two or three days. Nothing is left in the car, for my intention is to stay in the swim day and night and not move more than a few inches from my rods for 90% of that time! I will only move from that swim if I see fish moving elsewhere and am happy that I'd given the area a fair try, which usually means 24 hours with no action. My bed chair is normally placed to that the side of the front leg is no more than an inch from the left hand rear rod rest. The bed chair then stays in this position day and night until it is time to pack up. My stove and tackle bag are normally positioned close enough to me so that it is unnecessary to get off the bed chair for anything, except for the obvious reasons! For short rests at night and at a time when I think the fish will not be feeding I extend the bed chair fully and usually slip inside my sleeping bags. I position my boots standing up beside the left hand side of the bed chair and never zip up the sleeping bag further than waist level and in fact I purposely damaged the zips so that they cannot

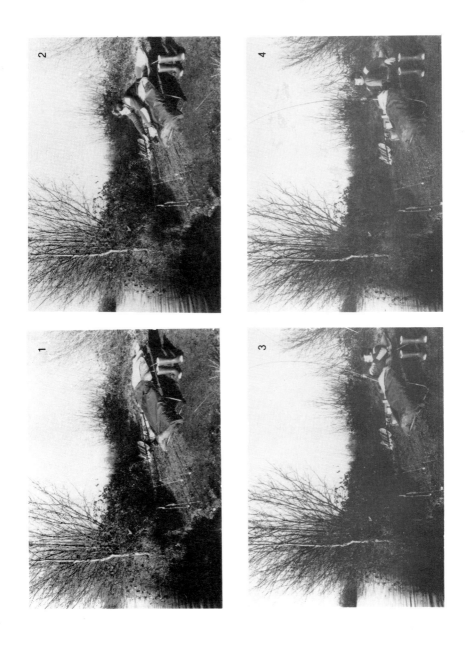

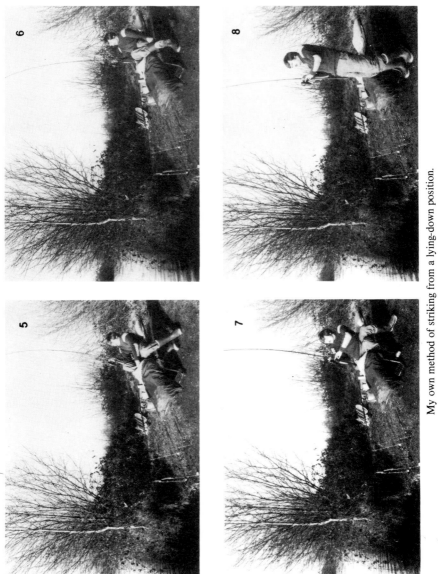

My own method of striking from a lying-down position.

travel any further than this. I also make a point of always keeping my head outside the sleeping bag, for two reasons. I do not put a brolly up unless it is raining as this can impede efficient striking, and as English weather is so unpredictable, by keeping my head outside I automatically become aware of any rain that starts. Secondly, I have always disciplined myself not to get too comfortable at night when in the sleeping bag as this can also lead to inefficiency. I expect some readers are muttering to themselves that you can't fish properly at night if you're asleep. This may be true with some people but I am fortunate enough (or unfortunate when I'm at home!) to be a very light sleeper and I claim I can hit a bite as quickly as any other angler who is sitting up by his rods all night, and in many cases quicker. With the rods about 18 inches high, from a lying down position, fast asleep, I can hit a medium speed take before the indicator reaches the butt – every time. My intention is not to sound big-headed but to demonstrate to those who oppose sleeping by their rods that there is nothing wrong with doing this if you are the right type of person and you discipline yourself. I have landed scores of fish, including two of the four thirties I caught in the 1980 season, that have picked up my baits while 'cat-napping'! I have fished like this for many years and have *never once* slept through a run. 100% reliable buzzers are of course necessary for this type of fishing. As shown in the photo sequence, immediately the bite alarm sounds I sit up, and, remaining in my sleeping bag, I shut the bail arm and strike. Once the fish is firmly hooked and under control, I push the sleeping bag (already half unzipped) down to knee level with my left hand and pull my leg out. I then pull the left boot on and repeat this with the right leg. Once both boots are on I then stand up and proceed as normal. At any stage it is possible to stop and then use the left hand to retrieve line should the fish come towards you; very easy and very efficient. If preferred you can keep slippers on while in bed but it is absolutely necessary to leave half the sleeping bag unzipped otherwise all sorts of weird and wonderful accidents can happen. Should the weather be wet, I fish in the same position in relation to the rods but I tilt the umbrella from my left hand side so that my top half is sheltered from the rain. As normal full size umbrellas cannot shelter your whole body length it is best to use a waterproof sleeping bag coverall or a dustbin liner over the end of the bed chair. Should the rain be blowing in from the right hand side then I will occasionally set my bed chair up on that side of my rods and swop the handles of my Cardinal reels to the other side. In any case I would never position the umbrella in such a way that it would interfere with striking. This is the way I always fish at night, summer or winter, when fishing a session of more than 24 hours. On rare occasions when the wind is variable with rain and it is impossible to keep dry then I set my umbrella up a short distance from the rods, put any non-waterproof gear under it and then sit out in the rain wearing waterproofs. Many people say I take things too seriously and that I must be mad for fishing in this way, especially in the winter, and they may be right, but for some reason I have always had this obsession about efficiency and I go to great lengths, frequently suffering hardships, to try to convert a very high percentage of 'takes' into fish on the bank. I do take my fishing very seriously while still enjoying myself and the company around me. Although I am fortunate enough to be able to fish two days a week my time is very much limited to that so I intend to make the most of it. Many of my friends fish for two or three times the number of hours I do and I suppose if I could do the same then perhaps I wouldn't be so meticulous about it all. I have dwelt on this point as I am about to mention my pet hate in carp fishing – the bivouac. A bivouac or brolly-camp, as they are also known, must be the most inefficient carp fishing accessory that has ever been made anywhere in the world. Its use leads to excessive inefficiency and any carp angler who owns one would catch many more fish if he threw it in the dustbin. 90% of all anglers who own a 'bivvy' admit to having lost count of the number of 'takes' they have missed simply through being inside a bivvy, let alone getting comfortable in one; takes that would definitely have resulted in fish on the bank if they had been attending to their rods in the proper manner. I am, of course, only referring to carp fishing; I can appreciate a bivvy being suitable for some other types of fishing. There is no doubt in my mind that even when using modern sophisticated rigs when the majority of bites are runs, it is better to strike a taking fish as soon as possible in most situations. On the other hand, an Aqua-Shed or storm sides which allow the angler to sit right next to his rods with the brollie in its tilted position is no real disadvantage.

b) *Opportunist.* The second type of fishing I practise is what I call opportunist fishing and this is my favourite form of carp fishing. It is a kind of cross between static fishing and stalking, and is extremely interesting especially on long sessions, but can be very hard work. Basically, it has two applications and when these are chosen correctly they will result in the capture of more carp than if you are fishing statically, even though static sessions should be planned to cover as many known feeding periods as possible. Waters where I have had considerable practice at this type of fishing are those which have areas that consistently produce fish only at certain times of the day or night and, surprisingly, many carp lakes fall into this category. One prime example of this is Duncan Kay's fishery in Northamptonshire. On this four and a half acre gravel pit there is a marginal area of the lake where carp will feed between midnight and dawn. This happens to be the quietest time in the most productive swims on the lake, where it is quite rare (throughout the main part of the season), to catch fish at these times. Although it results in a lot of hard work it is possible to capitalise on this opportunity, so I generally move into this area between ten and eleven p.m., with enough gear to fish the night, and then move back again at the crack of dawn. Fortunately, on many syndicate waters this is easily possible but on hard fished club and day ticket waters one would simply lose the main swim, making it impossible to carry out this type of fishing. Another type of water where opportunist fishing can pay off is on the large open waters which are generally understocked but where the fish are continually on the move in one or two shoals and can easily be spotted. In these situations it is a case of intercepting 'travellers'. I only know of two waters that fit into this category and on one of them, which is a large reservoir, very few fish will be caught unless you fish in this way. On this water most of the fish are continually travelling but the water is so large that even then many areas are not visited for several days. To spot the fish first on this water and then stay in that swim usually results in a blank, the fish having moved elsewhere a short time later. I cannot understand why the fish behave in this way because it is certainly not necessary for them to search for food as this is in abundance in most areas, and it is certainly not angling pressure for they behave like this throughout the close season. Perhaps they just enjoy it! On this water, where night fishing is allowed, you need to travel light and be willing to fish perhaps several areas in a day to catch a fish or two. There are various ways opportunist fishing can be applied successfully to many waters, such as intercepting fish cruising along their favourite routes, but one must not fall into the trap of over-chasing the fish as this is normally bad practice.

c) *Stalking.* On some waters stalking the fish individually is the best style. I have already discussed observation and location of fish and also their senses of detection so there remains only a little to say about stalking. Obviously you need to wear clothing that blends with bankside vegetation; all movements must be slow and quiet, consequently particular care must be taken with each footstep when nearing the water's edge. Considerable time should be spent in each spot, checking the water closest to the bank at first. No action should be carried out quickly especially when the fish has been spotted, before deciding on a plan of action. It usually pays to watch the fish for a little while to see what it is actually doing. It is impossible to say how best to present the bait to the fish for each stalking situation is different and consistent success will only come after considerable experience. Sometimes it is better to cast the bait straight at the fish or sometimes a little further out and then slowly retrieve it after a short pause. On other occasions a slow sinking bait in the path of a cruising fish will score. The right sort of tackle will also vary; one can freeline, float fish or ledger when stalking.

Although it is best to carry the minimum of tackle when stalking I usually carry two rods, one set up with a float on the line which can be used when indication of a take is required, whether a surface, mid-water or bottom bait is presented, and the other rod simply with a hook tied on the line for freelining. This, incidentally, is the only situation in which I would freeline – when I can actually see the bait, and here the use of polaroid sunglasses is beneficial. A smallish landing net with 32 inch arms is sufficient; anything much bigger tends to get heavy after a while and is also inconvenient when moving through undergrowth and vegetation. I find a lightweight trout fishing waistcoat very useful as several pockets are needed for hooks, baits, floats, and a spool of different line, etc. I always carry a catapult too as sometimes I like to see a fish's reaction to a free offering before casting the hookbait. This can be very helpful and often saves unnecessary disturbance of the water and fish. Wherever possible, climbing trees is a must and so is the use of polaroid glasses.

There are waters where carp feed at night on the surface, especially on warm, still nights. It is worth stalking these fish using similar methods to those described for day time stalking, but even more carefully and quietly. Crust or small multiple floaters are the best baits, and the fish will betray their presence by leaping, swirling or clooping. Tench, roach and other species also cloop at night, but make sounds which are higher in pitch and which can usually be distinguished from the deep sound of clooping carp, Even if you had intended to fish statically, it is worth putting a few floating baits out in the margins to see if they will attract feeding fish. There remains little else to say about stalking; the finer points are covered in various other parts of this section in detail.

As previously mentioned in the tackle section, different rods are required for the varying situations which present themselves. But not only are different rods required, many other variations of tackle and approach are necessary, and so it may be of benefit, especially to the newcomer, if we look independently at: margin and close range fishing, medium to long range fishing, and very long range fishing. The following descriptions

Almost there – a 29¾ pounder, caught in July 1982.

cover suitable tackle but are only rough guidelines. The choice really depends on the exact situation, how you're going to use such tackle and your ability to handle particular rods.

Margin and Close Range Fishing

By margin fishing I mean within three yards of the bank, and close range fishing up to about 15 yards. For this type of fishing an all through action compound taper rod is required of about one and a half pounds test curve. This soft rod will help absorb the dramatic reaction of a margin hooked fish. However, a soft rod is not all that is required in these situations as it will only cushion the initial lunges of the fish. A stretchy line of between eight and 15 pounds breaking strain, ten pounds being suitable for most circumstances, is also necessary to absorb the shocks which all the tackle, including the hook, is subjected to when a lively fish is being played at close range. One must also be prepared to give the fish line immediately when margin fishing so the clutch must be set on a fairly slack setting unless of course the intention is to hook and heave the fish out, in which case a more powerful rod and line is usually required. Although margin and close range fishing generally require the same tackle and approach, more attention to the finer points is necessary for margin fishing. Firstly, if the intention is to fish within three or so yards of the bank then the rods should be set up slightly further away from the water's edge than is normal. It is necessary to be seated well away from the bank otherwise the fish will easily detect your presence and also this will ensure that the line is resting on the bottom in the vicinity of the fish. A line, tight from the rod tip to the lead, will be subject to line bites caused by active

MARGIN FISHING (UP TO 3 YARDS)

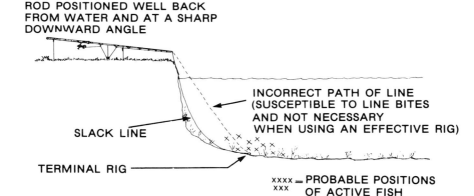

ROD POSITIONED WELL BACK FROM WATER AND AT A SHARP DOWNWARD ANGLE

INCORRECT PATH OF LINE (SUSCEPTIBLE TO LINE BITES AND NOT NECESSARY WHEN USING AN EFFECTIVE RIG)

SLACK LINE

TERMINAL RIG

xxxx = PROBABLE POSITIONS
xxx   OF ACTIVE FISH

CLOSE RANGE FISHING

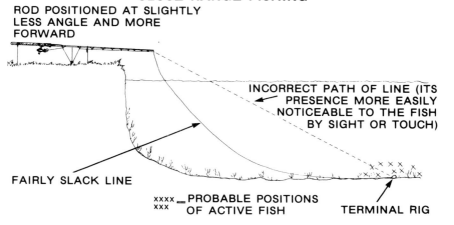

ROD POSITIONED AT SLIGHTLY LESS ANGLE AND MORE FORWARD

INCORRECT PATH OF LINE (ITS PRESENCE MORE EASILY NOTICEABLE TO THE FISH BY SIGHT OR TOUCH)

FAIRLY SLACK LINE

xxxx = PROBABLE POSITIONS
xxx   OF ACTIVE FISH

TERMINAL RIG

fish in the area of the hookbait. This tight line is unnecessary *if* the bait is presented on an efficient rig where immediate, sensitive indication is not what is required. Another disadvantage of a tight line in these situations is that the fish are more likely to detect the line either by touching it with their bodies or in some instances actually seeing it, in which cases most wary fish will be frightened off. The following line diagrams show what I have found to be the most effective set-up with regard to rod positions and angle of lines when used in conjunction with a suitable rig.

The diagrams show exactly how I would fish, which would be in conjunction with a carefully balanced rig, known as a bolt rig (described later). Using this type of set-up no twitches will occur from the fish caused by them either warily inspecting the bait or fouling the line. This is especially so when the angler has baited up, as considerable activity from the fish can be expected. Should the angler wish to fish with a more conventional rig then a tighter line will be necessary, but in the case of margin fishing this will then result in probably striking several times without the bait being in the fish's mouth thereby frightening the fish out of the swim.

Medium Range Fishing

For medium to long range fishing (30-70 yards) the tackle and set-up are different from that already mentioned. Rods will need to be either more powerful compound tapers, or fast tapers, depending on many factors. The most important dominating factor is the amount of force required at the 'business' end of the tackle to pull the hook free of the bait and with the same action set the hook to at least a sufficient depth so that the final setting can safely take place during the playing of the fish. Therefore, if one is using a small, soft bait on a large, well-exposed hook at say medium range, a compound taper rod of approximately two pounds test curve will be quite suitable. If, however, the angler is using a bait which is difficult to strike off, such as a hard boiled bait, then a fast taper rod of approximately two pounds TC is more suitable, especially as the distance fished increases. To help check that you have chosen the correct rod with regard to hooking efficiency, simply cast out to the intended distance, set the rod up as usual perhaps with a little slack line to simulate the typical set-up after fishing for a while, and in a sitting position with the indicator half-way up the needle strike the rod with medium effort. Then reel in very gently and check that the bait is not still partly on the hook. Repeat about five times and in every case the bait must be missing. This is a very good test when using boiled baits. Some anglers will say this is unnecessary but I do not think so for I believe more fish are lost through incorrect bait mounting and/or rod choice than are lost through the fault of the hook. I always remember an incident a few years back when a fellow syndicate member was using soft rods at a range of about 50 yards in conjunction with boiled baits. He proceeded to hook and lose three fish in a row and the came round to my swim to discuss the problem. He immediately thought the hooks were to blame which I suppose is understandable as he had had very little experience of using hard baits. I told him what I thought it was and he returned to his swim to hook and lose another fish almost immediately. I went round to his swim and got him to cast a bait out and test strike as I have previously described. On every strike, no matter how hard, the bait was retrieved in perfect condition and still firmly mounted, covering most of the hook. As he had no powerful rods with him the remedy was to mount the bait correctly, which a few test strikes verified. Fortunately for him, his action continued without loss of fish. The next time we met I noticed he had wisely purchased a more powerful pair of rods!

With regard to lines, when fishing at medium range, these are similar to those used for close range although the stretch needs to be considered if using a compound rod at distances over about 50 yards, where a fast taper rod should really have been chosen. Here, a line with less stretch would be better due to the rod's poor striking efficiency; examples of lines were given in the 'Tackle' section. No special set-up is required for fishing at these ranges and the rods can be positioned high or low, whichever the angler prefers, although it is not a bad idea to position the rods pointing roughly at the baits. Fishing tends to be more comfortable at these ranges as the angler need not be as careful of blending himself and his tackle with the bankside, nor to be so particular about noise, the necessary use of a shaded hand torch, etc, as with margin fishing, but consideration for other anglers is still essential.

Very Long Range Fishing

As carp fishing becomes increasingly popular, so the need to fish at very long range inevitably becomes necessary on some waters.

Anglers who are highly successful at long range fishing are often criticised and it is said that these anglers are unnecessarily 'over' fishing the majority of the time. While in some cases this is true, in many it is not. The critics are usually those people who cannot, or will not, try to fish effectively at long range when it becomes necessary. In my opinion it is most certainly essential at times and on some waters all of the time. It is however a common fault for many of us to get into a set routine and because we have caught well at long range on a particular water we tend to overcast unnecessarily. Although it may have been necessary to fish at long range initially, the situation can easily reverse itself and it is not uncommon to see an angler come along and score heavily from the marginal areas while everybody else is fishing at long range. Anglers should be aware of this and therefore be more flexible in their approach. Knowing the right time to start and stop fishing at very long range will undoubtedly result in the capture of more carp, but you should never fish at long range for the sake of doing so. The angler who can adapt to fishing successfully at any range from the margins up to 100 yards is a very good one for it is definitely a skill to be able to convert a high proportion of bites to fish on the bank, at ranges of over 70 yards.

In some cases it is necessary to fish at long range simply because of the excessive bankside disturbance. This is most common on day ticket and club waters; ones that contain good fish that everyone wants to catch! The other type of water that calls for fishing at extremely long range is the large gravel pits which are found mainly in the southern parts of England in counties such as Essex, Middlesex, Surrey and Kent. Many of these large waters are generally understocked with carp and as they do not have to rely on anglers' baits the fish prefer to frequent the areas out in the centre of the lake. This is, of course, providing those areas are not excessively deep and that they hold an adequate supply of food. On most of these southern gravel pits it is common to find areas of gravel bars with relatively shallow troughs running between them at long range. These areas harbour an abundance of all sorts of food and, being well away from anglers, the carp virtually live in these areas all the summer. It should be appreciated, however, that some large waters are very deep at long range and I have found that where depths exceed 25 feet, the carp prefer to feed in the marginal areas most of the time. Some reservoirs are typical examples of this. While carp can definitely be caught at depths of around 30-35 feet, in most cases such depths receive little light and therefore harbour little or no natural food.

In the tackle section I discussed in detail what was required of a rod for it to be suitable for long range use. Not only does the rod need to be capable of casting a lead and bait the required distance but it must be positive enough to transmit a reasonably powerful strike and yet be gentle enough to absorb the powerful lunges of a fish at close range. All experienced anglers will probably agree that for long range fishing the suitable rod needs to be fairly powerful, at least 11 feet in length and of a reasonably fast taper. Here one needs to compromise, for although many rods will cast the necessary distance, some are much better than others at performing the other two requirements. So, if a list is made of the rods that are capable of casting the necessary distance then the next consideration is their hooking capabilities. The following chart contains the results that I recorded while attempting to compare the hooking capabilities of some long range rods. Initially, my intention was not to publish these results but to confirm my findings from thousands of hours of using numerous rods of different types that particular carbon fibre blanks were the best possible rods for long range carp fishing. The methods used in the tests were rather crude and the figures must therefore only be taken as a rough comparison between those rods included. I do, however, believe they have some value and prove one or two points.

I have only included Simpson's rods in this test because comparisons with the rods of other manufacturers might cause problems and the intention was only to compare carbon fibre to glass fibre. The rods marked * are no longer made.

STRIKING EFFICIENCY COMPARISON
OF SOME LONG RANGE CARP RODS

Type of Rod	Material C = Carbon Fibre G = Fibre Glass	Force measured at hook	
		60 yds range	90 yds range
* 11' Simpsons KM Carp 1.2lb TC Compound	G	3½lb	2lb
* 11' Simpsons KM Carp 3. 2¼lb TC Fast Taper	G	3½lb	2½lb
* 11' Simpsons Hunter 2. 2½lb TC Fast Taper	G	3¼lb	2lb
* 11' Simpsons Hunter 3. 3lb TC Fast Taper	G	3½lb	2¼lb
11' Simpsons KMCF1. 2¼lb TC Semi-fast Taper	C	4lb	2¾lb
11' Simpsons KMCF2. 3lb TC Semi-fast Taper	C	3¾lb	2¾lb
11' Simpsons KMCF4. 2lb TC Compound Taper	C	3¾lb	2½lb
12' Simpsons KM1 DT. 2lb TC 'Dual' Taper	C	3¾lb	2¾lb
12' Simpsons KM2 DT. 1¾lb TC 'Dual' Taper	C	4lb	3lb
11½' KM Trident MPR. 2½lb TC	C	4lb	3½lb
12½' KM Trident MPR. 2¾lb TC	C	4½lb	4lb
13½' KM Trident MPR. 3lb TC	C	4½lb	4lb

The tests were carried out on dry land and a set of Salter scales measuring to the nearest quarter pound were fixed to the ground in such a way that the maximum force of each strike was automatically recorded. As it was impracticable to build a mechanical device to strike the rods with the same force on each strike it was decided to average out the figures recorded from four anglers striking as hard as they could, five times each. Rather 'Heath Robinson', I know, but I believe each rod had equal treatment. There was a light wind from behind the anglers making it necessary for them to strike the rod into the wind. The line was nine pound BS Sylcast and only a hook was attached, there being no other terminal tackle present. The figures are of course not realistic when one considers the true amount of force transmitted in a real situation using a lead on the line and considering water resistance compared with air, but there is no satisfactory way of tests of this kind being made in water. The figures are however a fair comparison between the rods.

You will notice from the results that all the rods chosen were between 2lb TC and 3lb TC and that there were variations of up to one and three-quarters of a pound striking pressure at 90 yards. While at a glance it appears that the carbon rods are generally only slightly better, the results prove beyond doubt that carbon fibre rods are far more suitable for long range fishing than fibre glass when one considers the action of the rods. Besides being approximately 20% more effective on hooking, the unique action of these rods gives the angler virtually all the advantages of a compound taper type action once the fish is close in, as well as the proven long range capabilities.

For most long fishing the normal arrangement of rod rings is adequate. There are cases, however, where anglers feel they need every possible advantage to get that little bit more distance. There is certainly room for improvement in the standard ringing arrangement and I put this suggestion to Roger Hurst, a rod builder and designer at Simpsons, with whom I have worked closely for a considerable time. Eventually we settled for the following arrangement:

STANDARD RINGING

SUGGESTED LONG RANGE RINGING

By using six rings instead of the standard ten (for an 11 foot rod) and by selecting models that allowed the line to run in a straight line from the centre of the spool to the tip ring, line friction was minimised and hence a greater distance was achieved than with standard ringing. The ring spacings, which are measured from the tip ring to the centre of the following ring and downwards towards the butt, are as follows: 9½", 9½", 14½", 18½" and 21". The arrangement we settled for is by no means the best – in fact it is far from it. Other improvements such as immediate coning down of the line by a series of butt rings were possible but we felt that a compromise between a pure casting tool and a fishing rod was needed and so we settled for the ringing shown in the diagram. The first ring was a fold down Fuji (FCG type, oxide butt ring) which, as mentioned, not only allowed a straight line from spool to tip ring but also eliminated line slap against the rod. It is not uncommon to see wear on the varnish and whipping under a standard butt ring on a rod which has been subject to long range casting and this is caused by line slap (oscillation). The remaining rings chosen were of the stand-off, low friction Seymo variety although these have since been superseded by Trinite long range rings.

For long range fishing the line should be as thin as possible to assist in better casting but must be strong enough to play the fish properly and of course to cast the necessary weight. In snag-free conditions a pre-stretched line such as Sylcast Bronze may be necessary to help transmit a more positive strike to the business end. I say 'may' because I do not find the need to use these types of lines myself. Many anglers feel it is essential to completely cover the hook with the bait and this often leads to fish 'falling off' shortly after contacting; even the combination of a fast taper rod, a pre-stretched line and a very powerful strike is often still not enough to pull the hook through a bait that has withstood the force of a cast and set the hook at extremely long range. All of my fishing is carried out with the point of the hook, its barb and the bend completely bare. At long range I go even further than this and fish with 80% of the hook bare and in some cases, all of the hook, and I believe it is for this reason that I have little trouble in fishing efficiently at long range. In fact I rarely have a fish 'come off' when long range fishing. I do not believe carp can recognise hooks by sight or feel (unless the point sticks into them) as they are frequently mouthing other hard and sharp objects such as stones and small twigs, etc. My preference is to use a stretchy line – my favourite being Sylcast (regular) in conjunction with a carbon rod such as the KM2 DT model. I find this rod and line suits the way I mount my baits. Other

SHOCK LEADER FOR LONG RANGE CASTING
CAN ALSO BE USED AS A 'SNAG LEADER' TO PREVENT LINE FROM BEING FRAYED OR CUT WHEN FISHING OVER SHARP GRAVEL BARS

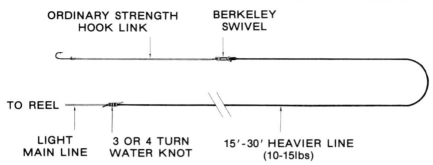

ORDINARY STRENGTH HOOK LINK

BERKELEY SWIVEL

TO REEL

LIGHT MAIN LINE

3 OR 4 TURN WATER KNOT

15'-30' HEAVIER LINE (10-15lbs)

anglers who are firm in the belief that carp can recognise hooks may not find this type of line adequate for long range; so really it is up to the individual to pick a line which suits his style of bait mounting and choice of rod. In waters where gravel bars or other types of snags are present, then pre-stretched lines are not suitable anyway and this situation is discussed in detail under 'Snag Fishing'. There are, however, odd instances when a pre-stretched line can be used when fishing among snags; this is when the snags are at long distance only and then a shock leader of a sufficient type and can be attached. One disadvantage of using a pre-stretched line for long range use without a 'softer' shock leader is the unsuitable combination of a stiff fibre glass rod and a non-stretch line when playing a fish at close range.

There are many other ways in which the angler can achieve greater casting distances. The combination of using a heavy lead, a shock leader and a light main line is a definite advantage. Where leads of over one and a half ounces are required to achieve the distance, a shock leader is necessary in most cases to prevent 'cracking off' during the cast. For maximum distance, a fairly light line of around seven or eight pounds BS but no less than six pounds (governed by the action of a long range rod) should be used when the situation permits. To this, a heavier line, which will withstand the continued casting of a heavy lead, is attached by means of a four turn water knot. The minimum length of the shock leader should be so that when the angler is in his casting position there remains at least four turns of the heavier line on the spool of the reel. This is the minimum acceptable length – I prefer a shock leader longer than this, usually about three rod lengths in length, so that when the fish is being played in the

TYPICAL LONG RANGE TERMINAL ARRANGEMENT

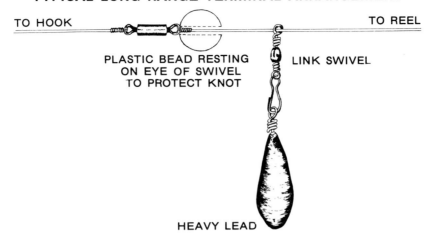

TO HOOK

TO REEL

PLASTIC BEAD RESTING
ON EYE OF SWIVEL
TO PROTECT KNOT

LINK SWIVEL

HEAVY LEAD

margins the shock leader knot is already on the spool instead of passing backwards and forwards through the rod rings. The type of ledger stop for long range casting needs to be substantial and I continue to use a small Berkley swivel in the line as I normally do. This also allows the angler to vary easily his type of line for the hook length. My usual choice for very long range casting is seven pound BS Sylcast for the hook length and main line and 11 pound BS Sylcast for the shock leader, in conjunction with a two ounce bomb. It should, however, be appreciated that a rod has a limit on its casting weight and only carp rods that are designed for long range use will handle leads of two ounces and over. I also find that while my long range carbon rods will handle heavier weights, best results are achieved with one and a half to two and a quarter ounce bombs. Continual casting with heavy leads causes wear and damage to the knot on the stop swivel. This is easily overcome by using a small plastic bead that will pass over the knot and rest on the eye of the swivel as shown in the diagram.

A small amount of wear may still take place on the line immediately above the bead so it is advisable to check for this from time to time.

Other factors which allow a greater casting distance are the use of small, hard, round baits. I favour a quarter inch to three-eighths of an inch diameter boiled baits as these cast much further than the larger conventional sized baits when a lead is being used.

Adjusting the terminal rig will also assist the angler to achieve greater distances if the situation allows. The nearer the lead is to the bait when in flight the further it will cast, so those anglers who favour long links and tails on their rigs will find it an advantage to make adjustments. 90% of my fishing is done with the lead straight on the line in conjunction with a relatively short tail to the hook and I am certain this helps me achieve long distance casts. Where the angler prefers to use a heavy lead on a link, the link should be very short and the line between the running swivel and lead should be of no less than ten pounds BS otherwise this could break after a number of casts.

Hook design and size is also an important factor with long range fishing. Hooks must be very sharp and, where possible, thin in the wire. Smaller hooks will penetrate better than large ones at long range and this is where I favour a size six or eight if the bait allows. Although I do not use barbless hooks I accept that they must penetrate more easily at long range and anglers who suffer hook-setting difficulties might do better using barbless hooks in snag-free conditions.

One problem that is always present when fishing at very long range is the tendency for the line indicator to continually creep upwards, caused by excessive underwater drag. This is easily overcome by using a line clip fitted onto the rod, positioned in front of the buzzer head when the rod is placed in its rests, as described in the tackle section. After casting I have found it best to wait until most of the line has settled on the bottom before fitting the line into the clip; this usually takes about a minute. During this 'settling down' period excessive drag occurs, and to use the clip before this takes place will result in a very tight line that is susceptible to false bites caused by gusts of wind, etc.

Snag, Weed and Gravel Bar Fishing

Snag fishing calls for a completely different choice of tackle and approach. Planning the downfall of the fish is essential but then only self-discipline will complete the success. Initially, the angler needs to assess the tackle required and this is determined by the nature of the snags and what the angler intends to do once the fish is hooked. This may sound obvious, but it is common for an angler to work everything out correctly knowing that he must not give the fish an inch of line, yet on hooking the fish he becomes worried about the tension on his tackle, gives the fish line and then loses it. For this reason it is absolutely essential to carry out one's plan to the end. Another factor which many anglers overlook is the size of the fish. It must be appreciated that any carp, once it is over ten pounds, makes very little difference to the choice of tackle, for an upper double is capable of anything a 30 pounder can do. In most cases the tackle chosen must be very strong and the angler must have complete confidence in it. If I am fishing an area where the fish must not be given any line, then I sometimes hook my tackle onto a nearby fence or similar beforehand and really lay into it, bending the rod double and jerking it from side to side; this gives me great confidence in the tackle. The type of line chosen for snag work must on no account be of the pre-stretched variety as these have little abrasive resistance. The most suitable line I have found is Sylcast regular and although the variations in the types of snags are many, the 11 and 15 pound breaking strains are suitable for 90% of angling situations.

One item of tackle which presents a problem when the fish needs to be bullied is the hook. This should be very strong and on no account should it be barbless, for once there is a snag involved the angler has less control over the pressure applied on the fish. Two such hooks which are suitable for close range snag fishing are the Au Lion d'Or 1545 and the Partridge Z2. For the majority of snag fishing no item of tackle should be permanently fixed to the line, excluding the hook of course! Freelining can obviously be an advantage here and if floats are used they are best attached by means of a single float ring close to the end of the float. If a weight is needed for casting then this should be attached in such a way that it can break free either after casting or, if desired, after the fish is hooked. Otherwise these easily get caught up and result in the fish being lost. If required, a small metal object such as a nut or bolt can be attached using PVA strip which will dissolve in the water after a minute or so. In the case of a permanent weight, a lead or other suitable object can be attached via a light line link of between a half to one pound breaking strain which will then break away should the lead get caught up. The link can be attached to the line by means of a miniature loop instead of a swivel and can be stopped using a form of breakaway ledger stop. Either a very loosely fitted conventional plastic stop can be used or a small piece of plasticine squeezed onto the line. Plasticine may be used as the main casting weight although I have on occasions had this taken by the fish instead of the bait.

On some waters carp spend much of their time in snaggy areas. Sometimes they feed in these areas but more often than not they visit these 'safe places' or holding areas simply to get away from anglers and their tackle. Having said that, I know of a lake which is hardly ever fished and not at all by carp anglers, which has many full size trees that grew before it was flooded. These have since died and although there are plenty of clear areas in the lake, the carp frequent the submerged trees as if simply feeling secure when close to them. Much of the fishes' time in areas of such snags will be spent just lying up and although they are not feeding, if the angler can present a bait there is always a good chance of catching fish. The behaviour of carp in safe places is completely different from normal. They are less easily scared and will often take any bait that is correctly presented within seconds, regardless of whether it has been well used or not. I have found slow sinking bread flake the most effective when the fish can be seen, but virtually any bait will work.

Areas that can be regarded as both snags and feeding areas are weedbeds. Lilies cause the most problems and when they are tightly packed it is essential to keep the fish out of them at all costs. This is not necessary if they are sparse for when the fish is under pressure the strong line will often cut through random stalks and leaves. This similarly applies for the underwater lilies although the exact extent of their growth is harder to imagine. When fish are being played among sparse lily growth it is an advantage to apply the pressure from above as this makes the cutting of the individual plants easier. The rod should therefore be kept high and a 12 foot rod is an advantage. I have found that you stand a better chance of landing a big fish than a smaller one among lilies as a big carp thrashing around tends to smash the plants up. In the case of soft weeds it is not so dangerous to let the fish enter them although in general this should be avoided. When the fish gets into the soft weed, keeping a steady pressure on it for a minute or so usually results in the fish gradually coming free. Where this does not work the line should be slackened off and the rod left in the rest for a while when it will be found on occasions that the fish will swim out of its own accord. As a final resort, gentle, steady hand lining often works.

On one water I occasionally fish, 90% of the lake is covered in various soft weeds. It is a shallow lake averaging three to four feet in depth and the weed grows from the bottom to the surface. The only clear patches are those where feeding carp root around the bottom in a small area of about two feet in diameter, uprooting the weed and leaving a nice clean gravel patch. The problem in this water is not so much getting the fish out of the weed as this is easy, it is placing a bait onto these patches, for a bait cast into the weed is usually a waste of time. As most of these patches are well aware from the bank the best way I have found is to place a marker by the side of each area. This is simply a reed stem with a stone tied to one end, and once thrown into the water it will stand up like the real thing. The carp seem willing to accept this and accurate casting is then possible. There is one drawback with this method: a boat is required and while we have found this doesn't perturb the carp, on many fisheries this would not be allowed. Fortunately, this lake is hardly fished and nobody is inconvenienced by the use of a boat.

With regard to sunken trees the fish must be kept away at all costs, for although a good line will withstand rubbing up against the wood, the fish will often swim a complete circle around the branches. The fight is then at an end, as no matter what the angler tries to do he will eventually have to pull for a break. In this case the fish will probably have broken its end of the line immediately it became entangled. Wherever possible, it is good practice to float fish next to sunken trees for this gives the angler the advantage of immediate indication as to the whereabouts of the fish once it is hooked. In fact, floats are ideal for fishing bottom or mid-water baits alongside any snag. The type of float I have described for presenting small floaters is ideal as a breakaway float for these situations.

One type of snag which is different from all the rest is the type which necessitates the angler fishing at long distance over shallow gravel bars. These can be very abrasive to line, especially when they harbour beds of mussels or small rocks etc. On some waters this is a severe problem for when the line rubs against such gravel bars while a fish is being played, it is cut every time. I have found in these cases that it is best to use a 'snag leader' of heavier nylon line and in the case of long range fishing an ideal length is usually three to four rod lengths. Under no circumstances would I use braided terylene line because of its poor abrasive quality. I usually use seven pound BS Sylcast to assist the longer casting and use 11 pound BS Sylcast for the leader. For most gravel bar situations this is adequate, but it is essential that the fish are played lightly. Giving the fish 'stick' in these circumstances inevitably results in the line being cut. In the unusual event of the 11 pound BS Sylcast leader proving unsuccessful then 15 pound BS can be used, or better still a wire leader. Although I have not tried many different types of wire for snag leaders it soon became apparent that many were unsuitable for casting. However, 'Pike Strand' is usable although a short distance will be lost on the cast. Pike Strand will resist all types of sharp objects. Again, generally I use three to four rod lengths although of course some situations require different lengths. It is essential that the wire has a reliable join to I attach this to a short piece of 11 Sylcast (which has been water knotted to the reel line) by means of a small knot tied at the end of the wire and the nylon whipped over the wire and up to its knot, as with tying a spade end hook. Whipping the nylon around the wire weakens it slightly so it is better to step up the reel line in strength or use a short heavier piece of nylon as described should distance dictate the use of light line.

One of my favourite fish – a magnificent mirror of 33 pounds 2 ounces from Ashlea Pool in September 1978.

As mentioned earlier, correct planning is quite often an essential part of successful snag fishing. The angler needs to choose a spot where he has the best chance of controlling the fish. Positioning oneself as close as possible to the fish is advisable for the further the fish is away the less positive control an angler will have. As the distance increases so the possible angles that pressure can be applied from decrease and this is exaggerated by line stretch. Once a plan of action is decided upon, it must be adhered to rigidly. If you've made up your mind to run up the bank for 25 yards then do so, or if you've decided to give not an inch of line then don't, for if you change your mind you will probably lose the fish. It is best to keep one step ahead of the fish – surprise it and you will probably win. The angler must have complete control over the fish and not vice-versa.

When baits are positioned very close to the snag the angler needs to allow for the distance which the fish can travel before you and your tackle gains control of the fish. This is most noticeable with soft compound rods or when fishing long distances with stretchy lines. Even with the bail arm closed and an immediate strike the fish can still travel several feet before the bend of a typical compound rod is taken up and this can easily make all the difference between catching or losing the fish. A remedy for this is to take a step backwards as the strike is made. This is not so important with a fast taper rod. Sometimes it is necessary to make special tackle for snag work. I have found a short, strong rod of about five feet in length very suitable for fishing within the confines of marginal bushes which overhang the water, or for general tree work. Once inside these bushes it is impossible to use a conventional landing net because of the limited room and this is when I use my converted trout net. Where fish are to be netted in thick weeds it may be necessary to construct a net with a very strong frame.

Finally, it should be appreciated that once a hooked fish swims round a snag there is quite often a different amount of pressure on the tackle at the fish's end from that of the angler's. While the angler might only be putting a pressure of one pound on his tackle, the fish could be exerting twice as much and it is for this reason that once the fish is around the snag it should be played lightly.

Night Fishing

I would like to start this section by repeating the best night description I know of. It is from Peter Mohan's book, *Cypry the Carp:*

> *"Night came. The darkening water cooled slowly, fish became more active. Sleepy day birds sang their evening songs before retiring and bank voles plopped busily in and out of the water, submerging at the slightest sound. Tiny pipistrelle bats, ugly but incredibly quick, snaked their sound-controlled flights under the trees, twisting and turning to catch the last insects as they dropped despairing with the sun into the black water. A big white barn owl, originator of many country ghost stories of the past, flew noiselessly up the track ready to pounce on the first scratchy mouse movement selected by his huge ears, while hundreds of light years away innumerable brilliant stars decorated the night sky. The air was still, the wood almost silent, peace broken only by the occasional hum and arced headlights of a car on the distant road. Across the lake, a dark figure flitted from tree to tree – the bailiff, alone now, checking for poachers, the only human shape in a microscosmic animal and vegetable world, adapted to move inconspicuously in it by long years of careful practice.*

Few people see the night. To most, it is but a passing incon-venience, a suspension of faculties long lost, an hiatus in time, to be passed in rapid sleep till new light restores vision and confidence. Darkness induces an elemental fear, fed by transmitted time-memories of snuffling hunting beasts and imagined horrific spirits whose horrid unreality haunts lonely unlit countryside with evil intent. Reality is otherwise. Night can be learned, for those who care to do so. Bailiffs and game-keepers, night anglers and naturalists study to enjoy the quiet dark hours, knowing that man has nothing to fear in them but other men. To the initiated, each identifiable rustle and squeak in the undergrowth is but evidence of the pullulating animal life which increases at nightfall, not the insubstantial foot-steps of some long-dead monkish phantom. The whisper of wings and the sudden splash of a joy-leaping carp punctuate the long hours of obscurity to the reclining angler, relaxed as never by day, petty troubles forgotten in a new awareness of a night-awoken life beyond his own."

One facet of carp fishing which is often badly practised by all but the experienced angler, is night fishing. If you are the type of person who is frightened of the dark or cannot do anything without the aid of a torch, then you should not go fishing at night. It is as simple as that, because people of this type spoil it for others. It is worth remembering that there is nothing to be frightened of in the dark except other people. Many animals make noises at night, and if you hear anything which appears strange, go and investigate it, and you will soon find there is nothing to fear. I am not saying that the use of a torch frightens carp because in most cases, excluding margin fishing, I believe it doesn't, but anglers should behave in a responsible manner and consider others who have gone to the effort of practising their night fishing in a quiet or orderly manner. I realise we all have to start somewhere and my advice for beginners would be to start at home. The first step is to set up the complete tackle in an almost dark room. The emphasis should be on the terminal tackle and tying the hook as this will need to be carried out more often than anything else, and has to be absolutely right. If you have problems in tying the hook, lay the eye of the hook against your tongue and then by prodding with the line you will be able to feel it go into the centre of the eye. By tying the rest of the knot bigger than normal it will be easy to find the loop for tucking the end. Once you have this right, instead of planning to fish a whole night, start by fishing a couple of hours into the dark and then gradually increase this time as you become more proficient. Try to have everything set up and the

Peter Mohan with a good twenty caught in August 1982.

baits cast out in daylight, at least at first. Remember that summer nights can be very cold so you may need winter clothing. Carry a small, weak torch but do not intend to use it, not even for putting the baits on the hook. This is for emergencies only and one day it will probably fail. If you rely on it and this happens you may have to go home. If you need to switch it on then do so in such a position that it is well away from the water and where other anglers cannot see it. By practising in this way you won't need to go with a friend and hence your night fishing will be quiet and well organised right from the start. Anglers who start their night fishing with friends tend to keep chatting to each other and this usually means sharing a swim or continually leaving rods unattended, which in carp fishing are both bad practices.

It is usually a good idea to put in a number of free offerings in the area in which you are going to fish just before dark. Doing this in daylight enables the baits to be placed accurately, although this should be left as late as possible. Also there is often less activity from other species once it is dark, so the baits may remain until the carp find them. I haven't said much about baits for night fishing, because I use the same ones as I do in the daytime. Anchored floaters do well on some waters although it is not always easy to be certain that the bait has risen to the surface. After casting, slacken the line and put a light indicator on it. When this stops rising, the bait will be on the surface.

Accurate casting at night can sometimes be difficult. On most lakes, silhouettes of the features on the opposite bank can be seen on the water even in the darkest nights. This will assist the angler to get the desired direction. Here, anglers who practice direct overhead casting will obtain more accuracy. In calm conditions the splash of the bait and terminal tackle can usually be seen and heard. When accurate distance is required, such as in the case of fishing into a hole in weed or close to an island, it is best to practise your method before dark. The angler can either choose to use a lead which is only just heavy enough to reach the desired spot with a fairly powerful cast, or use a lead heavier than is required, either fixing a small marker on the line, such as a piece of Sellotape, or in the case where you cannot afford to overcast, fit a rubber band around the spool. To use a rubber band, the bait should first be cast to the required spot, the bail arm opened and the spool removed, and the rubber band fitted over the remaining line lying on the spool. Keep the band on the spool, then reel in and rebait. You can then 'overcast' to the island margins or whatever and the rubber band will brake the cast at the desired distance. This method will need to be practised before darkness as varying rubber band tension slightly affects the braking distance. The rubber band can be left on while the fish is played, although if line from under the rubber band is pulled off it will need to be repositioned afterwards, the original spot having been marked with dye or something similar. This may sound complicated, or not worth the trouble, but I can assure you that I have used this method successfully on many occasions.

Efficiency is a dominating factor of successful night fishing and it should start with the arrangement of tackle. The angler should have every piece of equipment positioned exactly where he knows it can be found so that immediate location of any tackle item is possible by feel. Bite indication should be effective; I use an electronic system, which includes a light emitting diode (LED) in each buzzer head, in conjunction with a white indicator on the line. I find this adequate, but should you find it difficult to see a white indicator then a Betalight should be affixed, or silver paper formed into an indicator. The face of the buzzer heads are more easily located at night when painted white, while the sides and back can be left a less conspicuous colour.

Playing a hooked fish at night is a little different from doing the same thing in daylight. Sometimes it is difficult to imagine where the fish is, in relation to overhanging branches or other snags. I have found that practising the playing of a fish with my eyes shut in the daytime helps me to guess the position of the fish more accurately. When a fish is hooked in snag-free conditions in the daylight you can play the fish for a while with your eyes shut, guess where it is and then check to see if you are right. After doing this a few times an accurate 'feel' of the tackle will be experienced, thereby assisting the angler on those very dark nights when it is impossible to see the rod's position silhouetted against the sky.

A large landing net is essential for night fishing and I would never use one with less than 36 inch arms, a 42 inch model being my favourite. The netting of the fish requires more patience at night. Whereas I would net a fish at the first opportunity in daylight, at night I keep the net fairly close to the bank and crouch down a little so that I can easily see the spreader block of the net. I then pull the fish over the net until its mouth virtually touches the block. All that is required is a little more patience and then even on the darkest night a big fish can be landed with ease. On no account use a torch as this can easily frighten the fish causing last minute struggles. As with daytime fishing, net the fish yourself and never allow a stranger to pick up your net and land your fish. If someone else makes a mistake and loses the fish for you, you will always blame him, but if you do your own netting you only have yourself to blame if anything goes wrong. From experience I find it impossible to state the ideal conditions for night fishing, because it seems to depend on the water. On some waters I have done well on bright moonlit nights, while on others it has been best when it is overcast. Often conditions have remained the same, except that it got dark, and fish have been feeding well, so this was obviously not due to reduced light intensity. On the other hand, there have been times when I did start to catch after dark, while there had been no action during daylight and this may well have been because the fish were feeding because it was darker.

When weather and other conditions are right, the fish will feed, and on some waters I have fished this feeding will take place whether it is day time or night time. On the other hand, it does happen that fish on some waters will start to feed as soon as it gets dark, even though other conditions have remained the same as in the daylight, when they would not feed, so this must be due to the decrease in light intensity. I believe in most cases, however, that carp prefer to feed in the daytime rather than at night, for although about 60% of my fishing is in daylight, as many as 80% of my fish are caught at these times. This is not because I am fishing less efficiently at night, although if you are too tired to fish efficiently, it would be better to go home.

An immaculate 20 pound-plus common, taken on chick pea at close range.

Night fishing is certainly not essential to be successful. Most of the waters I fish produce fewer carp after dark when I am fishing sessions but I often wonder if I started my sessions at night instead of at dawn whether the results would be different. I have long been of the belief that on some occasions when you have chosen the right spot, you can catch some of the resident fish within a short time of starting, whether it be in daylight or darkness. If this is the case then my records are rather misleading as I rarely start fishing at night. It may also be worth stating that on many of my 50 hour sessions where I have remained in the same swim, the catch rate starts well and then drops off as the session progresses, which indicates over-fishing a particular area.

There are some waters, however, where night fishing is good from dark till around midnight, while on others just before dawn is best. In some cases there is no apparent reason for this – more carp get caught at night throughout the whole season regardless of weather conditions or angling pressure. In other cases there appear to be definite reasons for this; either night fishing is banned or the water accommodates far more anglers in the daytime than at night. This situation does not, of course, guarantee the water to be a better proposition at night for I know many waters which are 'hammered' in the daytime yet still the carp prefer to feed at these times. On other waters margin fishing is sometimes better at night. This, I believe, is mainly due to anglers making their presence obvious to the carp even when they have gone to the trouble of being quiet and less conspicuous. I am certain that carp keep away from marginal areas that have anglers lines drooping across them, but when the light fades the fish become less aware of the lines, probably because they cannot see them, and visit the margins more often. In other cases, margin fishing improves at night because the carp visit the margins to clear up all the baits thrown in by departing day anglers.

We are constantly told that weeds give off gases during the night which the fish find unpleasant and so move to unaffected areas. I have not found this to be so and it is certainly not uncommon to find, and catch, fish from weedy areas at night. One movement which may occur frequently during the night is from areas of sunken trees, which presumably harbour little food, to other areas of the lake. This is most common on the type of water where carp spend all day among these 'holding areas' apparently doing nothing in particular.

Use of Bait

First of all, you must decide exactly what type of bait you are going to use and be prepared to give it a fair trial. My own way of doing this may be different from the methods chosen by others; since I only want to catch carp, and I prefer these to be big carp, I use very hard boiled baits about half an inch in diameter on most waters. In spite of this I very rarely catch small carp, and in most waters I seldom catch carp of under ten pounds. For example, on two well known waters I fished recently I caught only doubles and 20s while other anglers who fished the same waters had quite a number of singles with their doubles. I am convinced this is because of the rock hard baits I choose, which not only keep me from catching other species, but which also don't seem to be taken by the smaller carp. In most cases I tend to select my baits regardless of what other anglers are using or have used, but I do relate my choice to the type of water I am going to fish. In a hungry water one can get away with almost any bait; in a richer water I choose baits that I know to be readily acceptable to the fish, such as those based on Munchies and other pet foods. I also prefer to use natural type flavours, rather than artificial, chemical flavours. Whether to select high protein or other types of baits is discussed in the bait section.

I rarely use soft paste baits, except for stalking, because they are taken so readily by other species and small carp. The reader may wonder why my boiled baits are so small; the reason for this is that I like to be different from other anglers, most of whom use either large boiled baits or multiple baits. I have found that in being different, it is best to have smaller rather than larger baits, as it seems to be the texture and hardness of the baits that puts off the small fish, rather than their size.

In one very large lake which contains only a small number of large carp, with no other species, I do use soft pastes as I think that carp may actually prefer them to the harder baits, and here there is no danger of being troubled by small carp or unwanted species. On this type of water I might also use a multiple, but since I believe that paste baits made into small pieces and used like a multiple are better than most peas, beans and seeds, I will take the trouble to roll the bait into tiny pieces and fish them as a multiple.

I don't use multiple baits generally, but if I am going to choose them I would not use one of a similar size and type to anything already being used. For instance, I would rather not use a seed bait, even of a different type, if a seed was already being used, nor would I use another type of bean if a similar bean was already being used on the water. In addition, I prefer to change to a different multiple if the fish appear to 'go off' the one I am using, rather than to dye or flavour one of the same type.

Where fish seem to spend a lot of time at or near the surface, or where floaters or suspended baits have not been used, these baits might well be your first choice. On one well-known water I was often told for two years that the fish could not be taken on floaters. In spite of this I eventually decided to try floaters and had seven doubles the first time I used them!

If you want to catch as many carp as possible, but are not too worried about their size, or you don't mind catching fish of other species, then a paste or multiple will probably be best. If this is the way you want to choose your baits, then try to find out what the carp are caught on, and use a similar bait, but make improvements to it such as a different bait colour, size or flavour, or a different amount of pre-baiting in a different area at the lake. If this fails, try something totally different. On some waters it is common to see many anglers use the same type of baits; here a contrasting bait or method may well succeed. For example, where everyone is using multiples at close range, a boiled bait fished much further out will often bring quick results.

If you want to concentrate on the bigger fish as I do, then hard boiled baits are definitely best. Although bites may be few and far between it pays to stick it out. Beginners may find this boring and prefer to get more action by using paste or multiples which will tempt a wider range of fish. It will soon become apparent that the more a swim is disturbed, the less chance there is of tempting a bigger fish and as already mentioned it will eventually pay to concentrate on one method in order to get the quality fish.

Once a bait has been chosen you will need to decide whether to pre-bait or not. It may surprise some anglers when they see that I would suggest there are times when pre-baiting is completely unnecessary; indeed, for many anglers, pre-baiting has become a sort of 'fashion'.

As I have said elsewhere I very rarely pre-bait, but in some cases it may be necessary. In a hungry, heavily fished water where many others are putting in large quantities of baits it is probably a waste of time to pre-bait, as the fish are likely to accept any good bait. If the baits are being taken by water birds and species other than carp you may also be wasting the baits, although in this case you might get through to the fish if you put in a very large number. It is worth remembering that very few baits last more than 24 hours or so on the bottom of a lake, for they start to break down and will dissolve or be eaten by small fish. Baits that are likely to stay intact for longer than this are potatoes and some multiple baits such as peanuts and tiger nuts.

It is impossible to make rules about the number of baits to be introduced or the frequency of pre-baiting, as this depends on the number of fish present, the type of water, and the amount of pre-baiting being done by others. If there are only a few carp, and no other fish, you won't need many baits. In one instance I know of a five acre water containing about 200 carp, 50 of which were doubles, was baited for the first time with trout pellets. No other anglers were pre-baiting. 400 TP baits were put in two or three times a week for about three weeks before the season started; five carp were caught on the first trip, and over 60 doubles were taken from the lake by two anglers during the season, while others using other baits had almost nothing.

It is not just a question of putting the baits in. Many things need to be taken into consideration, such as the feeding times if you can find out when they are, the number of carp, the other species present, the feeding areas, and any special rules and restrictions applicable to the water. In some waters other species such as tench and roach may take the baits during the day, so you are only helping to get them feeding on the bait if you bait up in daylight. In this case, put the baits in only after dark, and night fish, and you will have more chance with the carp. Alternatively, make sure your baits cannot be taken by other species by using hard boiled baits or similar. It is important to pre-bait with good quality materials, and to keep this the same quality, and the baits the same size as those you are going to use as hook baits. In hungry waters where HP baits are not being used the protein value of the bait is likely to matter less, and I rarely consider the HP value of my baits at any time, preferring to include a blend of individual ingredients each of which are liked by the carp. If others are using HP or HNV baits successfully in a water, it may well be best to pre-bait with baits of this type.

Where you know that other groups of anglers are pre-baiting with enormous quantities of HP or HNV baits, it is better not to compete with them. What usually happens in these instances is that the fish start to mouth the baits and most of the takes will only be twitches, and your baits will only make matters worse. I have found in these situations that it is best to rely on your angling ability without pre-baiting, and to use a good quality bait of your own in which you have confidence.

In very small waters of two acres or less you can bait up the whole of the water. In waters of from two acres to six acres or so I would suggest baiting up most of the lake where fish are likely to feed, but to concentrate much of the bait in selected feeding areas in which you can fish, while in waters much bigger than this it is impracticable to bait-up large areas, and it is best to concentrate your efforts only on the selected swims. If the baits are small, such as multiples, it is generally better to put more in, but it is quite impossible to suggest quantities. In mixed fisheries many multiple baits are taken by quickly by roach, tench and other species, and much of the bait may be wasted in waters of this type.

Not to be confused with pre-baiting, groundbaiting is carried out at the start and during a fishing session. When using paste or boiled baits I normally put in about ten baits near each hookbait, but not too close to them. This then encourages fish to search for food in the vicinity of the hookbait. It is impossible to say how many baits should be put in, as this depends on so many factors such as amounts of feeding fish likely to be in the area, weather conditions, feeding times, and other fish activity. I always try to imagine just how many fish might be in the area, and gauge my groundbaiting accordingly. After hooking or losing a fish I rebait with a similar number of baits on the theory that the odds are against it being my hookbait which was taken first. If I am getting twitches I don't put in any more free offerings as I believe that the fish have probably mouthed several pieces and are already suspicious of the hook bait. If the twitches are followed by at least half an hour of inactivity I will consider putting some more baits in but not if twitches are continuing, as the fish may be taking some of the free offerings and too many may fill them up and make it less likely that they will take the hook bait. On many waters fish will continue feeding while baits are being thrown in, but I do know of two places where the carp will leave the area immediately; you can only find out if this happens by trial and error.

When groundbaiting while fishing with multiple baits, then little and often is best but I still apply the same rules as already mentioned. It is usually better to spread the baits out a little, because if you overbait, especially in a limited area, the fish may become overconfident and much twitching and possible bite-offs may occur. Rigs are very important with this type of fishing and details of suggested methods and rigs will be found later in this section.

To bait up at very long range with boiled baits, I use an American hunting slingshot type catapult. This puts my small baits out to a distance of about 80 yards. Soft paste baits can be placed on the tip of an old stiff rod, preferably with the tip ring removed, and cast out at least the same distance as the boiled baits, although not with much accuracy. To bait up with multiple baits at long range a floating bait dropper can be used. When this cylindrical object is cast out the dropper turns over due to a polystyrene block fitted on its bottom end and the baits fall to the bottom.

Baiting up to a range of about 50 yards is possible with these multiple bait droppers although they require a very powerful rod to cast them. One of my favourite methods of baiting at long range with multiples is to use a short strip of PVA with the baits threaded onto it by means of a large needle. This is then attached to the terminal tackle and cast as usual.

Presentation of Bait

In many ways, I consider this to be the most important section in the book, following, of course, fish location. Prior to 1978, when Len Middleton and I invented the revolutionary 'hair rig', there had been very few developments in rigs and methods of presenting the bait, yet I consider these far more important than baits. In the heavily fished carp waters of today many of the fish have learned the difference between free offerings and hook baits, so we need to start thinking out new and sometimes unconventional methods of presentation. I am firmly convinced that this aspect of carp fishing will change radically in the next few years. My experience has led me to believe that the biggest problem today is to prevent carp from discovering that the bait is attached not to a hook, which they cannot recognise, but to any normal type of line used by the carp angler. While in daylight carp are occasionally frightened off by the sight of the line, in most cases they reject a bait because they feel the line across their lips as they mouth it.

There are a large number of actual methods which can be used to present a bait. Since most of my fishing is done in hard fished waters, and for big fish, I tend to use unusual rigs all the time, but I will start by listing some of the standard rigs.

STANDARD LINK LEDGER RIG

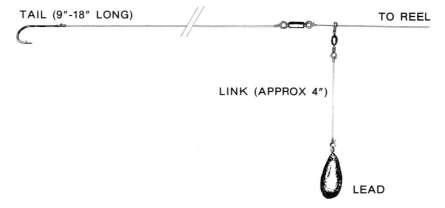

TAIL (9″-18″ LONG)   TO REEL

LINK (APPROX 4″)

LEAD

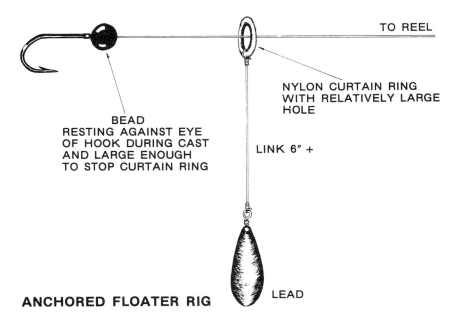

TO REEL

NYLON CURTAIN RING
WITH RELATIVELY LARGE
HOLE

BEAD
RESTING AGAINST EYE
OF HOOK DURING CAST
AND LARGE ENOUGH
TO STOP CURTAIN RING

LINK 6″ +

ANCHORED FLOATER RIG   LEAD

a) *Standard Rigs.* When using large, heavy baits, or at very short range, freelining can be used, and in this case only the hook and bait is attached to the line. Personally, I do not favour this type of fishing as it does not properly indicate an immediate pick-up of the bait or a fish picking up a bait and swimming towards the angler. Today most carp fishing is carried out by some form of ledgering, the most popular rig being a link ledger type. I don't use plastic ledger stops, and my stop is a small Berkley swivel, which is much stronger than an ordinary swivel, tied to the end of the hook length (tail) which can be from nine to 18 inches in length. The weight, usually an Arlesey bomb or pear lead, is tied to about four inches of line, to which another swivel is tied. The reel line is then threaded through this swivel so that it slides on the line. The end of the reel line is then tied to the swivel end of the hook link.

I would use this type of rig if the bottom of the lake was soft, hence the purpose of the lead link. In the very soft silt, the lead link should be longer to allow for the weight sinking into the silt, and this also applies in soft bottom weed, such as silk weed. With all standard type rigs I mount the baits in such a way that the point, barb and about half the bend of the hook is completely exposed. Anglers using hard baits but who bury their hooks inside the bait should ensure that they can strike through it or the fish may not be hooked.

Float fishing for carp is not as popular as it used to be but it can be a useful method in certain circumstances. Only one rod can be used properly and the eyestrain is considerable if you are fishing for long periods. It is often argued that the float will register even the smallest take but I feel far more confident, however short the range, using the more effective ledgering tactics of today. If you do wish to float fish for carp any standard float fishing methods can be used.

For fishing suspended bait, a conventional ledger rig can be used, but with a longer tail so that the floater rises in the water, to the desired height above the bottom.

Floaters can be anchored to prevent them from drifting in the wind, and for this I use the following method; a small plastic curtain ring is tied to a length of line, and the other end is attached to the weight. The length of this link varies from about six inches to a foot, depending on how soft the bottom is. When fishing over tall weed I use a long link and in some cases a small piece of sliding balsa or cork is necessary to keep the curtain ring above the weed. The reel line is then threaded through the ring and this is followed by a bead big enough to prevent the ring from sliding over the eye of the hook. The hook is then tied on, and the bead will rest against the hook knot.

b) *Unusual Rigs* In many of the hard fished lakes of today, and certainly in nearly all of those in which I fish, the carp have become so wary of baits that they are continually taking the baits into their mouths, but not moving off with them. This produces twitch bites and short snatches which are often too fast to be struck. On mixed fisheries, of course, not all takes are produced by carp, and some others may be line bites. Only experience will enable the angler to decide which missed takes are line bites, but if this is happening frequently try using one unbaited rod, and if you are still getting takes then obviously they must be line bites. Line bites are more common when fishing at long range and also in shallow water. If you are sure that the fish are actually taking the bait into their mouths, yet you are unable to hook them on the strike, because they are wary of the bait or tackle, the answer is the bolt rig, but if you feel sure that the carp are differentiating between free offerings and the hook bait, and few bites are experienced, then the answer is the 'hair' rig.

The purpose of the bolt rig is to enable the fish to feel resistance from the lead, or to prick itself, and in either case this should make it bolt. There are two ways of fishing the bolt rig set up; the lead, which should be a minimum of one and a half ounces, can be fixed or, alternatively, a running lead can be used but with the line pulled tight and fitted into the

BOLT RIG

(Also can be used as a conventional multiple bait rig when groundbaiting
in tight area.)

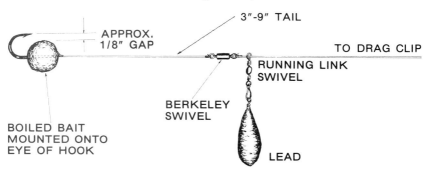

3″-9″ TAIL

APPROX.
1/8″ GAP

TO DRAG CLIP

RUNNING LINK
SWIVEL

BERKELEY
SWIVEL

BOILED BAIT
MOUNTED ONTO
EYE OF HOOK

LEAD

drag clip on the rod as shown in the diagram. When using a running lead I have found it best to mount the weight directly onto the line by means of a link swivel. This is then stopped by a Berkeley swivel tied into the line about six inches only from the hook. If this is not successful try varying the hook link from three to nine inches. If you lose fish, or catch one with the hook just outside the mouth, the hook link is too short, or the bait is mounted incorrectly. This is where the gap (shown in the diagram) is too large, so the fish will be pricked too soon. The mounting of the bait when using a bolt rig is vital. The most suitable bait is a small, hard boiled bait and it must be mounted on the shank of the hook, with the point, bend and barb exposed. If the hook is hidden in the bait you are wasting your time. As a guide, the inside of the bait should come to about an eighth of an inch

DRAG CLIP

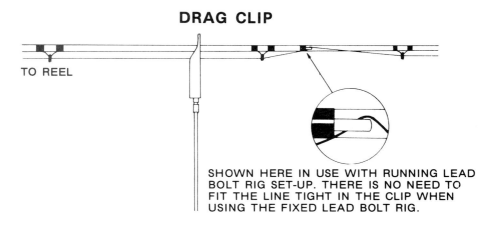

TO REEL

SHOWN HERE IN USE WITH RUNNING LEAD
BOLT RIG SET-UP. THERE IS NO NEED TO
FIT THE LINE TIGHT IN THE CLIP WHEN
USING THE FIXED LEAD BOLT RIG.

short of an imaginary line drawn from the point of the hook parallel with the hook shank. The finer adjustment of this gap (and the length of the tail) takes place during the fishing session.

If you are getting any sort of takes other than runs then the method is not working because the link is too long or the gap is too small. For this method it is better to use a sharp hook with a straight point rather than one with a turned in point. This rig is particularly useful when the carp are sucking in and expelling the bait very rapidly, as they often do with boiled baits, but it works in many other situations, although there will obviously be times when it will not work at all. It is worth remembering that the rig is only for use when the fish are very cautious, and should not be used in waters where confident takes are normally experienced, as it may soon spoil the fishing by unnecessarily scaring the carp. I keep the rods low to the ground and have the bail arms open at all times, as the runs are so fast whe using bolt rigs. Tangle-free bite indicators are essential because of these fast takes.

Nowadays I normally fish the bolt rig with a fixed lead and I make a point of not fitting the line tight into the drag clip like many anglers do automatically. There is no need to use drag clips when fishing a fixed lead set-up, even at long range (unless you're using Optonics, in which case you should not let an item of tackle dictate the use of clips; only the actual fishing situation should signify this), as the fixed lead does all the scaring that's needed, and what's going to happen will have already taken place before any indication is seen at the angler's end. In fact using a drag clip in these circumstances is detrimental and will cost you fish for there are many occasions when the fish will pick the lead up and move towards you. If the line is tight in the drag clip when this occurs the run will be missed unless you happen to be looking at it all the time, which of course is impossible. However, when no drag clip is used the sheer resistance of the line in the water is enough to set the buzzer off, even when the fish is moving towards you.

There are circumstances when I do not use a fixed lead with the bolt rig and this is when I'm fishing against snags or among weed beds. In these situations I use a heavy running lead (usually 2ozs) but fish with the line very tight in the drag clip – so tight that the rod tip stays bent all the time! A heavy lead is essential, otherwise runs that come towards you may result in a light lead being dragged along rather than the line being pulled out of the clip. The reason I fish 'running lead/tight in the clip' in preference to 'fixed lead/not in the clip' in these circumstances is because a fixed lead is a distinct disadvantage when a fish goes through a weedbed or some sunken branches. When the lead is fixed it invariably gets caught up and the hook link is then subjected to much abuse as the fish struggles for freedom. When the lead is running, the fish can still gain line despite the lead being caught up and it is then often possible to ease the fish back to the lead and eventually get it free again.

One of the main reasons why the bolt rig is not used extensively is because many anglers do not practise it enough when the time is right and hence have little confidence in it. A large hook must be used in relation to the bait size – I use a size 2 for a boilie of about ⅜″ diameter or a 1/0 for a bait of ½″ diameter. The hook should have a long straight point and not be off-set. The Au Lion d'Or is not suitable in this case; I use Sealey hooks model number 1715B but these are very difficult to obtain nowadays. However, Partridge of Redditch manufacture two models which fit the bill. As I mentioned in my chapter in Peter Mohan's book 'Basic Carp Fishing', one normally has to make various adjustments until every indication is a run and these are one, or all, of the following: length of tail, 'proudness' of the hook, use of line tight in drag clip or not, and the lead fixed or running. An ideal length hooklink to start off with is 6″ – 9″ with the lead fixed as shown in the following diagram, although there are many other ways of doing this.

For those who prefer not to use bolt rigs and in cases where bite-offs are occurring, I use what I call a 'frightener' on the line. This is a piece of stiff plastic tubing about one eighth of an inch in diameter and about an inch and a half in length. This threaded onto the line about four inches from the hook, and is prevented from sliding by pushing a matchstick into it, the male part of a plastic ledger stop, or a cocktail stick. As the bait is being passed back to the throat teeth, the frightener enters the mouth and alarms the fish, which bolts and is hooked. Other ways of preventing bite-offs are the use of very heavy, stiff nylon, or thin wire.

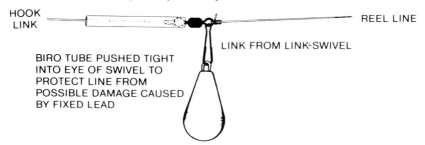

HOOK LINK

REEL LINE

LINK FROM LINK-SWIVEL

BIRO TUBE PUSHED TIGHT INTO EYE OF SWIVEL TO PROTECT LINE FROM POSSIBLE DAMAGE CAUSED BY FIXED LEAD

METHOD OF PERMANENTLY ATTACHING FIXED LEADS
(See Cassien section for alternatives)

Another problem which is becoming more and more common on hard fished waters is the ability of carp to learn to differentiate between free offerings and the hookbaits. Carp can be observed clearing up every piece of bait in the swim except the one with the hook in it, and I am sure that this will become even more prevalent as the fish are caught more often. In this case, the solution is usually the use of a version of the 'hair' rig and the following story explains exactly how this rig was invented.

By the summer of 1978 my fishing partners Len Middleton, Keith Gillings and I had become aware that on some waters carp were clearing up the free offerings, but were wary of the hook bait. I then decided to build a large tank in the sitting room of my house which we could use for experiments. The tank was stocked with carp of two to three pounds and I started off by testing baits in their natural forms. However, this proved to be of little value because the fish tended to eat all the baits that were dropped in and showed no preferences. So, from then on the baits were liquidised and fed into the gravel by means of a hidden pipe so that the carp were unaware of their introduction. Baits that caused natural stimulation could then be noted for they would have to search for them in the gravel and it would then be possible to see if there was any true reaction. I then tested various amino acids and at this point I felt that I had done all the bait testing possible. (The results of the amino acid tests can be seen in the bait section.)

Len and I then decided that we should have a look at the reaction of the carp in the tank to tackle. However, before doing so I felt it was necessary to hook each fish on line at least twice, and to play them and lift them out of the water in the same way as in a lake. Since Len lived half an hour's drive away from my house, and had no transport, I started to pick him up and take him home in my car. I made this one hour trip twice a night, many times collecting him at 6 pm and often not getting back from taking home until 3 am – sometimes we even stayed up all night testing! As soon as I decided the fish were prepared we started our tests.

When foods such as sweet corn were put into the tank, and a baited hook was introduced among the free offerings, the free baits would be eaten by the carp, but the baited hook was rarely taken and was always left until last if it was taken at all. Realising that this was probably because of the weight of the hook, I counteracted the hook's weight by attaching a small piece of polystyrene to the hook, so that the hooked bait was equal in weight to a free offering. This was done by putting the hook through different sizes of pieces of polystyrene until it appeared that the hook was weightless, when it remained suspended in mid-water. We then intro-

FRIGHTENER

(FOR USE WITH STANDARD RIGS OR FREELINING WHEN BITE-OFFS ARE EXPECTED OR OCCUR)

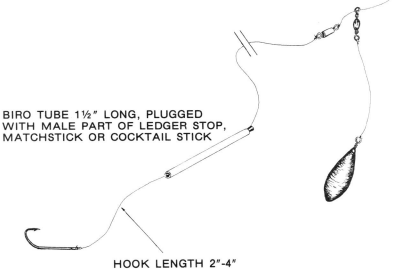

BIRO TUBE 1½" LONG, PLUGGED
WITH MALE PART OF LEDGER STOP,
MATCHSTICK OR COCKTAIL STICK

HOOK LENGTH 2"-4"

duced this 'balanced' hook with a bait attached, along with a handful of sweet corn, and the hookbait was taken at random by the fish on a number of tests and was obviously not deliberately left until last. This proved our belief that carp were not frightened of a hook; it was the *effect* that the hook had on the bait or the stiffness of the line that frightened them. Another interesting observation that was made at this stage was that the carp would eject the hook and polystyrene after chewing and removing the bait, on every occasion that the bait was picked up. We repeated this experiment many times with the same result. We then tied a hook to a piece of six pound line, put on a piece of sweetcorn, and dropped this into the tank wth the usual free offerings around it. Amazingly, the carp were obviously frightened of the line – so much so that they stayed right up at one end of the tank to begin with, well away from the line. It took about half an hour for them to feed, very cautiously, on the free offerings. On two occasions, but only after a long period, different carp took the hookbait into their mouths, but each time it was immediately ejected with great rapidity and each time the fish concerned shot off to the other end of the tank followed by the other carp.

BALANCED HOOKBAIT
(FOR USE WITH LIGHT BAITS AND LARGE HOOKS)

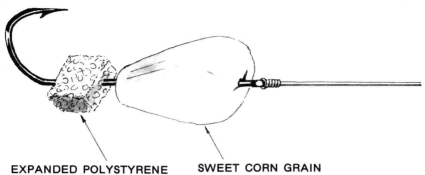

EXPANDED POLYSTYRENE   SWEET CORN GRAIN

Eventually all the grains of corn had been eaten *except* the one with the hook and line attached, which we left in the tank until morning, when it was still not eaten. Again, this test was repeated many times, but the baited tackle was rarely taken, and when it was it was only taken after many rejections, which would have produced the sort of twitches we had been having while fishing or no indication at all.

It was now clear that we had proved that the main problem was the line as we had suspected, and that we would now have to try to find some method by which the carp would no longer feel the line.

Now the hard work really started. Fortunately, the winter of 1978 was very unpleasant with most lakes being frozen for a considerable period and we had time to continue our tests several times a week for the next few months. We started by tying hooks to many different materials which we thought might be strong enough to land a carp, and which they might not be able to associate with danger. We used wools, cotton, string, wire, chain, braided nylon and many others, but even at the end of several months nothing seemed to work any better than the six pound nylon. The carp were still wary of any hook which was attached to any form of line.

At this stage I was beginning to wonder whether all the hundreds of miles collecting Len and all the many hours we had spent experimenting were going to be worthwhile. I estimate that we had spent 300 hours on tank tests and in addition to this I'd been at the driving wheel, to Len's house and back, for an incredible 80 hours!

We had discussed at length what we wanted to achieve, which was to get the carp to suck in baits thinking that they were free offerings. Our observations made us realise that carp take in the bait, then if they are not suspicious of it, they pass it back to the pharyngeal teeth for chewing. If they could do this without feeling the line over their lips, they would take the bait confidently as if it was a free offering. We were determined to succeed, and during the nights when Len was unable to come I continued to experiment alone.

We had both thought up and suggested dozens of ideas, one of which was attaching the bait to the hook by tying it on, with the bait not actually on the hook. This was a suggestion of Len's and when the hair rig finally evolved from this idea, both of us, at that time, automatically considered this a joint invention because we had done so much work on it, just as we would have considered it a joint invention had one of my suggestions solved the problem.

Since the attachment to the bait had to be much thinner and softer than six pound line, and as there was no really fine line in the house, Len pulled a hair from his head, tied one end carefully round a grain of sweetcorn and the other end to the bend of the hook and this was then lowered into the water. The distance from the bait to the hook was a little over an inch. The carp started to feed and eventually one picked up the bait on the hair in the normal way, and took it into its mouth without appearing to be suspicious. The hook and line followed. The carp then started to back away, and after a while ejected the bait and the hook, but had we been fishing we should easily have had time to strike.

We repeated this experiment also many times, and always with the same result – the carp treated baits on the 'hair' rig as they would have treated a free offering and the main line was always taken well into the mouth. The hair rig was born.

It must be clear from this account that we were both equally concerned with the development of the hair rig from the start, even though the initial tests took place at my home in my tank, and that those who have attributed the invention to one or other of us were incorrect.

It has been written that others were involved in the initial invention stage of the hair, but this was not so. We did invite our good friend and fishing companion Keith Gillings to take part, but because of work commitments he couldn't be involved in all of the tests. However, Keith did intend to help us with the trials under actual fishing conditions and I must emphasise that no-one else took part in the actual fishing trials. Between the three of us we emphatically agreed to tell no-one else about the rig.

Obviously, the most important point was to work out the correct distance between the centre of the bait and the hook. As the fish in the tank were relatively small we came to the conclusion that although this rig worked in the tank we should be unable to discover the correct length for the hair until we did tests under proper fishing conditions in lakes. We also needed to test a carrier rig for the method.

Now that the tank tests were finished we eagerly awaited the start of the '79 season but agreed not to use the rig until the opportunity arose. I was fishing crowded waters in June, so was unable to experiment and I first used the rig in July at Duncan Kay's water in Northamptonshire. I especially moved to a quiet part of the lake and put the hair rig on just after dark using a peanut tied to a two and a half inch length of my wife's hair which I had brought in a tobacco tin! We were not sure exactly what lengh of hair would be best but I had measured the distance between the lips and throat teeth of a big double and found it to be six inches. At first we thought a hair length of about half this distance would be best. I had a 10½ pound mirror in the margins during the night, and this proved it would work. Unfortunately, the next day there were too many people about for me to use the method.

A few days later Len rang me to say that he had also used the rig and had taken three fish on it at Darenth, compared with none using conventional methods. Keith, who was with him, also had four fish on the hair, and two of them were 20 pounders.

For the first time we began to get excited about the method, which was obviously going to be a success. We discussed how we had used the method, and Len and I agreed to do a three day session together at Leisure Sport's Darenth venue the following week, using one rod each with the hair and the other without. It was very fiddly using the method at first because the human hairs kept breaking on the cast and we had to use PVA to take the shock of the cast. Thin PVA strips were tied to the bottom of the hooks and were then passed through the bait by means of a large needle. I got run after run, and eventually had eleven fish, all on the hair, with only twitches on the conventional set-up. It was on this session that I first suggested the use of smaller hooks after I had caught a few fish. I told Len that I was going to use size 6 Au Lion d'Ors as I thought they would go into the mouth more easily. This worked well, though at first I played the fish very gingerly as it was considered very bad practice to use such small hooks for big carp. Then I hooked a 17 pounder, which I purposely gave a lot of stick, and the hook held without any problem and I landed it from 40 yards in less than two minutes. This was the first big step to sorting out some of the problems of the method and our catch rate increased.

STANDARD 'HAIR' RIG

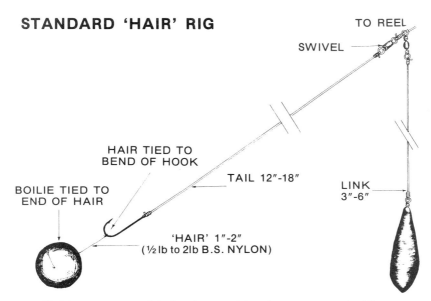

TO REEL

SWIVEL

HAIR TIED TO
BEND OF HOOK

TAIL 12"-18"

BOILIE TIED TO
END OF HAIR

LINK
3"-6"

'HAIR' 1"-2"
(½ lb to 2lb B.S. NYLON)

Keith was responsible for the next big advance we made. He suggested the use of light nylon, as used by match anglers, instead of human hair and PVA. Keith tried it and it worked perfectly – why we had never thought of this before I just don't know! Again our catch rate increased, using the one pound nylon.

We continued to fish hard throughout the summer and although Keith and Len concentrated most of their efforts on one water I fished a variety of lakes. Our results were quite startling at times and rarely did we blank using the hair rig. Often we fished the hair on one rod against another on conventional set-up but always we caught more on the hair. It worked on every water we tried, no matter whether we used boilies, pastes or multiples. Although we caught carp with the hair length from one to five inches, the ideal length varied from water to water but was always between 1" – 2½" and the rig seemed to work best on a standard-type ledger rig with a hook length of about 18 inches.

Boiled baits and multiples were attached by using the following method. The 'hair' was inserted into a needle and the needle was passed through the centre of the bait. The line was then pulled through and taken round the outside of the bait, where it was attached to itself by means of a slip knot. The other end of the hair was tied to the lower part of the bend of the hook, with great care being taken to get the correct distance between the hook and the bait.

A soft paste bait can be moulded round a small piece of edible substance, such as macaroni, which is attached to the bait end of the hair. We did try fixing the hook end of the hair to other parts of the hook, such as the eye, but the bend was found to be the best place. Tying up these hairs proved to be a fiddly job, especially in the dark, and I found it best to tie up about 15 before leaving for the water and place them in a tobacco tin ready for use.

By the time the winter had arrived Keith and Len had had their best seasons by far; at this stage Keith decided to stop carp fishing as he preferred to go shooting at this time of the year and I joined Len for the winter at Darenth.

I always thought hard about the set-up and I came to the conclusion that once the fish were running with the bait they would probably be unable to change the position of the hook because of the slight resistance set up by the terminal tackle, line and indicator, so that we might get better results by striking early. I suggested this to Len and we then agreed that I would strike my runs instantly in future, and he would delay his strikes. The instant strikes proved to be by far the most successful, catching many more fish than the delayed strikes used by Len. Until now we had been delaying our strikes for an agreed time of anything between five to thirty seconds, because we thought we would have to allow plenty of time for the hook to enter the mouth. This was very difficult as, for the past five years, we'd been hitting twitches as soon as possible. In fact, the only way I could stop myself striking too soon was to remove my reel handles and put them in my pocket! Then, each time a run occurred, I hurriedly spent the following 20 seconds fumbling, trying to fit the reel handles. As you can imagine I got some funny looks from the local anglers.

From November right through to the end of the season the weather remained very mild and this, together with the use of the hair, left me with what must be the best-ever winter results I shall ever have. In eighteen weeks fishing an average of 50 hours a week, I caught 84 doubles, of which 10 were over 20 pounds, plus a few singles. This brought my season's total up to 165 doubles which included two thirties and 17 twenties.

Len's results were nowhere near as good for the winter but this was not because of the hair; we later discovered the problem to be bait. Through November and December we both caught well using different baits but then our catches seemed to tail off a little. I'd been using a pilchard-flavoured Munchies boilie until our friend Geoff Kemp suggested I use

Keith Gillings with a nicely scaled fish weighing 26 pounds.

one of his baits. Geoff had been fishing the same water and had been getting a lot of action using his cream flavoured baits on a bolt rig set-up. As soon as I used Geoff's baits my catches picked up but Len's continued to decline using his original bait. This proved to us just how important baits can be despite the use of what was then a very effective rig.

But things were not all rosy that winter for we knew we had serious problems. We were catching lots of fish and whenever that happens in carp fishing it usually means trouble. Inevitably, other anglers want to know what you are doing and some will go to any lengths to find out, or get you thrown off the water. One day at Darenth I was just about to make a cast with my rod held behind me and the terminal tackle dangling, when I heard a rustling noise in the elderberry bush behind me. I lowered the rod and walked over to the bush to find a bailiff hiding in it! Somehow I don't think he wanted to check my permit. I learned later that this chap, along with some others, was spreading rumours about us stealing fish and I believe we very nearly got thrown out of the club. Besides all these minor problems that the hair had brought we had another serious setback. Because much of the fishing was at very long range it was necessary to use shock leaders, heavy leads and powerful rods, and occasionally our tackle would crack-off on the cast and land in the lake. This meant that any angler was likely to reel in the lost tackle and find a fine piece of nylon attached to the hook. We still wanted to keep the rig secret at this stage so I set about thinking of ways to overcome this. Eventually I came to the conclusion that the only positive way to ensure that the hair would not remain on the hook after a period in the water was to have a glue specially developed. I contacted a specialist company in the Midlands and told them exactly what I wanted: a glue that would attach a fine strand of nylon to metal, take a strain of at least one pound and remain at that strength for 12 hours in water after which time it should rapidly dissolve. I was informed that one of their adhesives used for attaching explosives to underwater objects was near to my requirements, and they set about producing the glue for me.

Unfortunately, the special glue, although perfect for the job, did not arrive until the close season by which time it was too late. A couple of anglers had reeled in our lost tackle, while others had spied on us when casting and were frantically trying to work it all out. Andy Little who had started fishing with Len towards the end of that winter got so near to guessing what it was that Len felt it fair to tell him. The following season, in 1980, Andy went on to make carp fishing history at Savay Lake using the hair.

Of course Andy was not the only angler to use the hair in 1980. A couple of Kent lads had discovered it at Darenth and it was now only a matter of time before the news spread through the carp angling 'grapevine'. Although the matter was now out of our hands we still agreed, during the 1980 close season, to keep it quiet as best we could. However, Len told me later in the season that he found it spoiling his fishing at Savay trying to hide the rig and that he had told several others who were fishing the lake. Until this time I hadn't told a soul, not even my closest of friends, but I completely understood the situation and agreed with Len that it was now right to tell everybody. Later, Len and I discussed the matter one day on the banks of Savay and we agreed that he would write an article about it and that I would mention it in this book, which I was writing at the time. However, before any of our writings were published, both Richard Walker and Arthur Clarke had written about our set-up.

In the meantime some fantastic catches of big carp were being made by other anglers using the hair rig, and our only regret is that we were not first to use the rig on other big fish waters. Having said that, Len, Keith and I did have our best-ever seasons so we've little to complain about.

Since then the hair rig has become so popular that it is now used with considerable success by the majority of specialist anglers in the country,

Ron Middleton with a magnificent 35¾ pound mirror.

BCSG member Dave Woods with his 36½ caught on floater from Silver End.

Kent angler Paul Regent,
with a mid-twenty common from Withy Pool.

This 31 pounder proves yet again that tiger nuts are a marvellous bait.

Catfish expert Bob Baldock with a Withy Pool common of 22 pounds.

A Savay 30¼ pounder caught from 'Alcatraz' at long range.

Cream RM30 boilies resulted in this terrific brace, weighing more than 60 pounds, from a very difficult water.

and there is no doubt that the rig represents one of the most significant technical advances in the history of angling.

Nowadays when I fish a 'new' water I know that there is a good chance that the hair rig has been used extensively by all and sundry, and if this is the case the first thing I do is to take note of the original position of the hookhold in the fish's mouth. If the fish is hooked on the outside of the lips, or you keep losing fish – they are 'falling off' for no apparent reason – then the rig is too sensitive. This means that the hook is not getting far enough into the mouth before the slack is taken up and some resistance is felt. If this is so I make the rig less sensitive by lengthening the hook length and/or the lead link. One point worth mentioning here is that a small adjustment on the lead link is equal to a much larger adjustment on the hook link, so for finer adjustments it is best to alter the hook link. In fact I rarely use a lead link at all nowadays. I try to use as short a hook link as possible which will give me a good hook hold – say one inch inside the mouth. Too long a hook link gives the fish too much freedom – the terminal tackle should tighten up quickly at the stage where the hook is far enough into the mouth. With too much freedom the fish can suck the bait in and eject it at will, giving no indication to the angler.

I prefer to keep the length of the hair between 1 to 1½ inches and then alter the 'carrier rig' as required. Some people are now shortening the hair in an attempt to get a deep hook hold to the extent that the value of the hair system is lost. I appreciate the fact that there are some advantages of a very short hair but it is worth remembering that the point of this rig is to give the fish confidence once it has picked the bait up; the fish will not have this confidence if it detects the hook close to the bait, or more probably, feels the stiffness of the line.

If there is any evidence to suggest that carp are clearing up the free offerings but not taking the hook bait, then the rig is not sensitive enough.

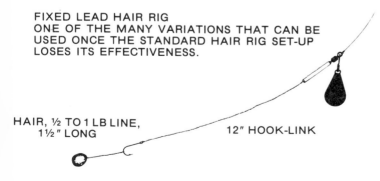

FIXED LEAD HAIR RIG
ONE OF THE MANY VARIATIONS THAT CAN BE
USED ONCE THE STANDARD HAIR RIG SET-UP
LOSES ITS EFFECTIVENESS.

HAIR, ½ TO 1 LB LINE,
1½" LONG

12" HOOK-LINK

RUNNING LEAD SET-UP WITH FIXED BACK STOP

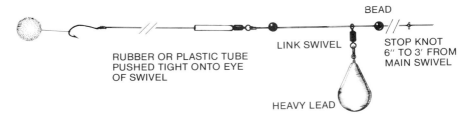

BEAD

LINK SWIVEL

STOP KNOT
6" TO 3' FROM
MAIN SWIVEL

RUBBER OR PLASTIC TUBE
PUSHED TIGHT ONTO EYE
OF SWIVEL

HEAVY LEAD

This is virtually a fixed lead rig except that the fish is allowed to take a certain amount of line (depending on distance stop is set from lead) before feeling the lead, thereby giving the fish more time to get the hook in its mouth. Do not clip up tight when using this rig as it defeats the object.

INDICATOR SET-UP FOR MEDIUM TO LONG RANGE FIXED LEAD TACTICS

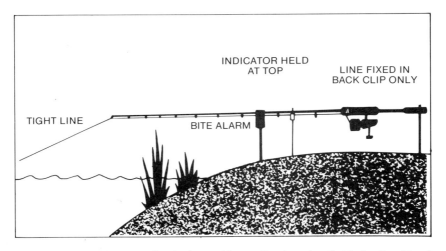

INDICATOR HELD
AT TOP

LINE FIXED IN
BACK CLIP ONLY

TIGHT LINE

BITE ALARM

The rod set-up shown earlier in the tackle section is not suitable for fixed lead (or back stop) fishing as a carp can easily move towards the angler, or sideways, taking the lead with it and not showing a lift on the indicator. By clipping the line tight, and with the indicator held up, all types of bite will show; if the fish moves away from the angler the line will pull out of the clip and if it moves towards the angler the indicator will drop. If a tight line between rod tip and rig is not desirable (fish are shy of mid-water lines) then it is better to clip up not so tight with indicator half-way up needle.

Once the calculations are correct, this system works very well – but as usual, the carp start to learn, and once more you may eventually be back to square one . . .

Now it is scare tactics instead of confidence tactics which are needed: you need a bolt-hair method! Since twitches are the first problem encountered the cure will now be the use of a fixed lead or drag clip which holds the line very tight to the lead. Resistance is then so great that either the fish prick themselves and bolt, or they become scared by the unaccustomed heavy resistance and go off at great speed giving the angler all he could ever wish for – a belting run. This will work well for a considerable time but then on some waters when using drag clips the fish start to become frightened of the tight line in the swim, especially when fishing at close to medium range. On waters where carp can be observed I have noticed this to be a common occurrence when using drag clips, so it is not unreasonable to assume that it happens more often than we imagine even in the more opaque waters. When I see this happening, or indeed when I suspect it, I have found it best to use a fixed lead and then after casting I pull several feet of line from the rod tip so that a slack line lies nicely on the bottom. The fish then enters the swim with confidence and the fixed lead set-up 'tricks' the carp that would not normally be hooked on the standard hair rig set-up. It should be remembered that this situation does not arise when fishing at long range because the last few yards of line near the terminal tackle will be lying on the bottom.

Although I have skipped through many stages in just a few paragraphs, in reality I have covered the progress of several seasons on many waters. Amazingly, though, on some of the southern waters which I fish, all these stages were surpassed in perhaps two seasons and a definite situation has been reached on the hard-fished waters – a situation which many other waters are heading for – when 95% of the anglers are all using the hair rig and fishing in exactly the same way and consequently are catching very little. I say 'consequently' because it is a certainty that if you become one

EFFECTIVE MULTIPLE BAIT RIG WITH BALANCED HOOK

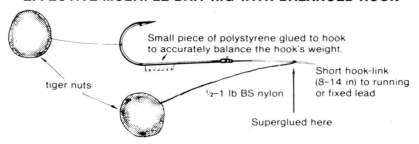

tiger nuts

Small piece of polystyrene glued to hook to accurately balance the hook's weight.

Short hook-link (8–14 in) to running or fixed lead

½–1 lb BS nylon

Superglued here

of the '95 percenters' you will end up with very ordinary results. On most of the waters I fish I do not automatically use the hair rig now simply because of the situation I have just described. The anglers fishing these waters seem convinced that the hair rig is God's gift to carp men, and won't use anything else, and the carp's job of differentiating between baits on the hair and free offerings is made easy because of the method's extensive use. Few anglers seem to accept the fact that a bait attached to a hair rig is still very different from a free offering. It should be appreciated that as soon as the fish moves the hair-mounted bait more than an inch, it acts completely differently from any free offering. While a few fish are still getting caught on these waters it is pathetically few considering the amount of hours being fished. Many anglers are oblivious to the fact that the fish are still continually mouthing the baits despite the obvious signs such as odd buzzes, short pulls, line falling slack at the rod tips and the free offerings being taken. Surely the most logical conclusion is to revert to using a bolt rig, but also to use your common sense, be flexible in your methods, and use the rigs which would seem likely to you to work, rather than copying what everyone else is doing.

Recently I have been fishing a great deal with multiple baits and have therefore been trying out all sorts of rigs. Presentation needs to be good once a multiple bait has been 'hammered' and I have found the following rig to be very effective on hard fished waters.

One bait (such as a tiger nut) is first tied further up the hooklink and is then pulled down until it hangs alongside the hook. A tiny dab of Superglue on the knot holds it in position for at least 24 hours and gives no real reduction in line strength. The second bait is then attached to the bend of the hook via the hair in the normal way. Prior to fishing, by trial and error methods, I glue a small piece of polystyrene to the hook as shown so that the hook is just about a 'sinker', i.e. so that it is *virtually* weightless in water. The use of two baits increases the chances of a fish picking up your hookbait among the hundreds of free offerings and the virtually weightless hook allows the hook baits to act more naturally. I have found the use of a fixed lead very effective with this presentation when fishing among the heavy carpet of free offerings. I believe the main reason why this rig is very effective is because it is more difficult for the fish to eject the baits and hook in comparison with the standard hair. With the standard hair set-up I have noticed from tank test observations that when the fish blows the boilie out, the hook automatically follows the same path, but this rig is completely unbalanced and therefore the hook tends to catch hold somewhere in the mouth rather than follow the flow of water with the bait.

POWER GUM RIG

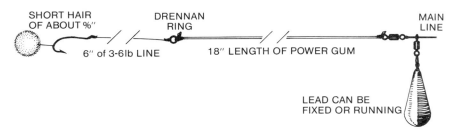

SHORT HAIR
OF ABOUT ⅜"

DRENNAN
RING

MAIN
LINE

6" of 3-6lb LINE

18" LENGTH OF POWER GUM

LEAD CAN BE
FIXED OR RUNNING

This rig must **never** be used in water where there is any weed or snags, nor should it be used by anglers who play their fish 'hard'. A weak hooklink of about 4lbs B.S. is used to overcome line shyness and this should be kept short (4"-6") to reduce the chances of it touching anything (such as stones) that would weaken it. Choice of hook is important as it must be small, sharp and as light in weight as possible, and I always use my own 'Kevin Maddocks Hair Rig Hooks', manufactured by Partridge of Reddich, as they are perfect for the job. I have always been reluctant to publish this rig because, in the 'wrong hands', fish could be lost quite easily, but since I invented it about 6 years ago one or two other people have mentioned it in print but have failed to describe its proper use. Therefore, I think the time is now right to describe it properly. It is a very good rig when all others have failed, but please be careful!

POWER GUM KNOT

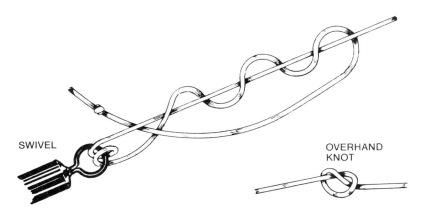

SWIVEL

OVERHAND
KNOT

Be careful when tying power gum as it is liable to slip. Tie an overhand knot in the end of line and pull it very tight. First attach the swivel by passing the gum twice through the eye, then use a three turn blood knot. Wet it and pull tight, allowing the knot to slip until the overhand knot pulls up against the main knot. This knot is very efficient and will never slip.

HAIR POSITIONS

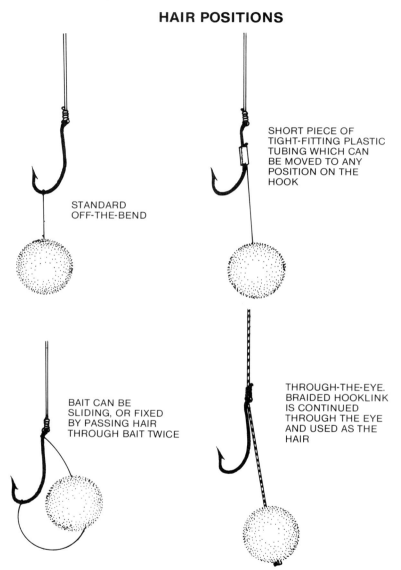

STANDARD
OFF-THE-BEND

SHORT PIECE OF
TIGHT-FITTING PLASTIC
TUBING WHICH CAN
BE MOVED TO ANY
POSITION ON THE
HOOK

BAIT CAN BE
SLIDING, OR FIXED
BY PASSING HAIR
THROUGH BAIT TWICE

THROUGH-THE-EYE.
BRAIDED HOOKLINK
IS CONTINUED
THROUGH THE EYE
AND USED AS THE
HAIR

The hair can be attached to the hook in any position and even now after using
the hair rig for many years I still favour the standard off-the-bend. I've not
found one position to be much better than another although this depends on
the water and what has been used there. Usually the best method of mounting
is one which the fish is not used to, so try all positions.

SLIDING HAIR

TIE WITH P.V.A. HERE

The object of this presentation is to give the fish complete confidence when first picking up the hook bait and to make it feel like a free-offering. On casting, the bait should be near the hook and the length of the hair, which is passed through the hook's eye, works best between 1"-3". Use in conjunction with a fairly long hooklink (18"-24") although this obviously depends on many 'local' factors.

STANDARD POP-UPS (SUSPENDED BOILIE)

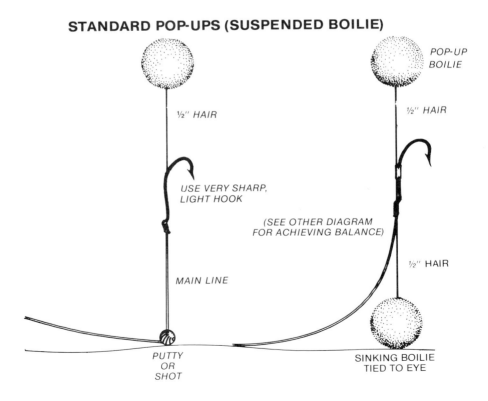

POP-UP
BOILIE

½" HAIR

½" HAIR

USE VERY SHARP,
LIGHT HOOK

(SEE OTHER DIAGRAM
FOR ACHIEVING BALANCE)

½" HAIR

MAIN LINE

PUTTY
OR
SHOT

SINKING BOILIE
TIED TO EYE

A standard suspended boilie (made to float by cooking in oven, grill or better still a microwave) can be fished singly as shown on the left using a small shot or piece of putty. Angler's putty is best for short to medium range fishing and only the amount needed to slowly sink the boilie should be used. The more time spent carefully balancing a pop-up, the more efficient the rig will be. Another method, shown on the right, is to use an ordinary boilie to hold the pop-up down, which again should be critically balanced. The easiest way to achieve this on the lakeside is to put one floating boilie and one sinking boilie on a needle and drop the lot into a cup or saucepan of water. By trial and error, using slightly different size boilies, you will be able to perfectly balance the two baits very quickly before mounting, and the weight of the needle is approximately equal to the hook's weight. (See diagram.)

BALANCING TWO BOILIES AT LAKESIDE
BEFORE MOUNTING

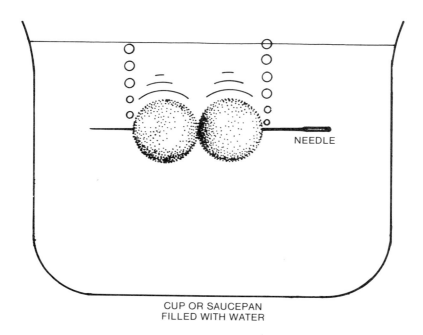

NEEDLE

CUP OR SAUCEPAN
FILLED WITH WATER

With one floater and one sinker on the needle the whole lot, if balanced correctly, should sink very slowly. Once this is achieved the baits can then be mounted on the rig. The needle is approximately equal in weight to a hook. This method is very accurate and will save time mucking about dropping mounted baits in the margins several times.

BUOYANT HOOK RIGS

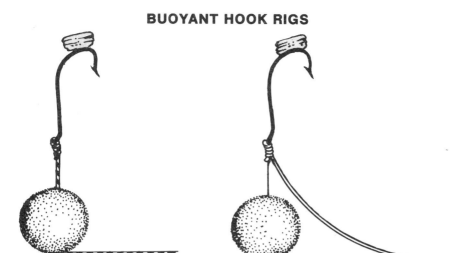

The idea behind this presentation is to make the carp suck the hook in first. Two things are very important here; the choice of hook, and relationship between size of bait and hook. Firstly, use as light a hook as you can safely get away with thereby allowing the use of only a small piece of cork or polystyrene – the larger the hook and the greater its buoyancy aid the more easily it is detected by the carp. Secondly, the width across the hook's gape **must** only be slightly less than the diameter of the bait because the carp normally adjust their suck and mouth opening according to bait size. The drawing on the left shows the set-up using a braided Dacron hooklink. An alternative, using a hair of ½″-¾″ long and tied to the hook's eye, is shown on the right.

ANTI-TANGLE DACRON RIG

BEAD

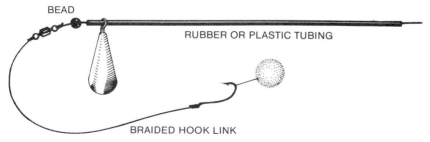

RUBBER OR PLASTIC TUBING

BRAIDED HOOK LINK

Dacron hook links are susceptible to tangling and this can be overcome by using a length of plastic or rubber tubing on the main line above the swivel. The tubing **must** be a little longer than the hook link and the eye of the lead should fit tight onto the tubing. Try to avoid using a link swivel on the lead as this can encourage tangles.

STRINGER RIG

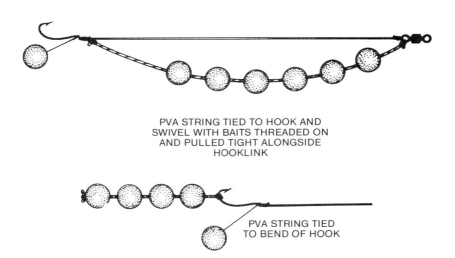

PVA STRING TIED TO HOOK AND
SWIVEL WITH BAITS THREADED ON
AND PULLED TIGHT ALONGSIDE
HOOKLINK

PVA STRING TIED
TO BEND OF HOOK

A stringer rig is ideal for fishing at range when only a few free offerings are
required very near the hookbait such as when fishing among gravel bars when
the tackle is pulled back to a particular 'hot' spot.

There is no doubt that in many hard fished carp waters today the fish
are very wary of rigs which are heavily used. Modern carp fishing is not as
super-efficient as many anglers think: if we were able to see what is
actually happening it would soon be found that carp are investigating and
rejecting the bait and hook many times without any indications that this is
occurring. It is best, therefore, to try a different type of rig from these
commonly used at the water, rather than copying others.

Many hooked carp undoubtedly adjust their feeding methods to the
rigs used. Some anglers claim to have invented foolproof anti-eject rigs,
but this is simply not possible. It would be a sad day for carp fishing if this
did occur, as, if a rig was genuinely anti-eject, every fish which took a bait
would inevitably get hooked. Naturally we should strive to try to improve
rigs, but they will never be perfect.

Some of the better rigs are illustrated, and some have never been
published before, but the good carp angler will experiment with variations,
as the rigs may have been previously used on the waters fished.

Other unusual methods used by carp anglers include the use of a fledger, which is a wooden ledger made so that it sinks only very slowly. This is used to rest on top of soft weed. You can also use a piece of cork which fits over the lead link, and which rises up the link to the swivel in order to keep the line above weed. A similar effect is achieved by a ledger stick, which is a straw-shaped piece of wood which fits over the line of the lead link and which, by standing erect in the water, has the same effect as the cork.

PVA (poly vinyl alcohol) has a number of uses, as it dissolves in water. I used a heavy bomb at Ashlea to get through the thick, underwater lily leaves (known as cabbages) and tied the terminal tackle into a knot using PVA strip so that the hook and bomb went through the heavy weed as one and came to rest on the weed-free bottom under the lilies. Another use for PVA strip is to fish at long range with a light bait, using stones tied up in a PVA strip to assist with casting. Once the PVA dissolves, there are then no weights on the line.

I have mentioned on several occasions that I have not found the use of a fixed lead an advantage over alternative methods for conventional fishing. There is, however, one application where I have found its use invaluable. While fishing in shallow water at long range among gravel bars the fish tend to 'kite' when hooked and this often results in the lead catching up on the snags. The angler's line is then running in a direction from the rod tip to the snag, while the fish is elsewhere and out of control. I reasoned that if the lead could be kept near the fish's head in such situations the problem would be solved – hence the successful use of a fixed lead.

On many waters, large floating baits don't now catch fish, so small multiple floaters are used. It is not easy to cast these very light baits without some type of controller on the line. The first type of controller I heard of was a small Arlesey bomb set into polystyrene to make it float. This can be cast great distances. Any type of weighted float will serve as a casting weight and bite indicator; these can be made of wood or some form of plastic. I use a piece of white peacock quill with a hole drilled into one end of it. Into this I insert a piece of welding rod in order to make it self-cocking. I fix this into the quill with Araldite. This is attached to the line by means of a single float ring. This is a good casting weight and also an excellent indicator; it takes very little to pull it under and will easily detach itself should it become snagged.

Mounting single multiple floaters is not easy, as the weight of the hook causes many of the cat food floaters to sink. A small piece of polystyrene

FLOATING MULTIPLE BAIT RIGS

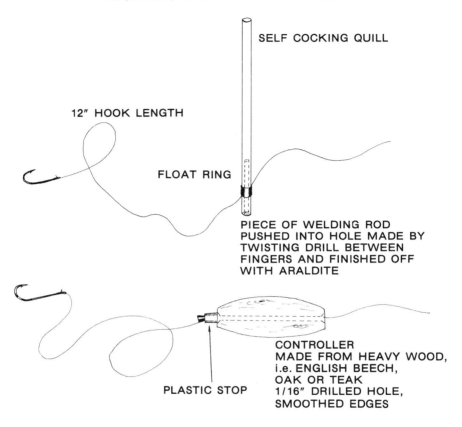

SELF COCKING QUILL

12" HOOK LENGTH

FLOAT RING

PIECE OF WELDING ROD
PUSHED INTO HOLE MADE BY
TWISTING DRILL BETWEEN
FINGERS AND FINISHED OFF
WITH ARALDITE

CONTROLLER
MADE FROM HEAVY WOOD,
i.e. ENGLISH BEECH,
OAK OR TEAK
1/16" DRILLED HOLE,
SMOOTHED EDGES

PLASTIC STOP

is inserted into the centre of the bait, and the bait is then glued to the back of the hook with Superglue as shown in the following diagram, along with other examples of how I mount baits.

Catching

The following are some useful tips for beginners. If I am fishing for runs I have the bail arm open and if I am expecting twitches the bail arm is closed. I keep the anti-reverse on at all times, but this may not be a good idea for anyone who sits away from their rods as they may lose a rod on a fast run if the anti-reverse is left on. In general, takes should be struck as soon as possible, with a high backwards sweep when fishing at long range, and less hard when fishing close in. When striking at takes on all types of

PROPRIETARY CAT FOODS
(GO CAT, MUNCHIES, ETC)

EXPANDED POLYSTYRENE
INSERTED INTO CENTRE HOLE
OF CATFOOD TO PREVENT THE
WEIGHT OF THE HOOK FROM
SINKING THE BAIT

HOOKBAIT SUPERGLUED TO SHANK
OF HOOK AS SHOWN (USED IN
CONJUNCTION WITH CONTROLLER)
ON HARD FISHED WATERS IT IS
BEST TO ATTACH THE FLOATER
TO THE HOOK USING A SHORT
'HAIR'.

SMALL PIECE OF FOAM OR
POLYSTYRENE PUSHED ONTO
EYE OF HOOK TO PREVENT BAITS
TRAVELLING UP THE LINE

SEED BAITS

SMALL PIECE OF MYSTIC PASTE
OR CHEWING GUM MOULDED
ROUND SHANK OF HOOK AND
THEN DIPPED INTO SEEDS

LENGTHS OF COTTON WITH
SEEDS SUPERGLUED AND THEN
ATTACHED TO HOOK

(Due to hookbait being so different from the free offering, it is essential in this
case to balance the hook's weight, as described in text, and to use relatively
small (light) hooks.

SIDE-HOOKED BOILED BAIT   PASTE BAIT

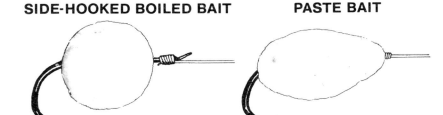

FOR THESE BAITS, HOOKS WITH LARGE GAPES SHOULD BE USED.

SIDE-HOOKED PEAS AND BEANS

CHICK PEA   BLACK EYED BEAN

It is essential that the bait be mounted in such a way that it does not impede the gape of the hook considerably. Oval shaped multiple baits such as a black eyed bean or kidney bean are best mounted as shown and pushed over the eye of the hook so that they cannot turn round. On hard fished waters it will be necessary to balance the hook bait, so that it sinks only very slowly, using cork or polystyrene.

floaters, watch the line, not the bait, and wait until the line (or float if you are using one) is moving steadily before you strike.

It is a good idea to plan your method of playing the fish before you hook it, especially when snag fishing, when you will have to hold on hard and not give line. I play my fish from the clutch and never backwind. Dare I suggest that backwinding has evolved as a method of playing fish because of the poor clutches on most of our reels? I am happy with the clutch operation on my Cardinal reels, so I don't need to backwind. I have often heard that playing fish on the clutch causes line twist, but I have never noticed this. Keep a cool head and be patient at all times when playing fish, especially at night. Avoid playing the fish heavily, especially when using fast taper rods, as this often causes permanent damage to the fish's mouth.

When landing the fish, bring it carefully over the net, and don't make stabs with the net at the fish. Lift the fish out by the mesh of the net, and not with the handle, and from this point the care of the fish should be considered. Always place the carp on soft ground or on a wet sack and handle it carefully, preferably with wet hands. Weigh the fish in a wet weighing sling or bag and when holding for photographs hold the fish low and over soft ground. A thumb in the mouth often stops the fish from wriggling when held. Get the fish back in the water as soon as possible.

I consider it very important to analyse both the reasons for a successful trip and the reasons for a blank. If you can learn from both, your fishing will improve.

Keep careful records of all your catches, the exact times and weather conditions, etc, and you will probably notice certain patterns forming which you can then take full advantage of. Unless you can spend the enormous amount of time at the waterside that many of the leading carp anglers do, don't try to compete with them. Fish your own way and for your own personal enjoyment, remembering that to catch the best fish there is in your waters is as good for you as the long strings of doubles and twenties may be for the more experienced carp man.

4 Winter Carp Fishing

This chapter contains the detailed results of several years of winter carp fishing. It takes into consideration a total of over 3000 hours spent at 24 lakes in 12 different counties over six seasons, giving my opinions, observations and conclusions on both the practical and theoretical sides of winter carping.

I have tried to set the results out clearly, without being too 'scientific', so that you have a chance to form your own conclusions on an aspect of carp fishing that seems to have very few hard and fast rules.

It is perhaps best to point out that all my winter carp fishing and observations have been on lakes in the southern half of England; therefore my results do not apply to 'typical' northern waters which, in comparison, are generally understocked and suffer colder temperatures, although I have little doubt that similar results, but on a different scale, could be obtained on northern waters.

The first of November is generally regarded as the start of winter carp fishing, but it is not until the first series of frosts, which usually come in mid to late November, that the water temperatures plummet and true winter fishing really begins. This first, sudden drop puts the carp temporarily off feeding and it seems that the more drastic this initial fall, the longer the effect will usually last. A short time after the temperature has levelled, the carp will usually resume regular feeding although throughout the winter they are generally less active than in the summer.

In most lakes there seems to be a considerable amount of food on the bottom during the winter months and I am sure that carp feed on natural food nearly every day throughout the average winter, except for the one or two really cold snaps. It is certainly not unusual to see carp feeding below the ice. Just how much natural food they eat on a winter's day is impossible to say, as their body temperature becomes lower; theoretically their food intake should be less, as it takes longer for them to digest it.

For a six year period my records show that some carp will feed on anglers' baits on most days throughout the winter, although usually only for short periods. For example, during the winter of 1979/80 I fished a total of 61 days from November to March on six different lakes. On 44 of those days I hooked carp, and on a further six others I had action from carp although none were landed, leaving only 11 blanks.

Get a group of carp anglers together and it won't be long before water temperatures become the most discussed aspect of winter carping. For the last few years, anglers seem to have attached great importance to water temperatures and some have even let the temperature decide whether they should fish or not on arriving at the water. I would be the first to admit that a still winter's morning with a carpet of heavy frost and cat ice around the lake margins is not very encouraging. However, having always kept rather detailed records of water temperatures and conditions I consider it worthwhile fishing whatever the weather. On checking records I did notice that my results always seemed to tail off during a severe drop in water temperature, although it usually takes a minimum of two or three days of falling temperatures to have any major effect on the carp's feeding patterns. Periods of steady water cooling have little or no detrimental effect on feeding and often improve one's chances of catching.

When I first started winter carp fishing I was already convinced that water temperature was the key factor and so the first couple of winters were spent dodging the colder weather and trying to time sessions for when the water was warmest. On each fishing trip I recorded water and air temperatures, weather conditions and so on. At the end of the second winter a definite pattern had begun to emerge. Much of what I had read or heard turned out to be somewhat inaccurate and often misleading. Initially I was catching carp when I didn't expect to, and in the sessions when I should have caught fish, I was quite often blanking. Besides the temperature aspect being unreliable, another theory, that fishing during the hours of darkness was best, had also misled me, especially as a good deal of my winter carp fishing was done in darkness. Fortunately, due to the distance these 'suitable' winter waters were from my home, I was forced to fish some daylight hours and it became apparent that darkness was not necessarily best. This, by the way, is something which contradicts all that has been advocated by several angling writers in the past. So together with the fact that I could not relate increased feeding activity with increasing water temperatures I now had a real incentive to do much more winter fishing; indeed, I have always said that an angler must understand why he is catching if he is to achieve consistent results.

It was after some considerable success in previous winter seasons that I decided, during the winter of 1976/77, to fish as many hours as possible. Despite some rough weather and low temperatures which frequently caused the lakes to freeze over during December and January, I managed to log a total of 561 hours. This was spent at five different lakes between mid-November and mid-March, all of which produced carp. I would, like, however, to exclude from these one very easy water which produced 30 carp in just 38½ hours. This was in fact a small two acre lake situated in the centre of the Gloucestershire town of Bourton-on-the-Water. Although it held a few double figure fish, it was basically grossly over-stocked with small fish. So crowded was it that the carp would fight for any food or bait even taking floating crust in mid-winter. From the remaining four waters a total of 23 carp were caught, of which 21 were doubles, including one of just under 30 pounds. I was elated at the capture of my first winter 20, especially as it was such a good fish. I well remember the long and dogged fight it gave me, and how, after a biteless day, the indicator crept slowly upwards. The evening was cold and windy and the sun had already set, leaving me alone to battle with a powerful carp. I can recall watching the outline of the rod curved against the slate-grey sky and how it would be suddenly jerked forwards as the fish plunged to the left or right. One sometimes feels so terribly alone and helpless in these situations, wondering how big the fish is, and hoping it won't come off. Then, in the fading light with the mesh of my landing net surrounding the fish, I lifted the leather from the water. It was a huge fish which pulled the spring balance down to 29 pounds 10 ounces. My next thought was to get some good photographs, although I was reluctant to sack the fish for the rest of the night.

When I took a closer look at the fish, however, I noticed an unusual number of leeches were attached to the underside of its body and head, with at least a hundred inside the mouth. It seemed likely that this fish must have been lying torpid on the lake bed for some time before it decided to feed. The leeches must have attached themselves during this time. I decided to sack the fish securely in some deep marginal water to my left and then examine and photograph it at first light. When morning came I picked off all the leeches and was able to get some photographs before returning it.

Two of the four waters I fished mainly at night, because of their locality and the limited time available. The other two I fished a total of 402 hours, fishing during both days and nights. It was only these two waters therefore that I could compare and determine what might be most productive and also at what temperatures one could expect most action. Listed below are the results from these two waters.

As can be seen from the tables, Mid-Northants produced 14 carp of which 12 were taken during the daytime compared with only two at night.

MID-NORTHANTS CARP FISHERY

DATE	HRS FISHED	FISH TAKEN	TIME TAKEN	WATER	WEATHER
Nov 16, 76	50 hrs	16-2 Leather 15-2 Leather Lost fish Lost fish 12-14 Mirror 13-1 Mirror 10-6 Mirror 6-8 Mirror 10-6 Mirror 19-9 Mirror 5-8 Mirror	3.10 pm daylight 4.15 pm daylight 3.30 am darkness 12.10 pm daylight 12.20 pm daylight 2.20 pm daylight 3.10 pm daylight 4.00 pm daylight 11.10 pm darkness 9.50 am daylight 12.35 pm daylight	43°F dropping to 41°F	Overcast, variable light winds, 46°F daytimes
Dec 21, 76	45¾ hrs	None	No bites what- soever, day or night	36°F constant, ice on edges of lake	37°F daytime frosty nights
Feb 9, 77	22 hrs	None	Odd bites daytime only	40°F	44°F day, strong winds, heavy rain
Feb 23, 77	48 hrs	Lost fish 15-12 Mirror 16-6 Mirror 17-0 Common	4.55 pm daylight 1.20 pm daylight 3.30 pm daylight 9.30 am daylight	42°F	48°F daytime, light winds
Mar 9, 77	55 hrs	29-10 Leather 11-8 Mirror	5.30 pm daylight 12.40 am darkness	46°F	52°F daytime 48°F night strong winds

MARLBOROUGH POOL, OXFORD

DATE	HRS FISHED	FISH TAKEN	TIME TAKEN	WATER	WEATHER
Jan 27, 77	41 hrs	10-0 Mirror	8.30 am daylight	42°F dropping to 40°F	strong winds & rain, frosty nights, 35°F daytimes
Feb 2, 77	41½ hrs	None	(Odd bites at night)	39°F rising to 40°F, ice thawing on edge of lake	46°F daytime strong winds
Feb 16, 77	43½ hrs	12-14 Mirror	1.30 am darkness	43°F	46°F daytime some rain
Mar 2, 77	43 hrs	Lost fish 10-8 Mirror 10-4 Mirror	6.25 pm darkness 10.15 pm darkness 12.30 am darkness	45°F rising to 48°F	64°F daytime strong to gale force wind
Mar 14, 77	12¼ hrs	11-8 Mirror	6.55 pm darkness	46°F	47°F at night, strong winds

There is no disputing that the fishing at this water was far superior during the daytime and the nights hardly worth fishing. In fact on most nights at this water no bites of any description were experienced and all the action was early in the day and during the afternoon. This was similar to my experiences in the summer.

In complete contrast Marlborough showed a marked tendency to fish well at night, although this was later found to be misleading. Out of five carp landed, four were taken during darkness compared with one fish caught in the daytime. Also one fish was lost in darkness. On this water most of the bites occurred between 6 pm and 1.30 am, the majority being between 10 pm and 1.30 am. Most days at this water were very slow, producing only the odd bite, and although I caught only a few fish here it is interesting to note that my friend Len Middleton who accompanied me, had very similar results.

The results for that winter were very interesting and again proved how difficult it was to determine what times of the day might be best. In addition, no positive conclusions could be made with regard to water temperatures. So, once again I was faced with the dilemma of catching carp, but not fully understanding why. I felt again I could just as well have been blanking! After some consideration I decided to fish as many hours as possible, for it would be necessary that I catch more fish and thereby hope to sort out some of the problems still hanging in my mind. In order that my activities could be assessed accurately it seemed best that I choose new winter venues, and to this end I continued to fish at least two totally new waters. Looking back I regard my decision as rather adventurous even though I shall always hold the opinion that to become an accomplished angler one must consistently catch carp on several different waters. Being successful on one type of water is no real guide to individual ability. Indeed, to this day I would consider my season incomplete if I have not caught carp from two or more new venues.

The 1977 season was a truly memorable one for me. I was again able to put in plenty of fishing time and this, together with a growing understanding of carp behaviour, enabled me to catch 21 fish over 20 pounds, the best weighing 31 pounds. It was in fact believed that this was the first time anyone had ever achieved this and was especially rewarding as most of these fish were caught from the 'new' waters.

My success throughout the summer had now given me some useful knowledge for the winter ahead. By the start of November that year I had landed 16 fish over 20 pounds, but I knew I would have to work extra hard if I were to reach my target of 20 by the end of the winter.

Not quite a winter thirty. This one tipped the scales at 29.10.

Despite the fact that the lakes I was winter fishing were frozen over for a complete month, I had a very successful winter, managing to land five 'twenties' and a good number of 'doubles'. Two of the 'twenties' came from 'D' lake, a day ticket water in Norfolk called Waveney Valley, and were caught within half an hour of each other. This represented the best ever winter brace of carp at that time, their weights being 27 pounds two ounces and 26 pounds four ounces. I did not gauge my success simply by the capture of such big fish, however. It seemed that at last I was beginning to understand winter carp fishing, and the veil of mystery which had surrounded it for so long. My theories and suspicions were in fact now becoming reality.

Throughout the winter of 1977/78 I continued to fish the Oxfordshire water Marlborough Pool for I believed I had fished the water badly the previous winter. Having had no summer experience on this water, locating the fish proved a little difficult. They never really showed themselves until the end of the winter and when they did, it was in an area about 80 yards from the bank. Typically, this was an area I hadn't fully exploited, mainly because of the size of the water and the time available. Had there been other anglers fishing the water I would no doubt have found this out long before, so I had made up my mind to fish this area before moving on to other waters. Most of the fish I had previously caught from Marlborough Pool were taken margin fishing or at short distance, and as they were caught at night I regarded fishing in the daylight hours as impracticable. As it happened, the fish were most active in the daytime but again right out in the centre of the lake, so had I not fished the additional winter I would never have known. Mostly I spent the winter fishing with two rods at long distance and a third rod in the margins, although at night I sometimes fished two rods in the margins. This resulted in catching the normal amount of carp during darkness but about twice as many again during the day on the long distance rods. I am convinced, knowing the

MARLBOROUGH POOL (THREE SEASONS WINTER FISHING)

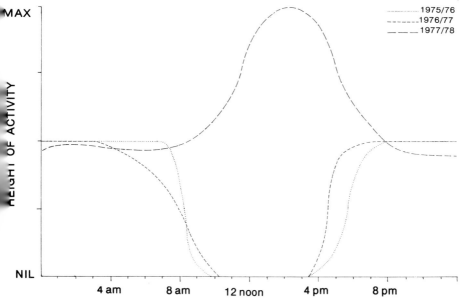

circumstances, that my results would have been the same the previous winter had I fished in this way. The following graph clearly shows the comparable results for the three winters.

So I had proved to myself this was not necessarily just a night water and my suspicions of activity in different areas at different times of the day were verified. Although I may not fish the water again I shall always remember it, for I really enjoyed my winter fishing there. On one particular night in January I experienced the most active night I have ever had since I started carp fishing. It was a clear, bright night with a full moon and no wind. Hopeless conditions for winter carp, many would say! The longest rest I had in the ten hour period was ten minutes without striking, casting or playing fish.

Several things were confirmed that winter on all the four lakes I fished. The initial, sudden drop in water temperatures put the carp completely off feed. On two lakes I measured this drop and found it to be five degrees F in 24 hours at its most crucial point. This drop from approximately 50 degrees F to around 38 degrees F with eventual freezing over, in a total period of little over a week, ruined any chance of a fish for about a fortnight. Fish were then caught on all of the waters once they had thawed out, or while their temperature remained constant for a few days. During the remainder of the winter the water temperature seemed to have little effect on the feeding of the fish, and the fish caught per hour was as good below 42 degrees F as it was when above this figure. This again confirmed the findings from previous winters. Also, no real assumptions were made with regard to barometric pressures, mainly because I hadn't really seriously considered them, although I did make a point of noting their effects, if any, in the future.

The following winter of 1978/79 proved to be rather unsuccessful after December, due to the continual very cold weather that seemed to hang around for a couple of months. It was in fact my worst ever winter as far as numbers of carp caught, as I took only 12 winter doubles, and a few smaller fish. I was fortunate enough though to catch two fish over twenty pounds, one of them being my best winter carp – a mirror weighing 30 pounds 12 ounces. This was a terrific fish that also fulfilled my dream of a true winter thirty, and was my third thirty of the season. For over half the winter the lakes were either frozen or a strong freezing wind kept water temperatures unusually low. I tried to fish every week and on many occasions had to break ice to wet a line, only to have it re-freeze a short time later. Once most waters were frozen I switched my efforts to a large North London reservoir. This is an understocked water of some 85 acres in size that had only ever frozen over once since the last war! At first, not being very hopeful, I spent a lot of time looking and was lucky enough early one morning to find some fish rolling in an area that was calm and away from the cold north-easterly wind. At dawn the following day I again found them in the same spot. Looking back I would estimate that a large proportion of the carp which inhabit this huge water were congregated in this small area. Strangely, the fish stayed in exactly the same spot for well over a month, until even this water eventually froze over. We did, however, manage to catch several fish, which helped to compensate

Fish like these make those cold winter trips all the more worthwhile – a fine winter brace weighing 27 pounds 2 ounces and 26 pounds 4 ounces, from a Norfolk day ticket water.

for the ridiculous weather we were experiencing. Nearly all the fish were taken in about 20 feet of water and the temperature remained slightly above 40 degrees F at this depth all the time, until the bitterly cold weather resulted in the reservoir eventually freezing over. On the days we landed fish, we were certain that no other carp could have been caught anywhere else in England as 95 per cent of the rivers and lakes were frozen and any remaining water would probably have been too cold. I must also point out that this is a very unusual water. As it is a reservoir, the Water Authority is continually altering the level, so a constant flow and exchange of water is always taking place.

I decided that the next summer I would spend a little more of my time fishing more difficult waters and, if the winter of 1979/80 would permit, I would concentrate my efforts on four waters with the majority of my time at two new waters in, this time, that most prolific of carp counties – Kent. This would then complete my plan to have winter-fished virtually every county in the southern half of England on a large variety of waters, ranging from a one acre pool to 100 acre lakes, some heavily stocked with carp and some understocked; some regarded as easy summer waters and others as hard.

My plan was completed in March 1980, after the most suitable winter for carp fishing I have ever known. From November right through to the end of the season there were no more than one or two periods of severe cold weather. This comparatively mild weather not only made the actual fishing more comfortable but provided the carp with almost constantly acceptable feeding conditions. These factors, together with my insatiable desire to catch carp, left me with what must be the best-ever winter results I shall ever have. In eighteen weeks fishing an average of 50 hours a week, I caught 84 doubles, of which 10 were over 20 pounds, plus a few singles. This brought my season's total up to 165 doubles which included two thirties and 17 twenties. On every winter trip I caught carp except for one, which was inevitably going to be a blank because of the thick fog that was present. These are conditions, incidentally, under which I have never caught a carp.

A total of six waters were fished, three of them on a regular basis throughout the whole winter, which all produced carp. The following table shows some of the statistics for each of these waters during that winter.

The most productive times and conditions on each water proved to be similar for both the winters. There are certain points to be considered when looking at the water temperature recorded. Firstly, the 'hours per fish': results for Waveney Valley are not a fair average as only two visits were made to this water. If we then exclude Northants and Nazeing which cannot be taken into consideration for water temperatures then the results again back up my belief that you stand just as much chance of catching carp when the water is 40 or 41 degrees F as you do when it is around 45 degrees F. On these mild occasions I have noticed, despite it being mid-winter, that fly hatches occur. This has prompted me to consider that other forms of emergent life become prematurely active and may cause the carp to transfer their attention towards the natural food, thereby neglecting anglers' baits.

It is interesting to note that on the three waters that were fished both day and night, feeding times remained remarkably similar throughout the whole winter, which again agrees with previous observations. This of

NOVEMBER 1979 to MARCH 1980

WATER	HOURS FISHED	FISH CAUGHT	FISH LOST	LARGEST FISH	HOURS PER FISH HOOKED Under 42°F water temp.	HOURS PER FISH HOOKED 42°F plus water temp.	FISH HOOKED DURING DAYLIGHT Fish	Hours Fished	DARKNESS Fish	Hours Fished	LOWEST WATER TEMPERATURE Fished	Fish Caught
Mid-Northants	209	16	4	27-4	N/A	10.5	18	65%	2	35%	42°F	42°F
Darenth, Kent	502	54	6	27-4	7.2	9.1	57	65%	3	35%	39°F	39°F
London Reservoir	30	4	0	20-0	7.5	7.5	4	100%	—	—	40°F	40°F
East Kent	104	9	1	16-6	9.8	11.0	1	30%	9	70%	39°F	39°F
Nazeing, Essex	9	1	1	14-1	4.5	N/A	2	100%	—	—	40°F	40°F
Waveney Valley, Norfolk	65	6	2	13-4	16.0	5.5	8	70%	0	30%	40°F	40°F

course is a great advantage as one knows exactly when to expect action and if one is fortunate enough to live close to the water, visits can be timed accordingly. In fact, had I been living near to Darenth I would definitely not have spent a total of 14 long, boring nights just to catch three carp. It was therefore impracticable to travel the long distance just for a few daylight hours, so I arranged my visits to last over two days on most occasions. At one stage I was fishing at Darenth in the daytime and then going straight to another water in East Kent at night, on a three day/two night session. You can imagine this was very tiring; constant lack of sleep, continual packing and setting up of gear, and the driving was beginning to have its effect. Health must take precedence overall and I therefore had to give it a break.

Looking at my results for the 24 different waters that I have fished in the winter it seems that daytime fishing is better than night fishing by a ratio of about 2.5 to one. Other carp anglers have found the opposite!

There do, however, seem to be definite day waters and definite night waters, where the majority of all carp caught are either during one or the other, with little chance of a spread-over. It is also noticeable that although feeding times usually remain similar throughout a whole winter, these can change from year to year on the same water. Because of this, it is advisable to fish an occasional 24 hour session to ascertain the current feeding times at the beginning of each winter and also when a change during the winter has been suspected. Otherwise feeding times can be relied upon until mid to late February.

The length of feeding periods can be slightly affected by a number of factors, but they usually range from half an hour to three hours in length and can come at any time during 24 hour periods. Carp can feed all day although this is generally rare. Most winter feeding periods are usually very active ones and it is not unusual to get two takes at more or less the same time.

Over the years I have enjoyed recording air and water temperature readings. From experience one cannot state an accurate water temperature at which carp generally stop feeding, although it is probably somewhere just under 39 degrees F. It is very rare to catch carp in water below 37 degrees and the lowest temperature in which I have ever caught a carp is 37.5. I have fished on a number of occasions with the temperature lower than this and had no action whatsoever. One hears occasionally of carp being caught in lower water temperatures than this but my experience suggests that the temperature readings have been taken in the margins and not where the bait was. Frequently I have recorded temperatures in low 30s in the margin areas and have caught carp, but the temperature has been considerably higher out in the deeper water, although it is quite rare for the water temperature to drop below 39 degrees F on the bottom more than a couple of times throughout an average winter. One must exclude, of course, shallow lakes of less than eight feet and the marginal areas of most other lakes. Taking this into consideration it is therefore possible to catch carp 90 per cent of the time throughout the winter in relation to water temperatures. Having now drawn these conclusions I propose to stop using a thermometer on a regular basis in the future.

In the past, various angling writers have suggested that we take water temperatures all over the lake and then fish the warmest part. I have found this to be useless advice and rather misleading and have again proved this to myself.

It must first be considered that no real thermocline exists throughout most of the winter as there is insufficient temperature variation to create one. It is quite rare to find a severe contrast in the temperature on the lake bed. I have spent countless hours on many lakes recording figures onto a map of the whole lake and still found a constant temperature. Even when a cold or warm wind is blowing onto one end of the lake there is rarely a measureable difference for very long. This is for two main reasons. Firstly, there has to be several degrees difference between the water and air temperatures before it can have a 'temperature change effect'. When this situation arises, if there is no wind, then the whole lake will be equally affected. In the case of a strong wind, the stronger it becomes the greater the sub-surface current; consequently it doesn't take very long, on the majority of waters, for the temperature change to be equally distributed throughout the whole lake. Remember also that the air is already having an effect, although more slowly, on the calm end of the lake. On the rare occasions that a slight temperature difference occurs this has been of little benefit as carp will feed where the majority of food is, regardless of water temperature. I also find this the case where springs enter a lake, for although spring water is usually around 50 degrees F, it is yet another example of something that is theoretically correct, but not so in practice. Many anglers presume that fishing into the wind is best in the winter. On some lakes certain wind conditions may influence the movement of the carp, but on the majority it has little or no effect. I am not stating that the fish will not follow a warmish wind as they quite often may do so, but they may follow a cold wind and on many occasions can be caught fishing into a wind that is colder than the water. Obviously it is not just water temperature they are influenced by. On these occasions, whether the wind 'blows the food' into the area or not, actual water movement or current acts as a stimulus for the fish to feed. I do not think that carp are 'turned on' by higher oxygen levels as often as they are in the summer, for the oxygen levels throughout the colder months remain quite high. Having caught many carp at the calm end of lakes regardless of wind conditions there is no doubt in my mind that a known feeding area is a better proposition than relying on wind direction. Results do show, however, that a gentle ripple will often prolong a feeding spell.

Practically the only time water temperature can drop very low on the bottom, in depths exceeding ten feet, is when the air temperature is freezing and a very strong wind is blowing continually. This stops ice from forming on the surface. It is in these rare conditions, when the water on the bottom can drop to as low as, say, 34 degrees F, that carp definitely do not feed. The depth of the lake obviously affects this and in areas of over 15 feet is far less common. You do in fact have a much better chance of catching carp by breaking a hole in the ice and fishing through it, as the water temperature never drops below 39.2 degrees F on the bottom (excluding shallow lakes) once the lake has frozen over. This of course excludes the thin layer of water immediately below the ice which we need not concern ourselves with.

I have occasionally smashed the ice and caught carp, but usually only when there is a light wind to stop the hole from re-freezing very quickly.

The following graph shows the average relation of carp caught against water temperatures.

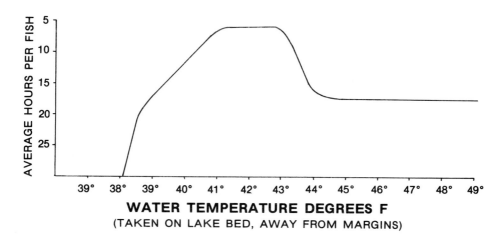

WATER TEMPERATURE DEGREES F
(TAKEN ON LAKE BED, AWAY FROM MARGINS)

From this we can ascertain the most productive water temperature by the average 'hours per fish' at various temperatures. As can be seen there is a sharp rise in activity between 38 degrees F and 41 degrees F. This holds good for a couple of degrees and then activity falls off to a steady level.

One of the most difficult times to catch carp in the winter is when mild weather has occurred for a considerable length of time, causing the water temperature to level off around the middle to upper 40s. The fish caught per hour is certainly less than when the temperature is dropping from, say, 42 degrees F to 39 degrees F, or rising from 39 degrees F to 42 degrees F. Why this temperature range of between 44 degrees F and 50 degrees F has no noticeable increased effect on the amount of fish caught I'm not sure. Certainly it is only when the water rises above 50 degrees F that any real relation between rise in temperature and increased feeding is noticeable. Once below 50 degrees F carp activity is definitely reduced. Several carp anglers in the past have speculated on why the carp are more active at the lower levels. The most common assumption is that the carp have a good feed if they sense a freeze-up is on the way. While there may be a little truth in this I somehow doubt it, especially as I have seen carp go on feeding under the ice for quite long periods after the lake has sealed over. This is always providing that the dissolved oxygen level is adequate. Throughout most of the winter the oxygen levels on most lakes remain acceptable while they are frozen over, except in the case of an early November freeze-up when the autumn leaves or dying weeds are rapidly decomposing.

Quite considerable temperature differences can occur from the bed of the lake to the surface. It is throughout February and March when this is most noticeable. The variation, which is not enough to be regarded as a thermocline, occurs on windless days, when the water temperature is around 40 degrees F and the air rises to over 50 degrees F. It is quite common in these conditions for the carp to rise into the upper layers and bask there. This is most usual in the afternoon after several hours of sunshine when they can be very hard to catch. Usually, however, before the carp sink back down to the bottom they can become active and will often roll on the surface paying no attention to the bottom baits directly below them. This is when a suspended bait can score. If you are fortunate enough to have a floating bait which you can suspend and are able to decide when is the right time, it is possible to take several fish in succession. This is much more difficult in practice than it sounds. You may not have floaters with you and the carp are rolling too far out to fish a normal bait in mid-water under a float. The other main problem is that unless you are previously aware of what could happen, you might sit there throughout the active period expecting a bite any moment and before you realise it, the fish have ceased activity. Wherever possible, if I think this situation is occurring, I like to put two baits among the fish, one on the bottom for when they may eventually go down and one suspended somewhere between mid-water and the bottom. Although the fish will occasionally take a surface bait in this situation a suspended bait is usually better. I always carry some expanded polystyrene with me as this is far more convenient than making floaters, which may not get used. A large piece is put on the hook alongside the boiled bait or in the case of a soft bait, the paste is moulded around the polystyrene. A quick test in the margin will check all's well, although it is difficult to get a modified bottom bait to suspend when fishing at long distance. My winter baits are usually very light so are not too much of a problem to suspend.

On some lakes one of the best times to catch winter carp is during the 24 hours immediately after a freeze-up. But once the water temperature hits the low 40s then both air and water temperatures, whether falling or rising, seem to have little effect on their feeding patterns.

Once the water temperature becomes suitable for the carp to feed, other factors can then be considered. One aspect that I am becoming more aware of is the change in air pressure and its effect on the fish. There is some evidence to suggest that fish react to a change in barometric pressure. The normal range of pressure to be experienced in southern England is about 970 to 1,030 millibars, a maximum change of

A true winter fish, this one; 28¾ pound leather taken in bitterly cold conditions on 11th February 1981 from the School Pool in Kent.

approximately 6 per cent. This difference in pressure, which is transmitted through water, is equal to that experienced by a carp changing its depth by two feet or so, and as fish undergo such depth changes frequently, it seems strange that a change in air pressure would affect feeding activity. My observations do suggest less feeding activity during sustained high pressure. In winter, high pressure usually means calm, sunny days and clear, calm, frosty nights, conditions under which I have often had poorer results. In severe misty or foggy weather, which is associated with high pressure, it seems practically impossible to catch fish. Although low pressure, which generally means unsettled weather, appears favourable, it seems very difficult to judge from a barometer when carp can actually be caught.

One very important aspect of successful winter carping is the right choice of water. Although carp can be caught from most lakes during the winter months it must be accepted that results would normally be considerably poorer in comparison with the summer. Something like one and a half to four times the number of hours per fish can be expected in the winter, so you need to evaluate your fishing. A decision has to be made on whether you are prepared to put a lot of time in on a hard water to catch few, if any fish, or whether you want to catch a quantity of fish regardless of their size. Both have their merits and I think one can be just as difficult as the other to achieve; either can be equally satisfying. Personally, for my winter fishing I nearly always decide to fish waters that contain a good head of doubles so that I can expect a fair amount of action. I must confess, I don't enjoy biteless winter sessions and I get great enjoyment from every winter fish I catch, especially when conditions are really severe and 90 per cent of the anglers have written off any chance of a fish.

Once a water has been chosen the most important part of winter carp fishing presents itself, and that is precise location of fish. Not only is exact location the most important factor it is also the most difficult, as visible signs of carp are quite rare on most lakes when the really severe weather sets in. Here, previous knowledge of the water is invaluable, as quite often summer hotspots are also the best areas in the winter. Initially, all efforts must be concentrated into finding the fish. Naturally it is a waste of time trying to attract the fish into an area which they would normally ignore during the winter months. On most lakes there are only one or two areas where fish can be taken consistently, the rest of the lake producing very little in comparison. If the carp are not located, then fishing will be

Part of an amazing catch made one session in January 1983. The two carp shown in the photograph weighed 26½ and 25¼ pounds. Two other commons weighting 30½ and 21¼ pounds were also taken, making the catch an historic one.

virtually 'blind' and several blank sessions can be expected until by persistent coverage of all areas you eventually find where they are feeding. This is where several carp anglers fishing the water at the same time becomes an advantage. More areas are being covered and generally the sooner the feeding areas are found. An invaluable aid for speedy location of fish is the use of bite alarms. When using buzzers, no matter how short the session, it is possible to look for fish from your pitch practically all the time. The sight of one carp can be, and quite often is, responsible for the capture of several fish over a number of sessions as there is a tendency for the carp to stay in groups and move around very little. To see just one sign is so important, so it's worth conditioning yourself to be always studying the water instead of your bobbins. A tell-tale swirl or silent rise can indicate a confidently feeding carp. It is also worth noting the capture of any carp by other anglers, as a certain pattern quite often emerges and their results can help you.

Once the carp have been located by one means or another, then consistent baiting on a regular basis usually encourages activity and feeding. Carp soon become accustomed to the availability of food in certain areas. The amount of bait being introduced is not as important as the regularity of the pre-baiting. However, the amount of ground bait introduced while you are fishing must be considered with great care. Too much bait can completely ruin your chances of catching a fish. Here the subject becomes rather involved. First, it must be appreciated that there are only a certain number of fish willing to feed on your bait; it might be three or four fish, or just one. Despite the availability of food, each fish will only eat a certain amount. If there are a lot of free offerings on the bottom, there is a greater chance of fish becoming satisfied before taking your hookbait. The majority of all the baits will be mouthed suspiciously before one is accepted. The chances are that your hookbait will also be mouthed, then left temporarily, for the carp are usually able to differ-entiate between free offerings and hookbaits. Fish will gradually accept free offerings as being safe and after a few of these are taken the fish become satisfied and stop feeding. It is here that you have to make a calculated guess as to how many active fish are in your area. Knowledge of the water, any visual activity of fish at the time, and all action with regard to bites must be considered. If you are getting bites on both rods at the same time then it can be assumed there may be several active fish, but if you are getting action on one rod, and then the other, it may be the same fish moving from one hookbait to the other as they quite often do. If the fish are continually moving from one to the other then the chances are that the carp wants to take the bait but is suspicious. The introduction of further free offerings will usually spoil the chances of catching that fish. So, in conclusion, one has to decide what amount of groundbaiting is best. There is little doubt in my mind that some groundbaiting is beneficial.

Generally, the more anglers there are fishing the same lake in the winter, the better. This can be beneficial to the quality of the fishing in several ways. First, it is an assurance that the lake is being baited up regularly, thus enabling the carp to become accustomed to finding food in certain areas and encouraging regular activity regardless of conditions. Secondly, the regular catching of carp also helps and the more fish that are put on the bank in the winter the better. This seems to encourage fish to resume feeding quite soon after capture, presumably to recover the energy lost. One feeding fish quite often tempts another to feed, and so on. The other main advantage is that a great deal can be learnt by noting the approach and results of other anglers, things that would possibly not have been discovered by oneself.

Generally, anglers overdo groundbait in the winter while they are actually fishing. If I think the area I'm fishing has been overbaited at the time or prior to my arrival, I rarely put any free samples out at all. For

A male fish of 24 pounds 6 ounces, taken in March. Note the breeding tubercules on top of the head; this fish took a maple flavoured black eye bean two yards from the bank.

instance, during the 1979/80 winter, one of the waters I fished at Darenth was being heavily fished and heavily groundbaited on most days. Because of the large amount of bait the area was receiving I decided to rely completely on the attractiveness of the bait and fished on hookbaits only. This resulted in the capture of 54 carp from that water without ever putting *one* free offering in. I am convinced that had I baited up while fishing I would have caught less. This is of course only one case, for on the Northants fishery that same winter I felt the need to groundbait a little on each visit; therefore it is fair to say that each water must be treated individually.

Sometimes during the winter, occasions arise when twitches are experienced immediately after casting and then the bait is ignored. When this happens the carp may not be feeding properly, but are attracted by the appearance or splash of a new bait being cast in. They may also be feeding, or lying in the middle layers, and follow the bait down, although they are not really interested in feeding on the bottom. In these circumstances two things can quite often lead to the capture of these fish. Continual re-casting can result in the capture of one or two fish. If the twitches are experienced soon after a cast it pays to cast each rod every half-hour and one rod about a quarter of an hour after the other. One can then sit behind the rod immediately and strike when the 'improved take' comes. It is not unusual for one of the many casts to produce a really positive bite. Another worthwhile ploy in these circumstances can sometimes pay off. Try catapulting in one or two stones, of similar weight to your terminal tackle, over the exact spot that your bait is lying. This can fool the fish into inspecting your hookbait again, but only do this when twitches occur regularly soon after casting.

I have found that some slight changes from the 'ideal' summer baits lead to improved results. Although there are fewer active fish during the winter months, these fish are far less careful of the sight and smell of baits. Because of this I like to take full advantage of the carps' powers of detection and I very often aim for a more visible and stronger smelling bait. First, with regard to specials, I increase the lighter ingredients of the base mix so that the finished bait is only slightly heavier than negative buoyancy in the water. I then make up some lighter baits that only just sink when the hook and line is attached. This ensures that the hookbait will rest lightly on the bottom and is especially worthwhile when fishing over a soft bottom. If it is so silted that a ledger weight buries the bait, then I have found it best either to float fish or freeline in the case of margin fishing. If the depth is accurately set then the float will hold the bait on the top of the silt. Provided there is not too much drag, one can sink the line between float and rod tip and use a bite alarm for night fishing, or when scanning the water for signs of active fish. I prefer to use an alarm in conjunction with a float at night, rather than a betalight float only, as long biteless periods can be expected.

These observations take me back to a tiny water in Herefordshire. I was never able to enjoy a summer's fishing there but it was during the winter of 1976 that I experienced the difficulties of fishing this unusual old water. Imagine an old moat, the sort that once surrounded a manor house or castle in medieval England, then scale it down to a tiny watercourse no more than 25 yards square.

Most of my fishing was done during the night-time and here above all things, stealth was essential. It was not easy to locate the carp on this quiet and deserted fishery. They seldom rolled or showed themselves but I knew they were there. It wasn't long before I found a tiny patch of firm bottom among the silt, and here I also found the carp. An inaccurate cast and the bait would lie in dense foul silt, something I knew the carp disliked. Having found an area in which the carp would feed I set about a small pre-baiting programme and as the fishing wasn't far from my home I found no difficulty in visiting two or three times a week to bait my pitch. In the following trips I not only caught carp but learned a valuable lesson

An autumn fish of 31 pounds.

too. Any standard ledger rig would catch carp from the small three foot square spot, but any bait cast into the silt never produced fish. Only when a bait was carefully suspended over the bottom in these silty areas did a carp find it attractive.

Delving into the history of the moat I found it is possible that it could date back to the 16th century or before. It seems likely that it was once much deeper than its present average of three feet and it is probable that several feet of silt has accumulated there over the years. I was fascinated by this unique place and, alone on the fishery on a winter's night, could easily visualize how it must have looked as the moated defence to a medieval country house.

I find that light-coloured baits tend to be better in the winter and I generally aim for a whitish colour. This, together with the weight balance, ensures a bait easily visible to the carp. In fact, sunken bread crust which is a good winter bait offers both these advantages. Wherever possible I like to increase the smell of the bait and have achieved better results by approximately doubling the smell of the 'ideal' summer bait for that same water. So we end up with a far more visible bait, one that will actually move if the carp is active close by, and one that can be located by smell from a greater distance, besides making precise location easier for the carp at close quarters.

Undoubtedly the best ready-made winter carp bait must be luncheon

A 27¼ pounder, one of a brace of winter twenties taken one afternoon in January.

A January fish weighing 27¼ pounds from Redmire Pool.

meat and this has probably accounted for more winter carp than any other bait. It's not surprising really, for it has all the qualities previously mentioned. It is light in weight and colour, strong smelling and is the perfect consistency for being small fish proof, and good for casting. It also has a very long effective life. Spam and Bacon Grill varieties are best.

With regard to the use of multiple baits in winter, sweet corn is without question the best and is always my first choice, regardless of how many carp have already been caught on it. It has all the necessary qualities of a winter bait and is one of the few multiples that has a naturally good smell. Other multiple baits do not seem to give any better results than the next. Personally, I have found the use of specials far more successful than multiple baits, especially the smaller seed baits, and therefore very little of my fishing is with beans or seeds during the winter.

Many people advocate smaller baits in the winter while in complete contrast a minority recommend a very large bait. But what exactly is a large or small bait? I would call a special of one inch in diameter a large bait whereas some of my friends would say it's average! It seems people who advocate the use of smaller baits mean about half an inch in diameter for a special and I like to use between quarter and half inch baits. Even my summer baits are not much bigger than that. Basically it is just down to what you have most confidence in.

While the effectiveness of the bait relies somewhat on its amount of pre-baiting, a good quality bait is very important in the winter. By good quality I mean very attractive to the carp. This is important if, as in the example of the Darenth lake in 1979/80, one is not introducing any free offerings whether beforehand or while fishing. When a bait of better quality is used in these circumstances, one is making full use of other anglers' groundbaiting schemes. Yet when the carp eventually has the choice of which hookbait to pick up, it will not necessarily take the type it has got used to. Some excellent resuls can be achieved if you are fortunate enough to be using the most attractive bait.

There remains little else to say in respect of winter carping. One would perhaps mention that fishing in areas of dead lilies, weed or reed beds is beneficial and undoubtedly a worthwhile ploy.

To finish this winter fishing section, it is best said that I prefer to get on with catching carp regardless of theories, which is why I have tried not to give long technical explanations. It is no good trying to baffle anyone with science about what happens to a carp's internal system, or what its exact requirements are through the winter, or even what happens to the lake, because I'm sure I would only baffle myself. Perhaps I am more of an angler than a writer, but all the contents of this section are my own findings and the facts and theories have been obtained through simply catching true winter carp.

If you're like me, then the summer season is just not long enough for catching carp. My love for the sport is simply too strong to sit at home while the carp are feeding just because it's cold outside. Get the right clothing and equipment and you soon forget it's winter. Remember, winter carp fishing is not just fishing a couple of sessions when weather conditions are favourable. It is a whole winter, fishing virtually every week from mid-November through to March. You will then find that your ideal fishing conditions will not always be the same as the carp's. If you have not yet caught carp in the winter, you will be surprised at their good condition, their fighting ability and their improved weight for length ratio compared with the summer. If the winter is suitable for the carp, then they will probably reach their peak condition sometime around February and, like me, you may well catch your best fish from that water at that time, perhaps with snow around your feet!

Since writing this chapter I have fished several more winters and although these have been very successful with many twenty pound plus carp being caught, including four winter thirties, I have nothing new to add. The observations and methods described still hold good.

5 Bait

Initially, my intention was to write about the baits and bait ingredients with which I was familiar and relate these to my own angling experience. I soon became aware however, that to cover the whole spectrum of modern carp baits would require a considerable degree of effort and research. Although I do not believe bait to be of number one importance in carp fishing, to provide the sort of comprehensive coverage I think a modern book on carp fishing should contain, I was able to draw on the resources of my friend and angling companion John Baker. We discussed the matter at some length and agreed that no one has previously written a complete guide and history of carp baits. The decision was to combine our experiences and hopefully provide the sort of reading that would remain as a reference to this most complex of angling subjects.

At this stage it is worth mentioning that John has spent what must amount to hundreds of hours in researching and experimenting with various ingredients and ideas. In my opinion his appreciation of the whole subject is above average and I value his advice and assistance in writing this section of the book.

*   *   *   *   *

The natural progression towards more sophisticated baits is really a matter of course. As we all become more and more aware of new food substances it follows that the inquisitive and adventurous amongst us will constantly strive to improve on our methods and baits. We should not,however, let bait determine our success but use it as an extension of our own basic angling ability. It is important that we examine all aspects of our approach equally. There is no single key that will unlock the door to consistent results. It is a combination of many things like perseverance, drive, confidence; the list is endless. Try to give your bait fair and due consideration and draw your own conclusions as to the degree of importance you must place on the subject. One of the most important factors when following any interest is self confidence. If you are convinced that the carp like your bait and you are fishing effectively, then your results should give you the confidence you require.

Many fish have external whiskers or feelers which are usually located near the mouth. Carp have four of these small appendages or barbules situated near their lips. These are in fact believed to be a form of external taste receptor, although carp rely to a greater extent on taste zones inside the lips and mouth. Before passing a likely food into the gut they will thoroughly feel and taste it. In doing so, they have been observed taking quite large quantities of seemingly valueless material into the mouth, such as mud, gravel and sand. For some reason they will often swallow this debris although it can be of little nutritional value. Perhaps an occasional intake of mud or sand asists in some digestive process, or maybe the carp sometimes become a little over enthusiastic when filtering out shrimps or blood worms from the silt.

When preoccupied by a sudden abundance of food, carp may be seen to dig and root with abandon, often burying their heads and even half their bodies into the lake bed. During these periods of intensive feeding activity, carp seem to rely almost entirely on smell and touch to find their food, often ignoring a bait which is placed nearby. Many people believe that the coating of protective slime on the fish can act as a means of transmitting taste and that a food morsel touched by the tail for example will cause the fish to turn and investigate. Although there is little evidence available to support this theory, there is no doubt that carp are perfectly aware of anything that touches them. Their reaction on coming into contact with line, especially on hard fished waters, can be very severe, often causing them to bolt. This reaction does not of course apply on all occasions.

Carp can and do feed at any time of the day or night and at any time of the year. It is up to us to determine the best feeding times. One cannot assume exactly which sense carp rely on most of all when selecting food because there are too many things to consider in any given situation. During periods of low light intensity, location of food is obviously by a combination of smell and touch. Carp are more likely to be attracted to an area if the food source is abundant, bloodworm and snail beds for example. These will hold them for a while, as the degree of preoccupation depends on the quantity of food present, for even carp of fifteen pounds can eat a great deal of food. It takes a lot of food to preoccupy a group of fish. During the hours of darkness individual food items such as anglers' baits or the odd snail would only be found by a travelling fish. A single bait or food particle would be more likely to be found under these conditions if it had an attractive smell. In daylight, carp still rely heavily on touch although sight plays a greater role in food finding. Out of pure

John Baker looks thankfully at a 30½ pound mirror which took 45 minutes to subdue.

curiosity they will examine all sorts of debris, from the lake bed to odd items suspended in mid-water or floating on the surface. Most fish including carp will copy each other, often seeming to play a sort of fish version of follow-my-leader. This is apparently beneficial for one carp will often lead another to food. Carp rely heavily on this and will often allow other members of a shoaling group to test a food source out first before they consider it safe. Usually the more members of the shoal there are feeding, the more confident that group of fish is. If the carp becomes confident in feeding on an angler's bait and sufficient free samples have been introduced into the water, then an almost ideal situation, from the angler's point of view, has been reached. What he has created, possibly without realizing it, is a situation of feeding security. All wild animals tend to drop their instinctive defences a little when provided with a plentiful and easily accessible food supply. What the angler must try to do is to fish effectively so that even the individual larger specimens can be caught off guard; after all, they require more food to live and are probably greedier fish.

If we now accept that carp, either in groups or individually, can be deceived into eating what are basically foreign food items, one question must now be asked: what type of food or bait will interest them most?

This question presents numerous problems because again there are so many factors which must be taken into consideration. Apart from the obvious problems such as good presentation, location of fish, etc, a bait must be found that the carp like.

In the name of sport, we as anglers return our catch, which obviously, even to the carp's primitive brain, is lesson enough to be wary of unusual food items and fishing lines. We can perhaps go a little further with this theory by comparing the method by which trout are often bred and grown to a catchable or eatable size. Then, on being released into lakes or reservoirs, they are left to fend for themselves, having no experience of anglers' baits. Although reared under artificial conditions they are basically wild fish, and when caught they are killed for food. A proportion of trout will be hooked and lost, or learn in other ways to be wary of anglers' baits and it is these individuals that are then the hardest to catch.

There are numerous reports of carp being caught on fish baits over the years and again these are usually fish which have taken a bait intended for other species. Besides confirmed records of carp caught on fish baits, one such case was witnessed by us in the December of 1977. The fish, an 18 pound mirror, was hooked fairly in the mouth and had taken a sprat to a wired snap tackle presented by a pike angler. These odd instances will still prompt some keen carp anglers into at least thinking about using fish baits.

With all natural type baits the same problem arises with presentation. If we choose to offer a carp a food substance with which it is familiar, we are immediately creating an area of suspicion because the carp is bound to know how the more natural and familiar things around it are likely to behave. All creatures are extremely curious at certain times. The carp is no exception and will frequently take unusual or new objects into its mouth. This is the best way a fish can learn and become used to its ever-changing environment. It is constantly on the lookout for food and is quick to capitalise on any new source.

It would be hard to say exactly when the first serious experimentation took place regarding carp baits. Certainly the Chinese were amongst the first to breed carp so it follows they were probably the first to put any serious thought into what a carp might like, or be persuaded, to eat.

Carp were reported to have been first introduced into the British Isles by monks, in the 14th and 15th centuries. Being self sufficient by choice, the monks somehow learned that by stocking nearby ponds and lakes with carp, a fish which seems to require little outside help to survive, they could then be easily caught and eaten. For what in fact was only a little work, they were providing themselves with a constant supply of fresh nutritious food. Perhaps then, it was the monks, who first began to think of ways in which to both feed their fish and find a simple way to catch them. Maybe a piece of bread, casually thrown into the water, was seen to be taken by a passing carp and the whole story began.

To many of us, early angling perhaps starts with the exploits of Isaak Walton, whose activities can be read about in that most famous of all angling books, 'The Compleat Angler'. Walton advocated what appears to be rather lengthy procedures in the preparation of carp baits, although when compared with the efforts we now go to, his ideas are much less involved. One cannot however disregard his suggestions, for they are undoubtedly based on a great wealth of experience. It must first be remembered that Walton's bait ideas are based on the capture of fish intended for the table; there are no allowances made for a carp which has been returned several times after capture and is aware of the danger of anglers' baits. Indeed, it must be stressed at this point that we would not need to find new bait recipes if the carp were not allowed to learn by the experience of capture.

Isaak Walton wrote 'The Compleat Angler' in 1640, so we may reasonably assume that if carp were first introduced to this country one or two hundred years previously, they must have been fairly well distributed in our rivers and lakes by the time the book was published.

Popular baits of the day were often quite complicated, like one recipe which involved mixing the flesh of rabbit or cat with bean flour, adding sugar or honey and beating together into a paste. Maggots were used and were thought to be especially effective when soaked in Oil of Peter or anointed with honey. Breadcrumb was thought to produce the best results when soaked in honey and mixed into a paste.

Of all the many angling books written since that early classic, there seems little reference made to the types of bait employed over the years. Whilst much has been talked of the methods by which carp can be caught, there appears to be no conclusive evidence of any major inroads into the

Many carp anglers prefer to use ready-made boilies nowadays. The Kevin Maddocks Maestro Boilies and Floaters are available in large and small packets, require no freezing, will remain fresh in an unopened bag for at least six months and are date stamped accordingly. Maestro Boilies have caught countless big carp of up to 40 pounds in England and up to 60 pounds in France. They are available in the following flavours: Mellow Lobster, Cream RM30, Honey Syrup, Smokey Maple, Gorganzola, Nice Spice and Peaches & Cream. They are relatively strong-flavoured baits and therefore require no pre-baiting and very little ground-baiting — just a few free-offerings around each hookbait is usually sufficient.

bait scene. Traherne and Sheringham, both noted carp catchers of their day, have mentioned baits which might best tempt a carp. There appears to have been little deviation from the use of breadcrust or paste, worms, maggots and wasp grubs. Fleeting reference is made to the use of strong cheese, coagulated sheep's blood, raw liver and other such delicacies. The use of small potatoes, lightly boiled, is a bait which has remained popular and effective to the present day.

On examining the observations of angling writers there does appear, more frequently than other baits, the use of bread in all its forms as being the most effective bait for carp. It is interesting how much importance is attached to the method of adding honey to bread paste to improve its taste. How ironic it is when one thinks of the exotic flavours we now use in baits; perhaps our ideas are not so original as we might think.

By the late 40's and early 50's carp angling, in its more specialised forms, began to grow in popularity. Anglers sought for new methods and baits when they began to find the carp were growing suspicious of the usual bread or potatoes.

There was now more information available on the subject. The 'Fishing Gazette' was a popular periodical. Here could be read the exploits of such anglers as Albert Buckley who caught a massive mirror carp that weighed 26lb from Mapperley reservoir in 1930.

Certain anglers became well known for their angling prowess or writing ability. Most notable of these was a Mr. Watkyns-Pitchford who still writes, under the pseudonym of BB. His most famous of books 'Confessions of a Carp Fisher' was eventually to become a carp fisher's bible, with its highly creative and informative passages and excellent illustrations.

There can be few of us however who have not heard of Richard Walker, who in the September of 1952 caught a huge common carp of 44 pounds. This fish far surpassed the estimated maximum weight for the species in this country and was to hold the record for many years. Its capture rocked the angling media and perhaps served as kindling for the growing fire of carp specialists ever since. Not long after the capture of his record fish Richard Walker and a few friends went on to form the Carp Catchers Club.

Despite the increased activity in carp circles, there was still little progress as far as baits were concerned. Great strides were made in methods and tactics but the old bread and potato routine still held good. One interesting trick was thought up for use when fishing over soft weed or silt. This was known as balanced baits. The usual method was to place a piece of crust on the bend of the hook and mould paste round the shank. The effect, after the bait had settled, was to counterbalance the bait to ensure that it lay lightly on top of the weed or silt, instead of being pulled into it.

Gradually, the carp angler was becoming more inventive. By now the carp in most waters were 'educated' fish, quick to realize that a large white object, lying on the lake bed or floating on the surface, spelt danger. Now, to catch his fish the carp angler began to fish regularly during the night-time. This tactic was favoured by the late Bill Keal who originated the use of a bedchair for night fishing. Now fishing sessions would often last a couple of days and sometimes great quantities of groundbait were used. Of course, more carp were caught but other fish were being caught too. Fish such as tench and bream would perhaps be eating most of the free samples and not allowing the carp to become used to the bait. Small tench and rudd, often abundant in carp waters, would constantly whittle away at a piece of crust or ball or paste, thereby leaving a bare hook when the carp came along. In order to overcome these problems it became apparent that new baiting methods should be employed. Breadpaste was made small-fish proof by immersing in boiling water for a minute or two, a method to be used later when making some special baits. Potatoes, instead of being boiled until quite soft, were only lightly boiled, making them harder for tench or bream to take. Other types of improved baits included flour and water kneaded to a stiff paste and immersed in boiling water, or semi-ripe banana, which is quite hard and effective although it does float to the surface in a rather unappetising brownish mass if not eaten. Cheeses also worked well, especially in the harder varieties. The idea was, to cut down the attentions of the unwanted species to allow the carp a better chance of finding the bait. After all, to be successful, is to catch carp, which is made easier if the swim is not disturbed by the constant striking, playing and casting caused by small fish eating the bait.

By the early sixties many hard-fished carp waters had been almost fished out on conventional baits. The occasional carp were caught on random baits and by good presentation, but usually at the beginning of the season when the carp were least suspicious.

It was in that most prolific of carp-counties, Kent, that the first real inroads into the bait-scene were made. One angler in particular who began to create a minor stir with his catches was Gerry Savage. Gerry and his friends considered using baits which had never previously been used for carp, and their results were staggering. They tried luncheon meat, already a proven bait for barbel and chub, which was stiffened to a paste with groundbait. It was deadly; the carp loved it. It was strong smelling, easy to use and completely different from anything previously tried. Gerry was catching in the region of one hundred carp a season and his angling ability and personality brought him instant recognition. Fired with enthusiasm and keen to catch more carp he helped pioneer the start of advanced carp baits. Articles appeared in the angling press by Gerry on such subjects as floating potatoes and pre-frozen baits. Other exotic ingredients were used such as grilled sausages, cat food and luncheon meat. Secret names were used on the bankside in front of other anglers. So effective were his methods that in the opening fortnight of 1968 Gerry caught 50 carp; a tremendous feat.

News travels fast on the carp grapevine and it wasn't long before hundred of weird and smelly baits were being used. By the early seventies the standard carp bait had now become catfood mixed to a paste with flour and crumb, but other minor alterations were made too. Flavours were added such as Bovril, Oxo or curry. The idea was to use anything that the carp might think was new or better. Anglers probably confused themselves as much as they did the carp.

In another area of Kent during the late sixties, adopting the usual low key activities now associated with specialist carp anglers, another carp fanatic had been doing some research. His theory was that carp, like other animals must have a balanced diet in order to survive. In other words carp must obtain all the nutrients essential to life: protein, carbohydrate, fat, vitamins and minerals. He considered that if it were possible to educate the carp into taking a bait which provided all these compounds in one go, then perhaps it would also be possible to convert the carp into taking an exclusive food. In other words, a bait which provided them with a perfect balanced diet. Admittedly, these ideas were rather far removed from the humble breadpaste. But, like many fanatical carp men Fred Wilton pursued his theories with the single minded determination that only a carp specialist knows. In 1972 Fred's theories and results appeared in a magazine issued by the British Carp Study Group and this marked the start of High Nutritional Value baits.

With all the organisations, clubs, syndicates and specimen groups dedicated to the pursuit of carp, one would perhaps be excused from assuming that there could now be little progress made to improve our sport. How wrong we would be though. Even now it is certain that there are activities afoot, especially in the bait scene, to find even more effective methods. Perhaps the answer is a purely chemical bait containing some secret drug which is irresistible to the carp, or perhaps the would-be chemists have had their day and it's all back to basics.

*   *   *   *   *

Before we become too involved in this complex subject it may be worth outlining a few salient points by way of preparation for what is to follow.

Rather that to attempt to delve into every single aspect of baits and cover them completely, the idea is to list and describe as many known carp baits and ingredients as possible. The sections will contain methods of preparation and the relative advantages of certain individual ingredients. All the information has been prepared as carefully and as accurately as possible. Whilst there are bound to be certain omissions it is fair to say that all substances mentioned have either individually or in combination accounted for the capture of carp in the British Isles.

Standard Baits

Bread	Cheese	Luncheon Meat
Worms	Potatoes	Sausage Meat
Maggots	Sweet Corn	Trout Pellets

Ron Middleton with a nice double.

The baits that appear under this heading are now accepted as standard in carping circles. They are those baits which are recognised by both the average and specialist angler alike. Each of these could be perhaps described as the most effective without being too complex. They have stood the test of time and so they may be used with confidence under any conditions. There are three common factors which determine their inclusion:

1) The most consistently effective.
2) The most easily obtained.
3) The most easily prepared.

Whilst there are numerous other baits which seemingly fit into these three categories, those listed above are considered to be the best. One could be excused for questioning what can be written about bread which has not already been said,but there is, still, most definitely, a place for it in modern carp fishing. It is cheap by most bait standards and very versatile; breadflake is unique in texture and difficult to reproduce. Flake is buoyant, and depending on how hard the hookbait is compressed it can be made to sink slowly and rest on a silty or weedy bottom. Crust is especially effective for suspended or surface fishing. Its attraction can be increased by dipping it into an additive such as honey, treacle, jam, Bovril, Marmite or your own special 'dip'. Small squares of bread may be made into a good bait by frying in deep fat, especially the fat you've just cooked your breakfast in!

Worms are especially good on richer waters, those which are often clear and heavily weeded. In these waters worm as a bait may often succeed when you least expect it to. Large lob-worms are not necessarily always the best to use; medium size 'blue-heads' or bunches of brandlings are ideal as 'intercept' baits for cruising fish. Try using a fine needled syringe for injecting air into the worms which can be made to float enticingly in the surface film or sink slowly through the water.

There can be few baits more universally used than maggots. Carp love them. When confronted by an appetising carpet of these white grubs few fish can resist gorging themselves. Some good catches of carp have been made by using maggots especially after heavily pre-baiting with them. However, it is the attraction of maggots which draws other fish too, so their use is usually limited depending on the types and quantity of other fish present. Dead or scalded maggots are believed to be equally or occasionally better than live ones. Chrysalises or casters are a good carp bait and seem to work well in winter.

Cheese and bread paste is standard mixture as this tends to keep the cheese softer in water and makes it go further. Many different types of cheese are effective as baits, but most recognised success has been achieved with Cheddar, Red Leicester, Edam, cream cheeses and some smoked varieties. Stilton and Dolcellate are really powerful but at nearly £2 a pound, are too expensive for the carp. Cheese can be used in many ways and can be moulded or cut to size. A good method is to dice it into tiny cubes and use it in multiple form. Small ¼" cubes work best.

Many carp anglers caught their first carp on potato, yet despite the length of time for which they have been used, potatoes will still catch carp. For some reason, potatoes can completely fail on certain waters yet on others their initial use or 'revival' can be very worthwhile. Tinned potatoes are easier to use as they are soft and about the right size. Fresh potatoes should be boiled until they are soft enough to be eaten, yet hard enough to stay on the hook. They can be used with or without skins or even partially peeled. They can be cut into any shape or size, made to float, or even made into chips; all these variations can be good baits.

It is always a good idea to carry a tin of luncheon meat, which is an excellent bait at all times of the year and rarely needs to be introduced in large quantities. Some varieties have a spicy strong smell, others are very meaty. There are certain brands, especially the unwrapped sorts, which have a very high fat content and which float. Others are hard and rubbery and all are different colours and prices. No two brands are the same. Listed below are some of the best varieties:

| Bacon Grill | Unox Chopped Ham & Pork | Dana |
| Spam | Unox Pork Luncheon Meat | Tudor Queen |

Pork sausage meat, not unlike luncheon meat, seems to attract the carp by its powerful 'porky' smell. Pure sausage meat works best although the meat squeezed from the actual sausage can be equally effective. This does contain other ingredients such as rusk, crumb and spices. On its own sausage meat is far too sticky for a hookbait, although one bait may be made from it without adding anything. Flatten out the meat to about half an inch thickness in hamburger size pieces. Then simply fry them until firm. A light dusting of flour will help to prevent them sticking to the pan. When cool, they can be cut into the desired baitsize pieces. Some sausage meat will contain pieces of gristle which can impede hook penetration. Although it is a bit messy picking them all out it is worth doing so to ensure the hook-bait is smooth and consistent. This is not necessary for the free offerings.

During the winter time when water temperatures are low, sausage meat baits tend to go a bit hard. Unfortunately, this is difficult to prevent and is caused by the fat content. It pays to buy the best quality you can, and this is the sausage with the highest meat content. There are numerous ingredients which can be added to sausage meat to make it into a good paste, but the more things added, the less attractive the smell is. Any dry powder or cereal binder will work. Below are three recipes which have caught carp.

1lb Sausage Meat	1lb Pork Sausage Meat	1lb Sausage Meat
5oz breadcrumb (approx)	stiffened with	¼ cup ground cloves
½oz Vencat curry powder	Pomenteg	1oz flour
½ teaspoon salt	groundbait	4oz breadcrumb

Of all the many carp baits, there can be very few that surpass sweet corn. Here is a bait which consistently catches carp at any time of the year. Sweet corn has everything in its favour: size, shape, colour, smell and taste. Admittedly it is attractive to other species, but, like so many other baits, when the carp decide to feed it is very good. Some anglers believe the fish are drawn by the amino acid content (sweet corn has a high lysine content) but this would be difficult to prove. Depending on your requirements it is best to try and buy corn in bulk packs. Twelve 12oz tins can be bought at a reduced price from small shops or a cash and carry store. If a long session is planned, the 7lb tins are good value. The three best varieties are Jolly Green Giant – Niblets, Sainsburys and Del-Monte. Some anglers use the frozen variety but these do not seem as good as the tinned sorts which keep smelly and moist in the milky juices of the tin. Even if you are transferring corn to a different container it is a good idea to keep it covered with the juice. On a long session this begins to ferment, a condition favoured all the more by the carp.

Trout pellets are a scientifically designed fish food and are therefore certain to be a good bait for carp. The strong smell attracts fish and the balanced food value satisfies them. TP is very popular, fairly cheap, and easy to use. They may be made into a soft paste by mixing with boiling water, or ground to a powder and used 'neat' with eggs as a form of HNV paste. By far the most effective method is the T.P. boiled bait which is made as follows:

You will need a coffee or food grinder to grind the pellets into a powder. This powder can now be added to other interesting powders or used as it is. If used alone, simply mix in enough eggs to make up a good dollop of stiffish paste. Then pull off small bait size pieces and roll into small balls between the hands. When all the paste has been used, the baits will be ready for immersion in boiling water, which can be done by lowering a few at a time in a wire chip basket. This process gives them a rubbery outer skin rendering them less susceptible to the attentions of small fry, easier to cast and longer lasting. Immersion time varies according to how hard a skin is required, how hard the original paste was and how many are lowered into the pan at once (too many makes the water go off the boil); 45-90 seconds is average.

'Special' Baits

'Specials' are baits made by using a number of ingredients which are mixed to form a food/bait attractive to carp. If high protein substances are used combined with balanced vitamins and minerals, they will be baits of high nutritive value (HNV), but if materials high in carbohydrates are used they will be low protein baits. Either can be equally effective, and it is worth remembering that you won't necessarily produce a good bait by using many different, expensive, and rare ingredients.

Choose one of the bait recipes suggested in this book, or make up your own from the materials listed, and try it in your water, having first attempted to find out what kind of baits have already been used at the chosen water. If there seems to be definite evidence to indicate that the carp no longer take a particular bait, it would be better to try something different, although bearing in mind that your information may not always be correct.

Pre-baiting is not always necessary, especially in waters which already receive large quantities of baits from other anglers.

A hard-fighting Cambridgeshire common weighing a little over 20 pounds.

After some observation at the water, you may find that it would be better to use a multiple bait instead of paste, especially if it appears that other anglers have not been using multiples.

You will have to make a decision on whether you will use a 'soft' water-based paste, or whether you will use eggs instead of water, and boil the baits. Soft pastes usually give off a stronger smell and taste and may attract more fish as they break down in the water. This is especially useful when the water temperatures are low. The main use for boiled baits is to prevent unwanted species from taking the bait, and this may also include small carp in carp only waters.

Paste Baits

Paste baits are simply made by the inclusion of two principle ingredients; a bulk ingredient and a binding agent. For example a simple special could be tinned pilchards, mashed with a fork and kneaded together with wholemeal flour. Here, the fibres of pilchard flesh are held together and carried by the flour which has a glutinous (wheat gluten) content and allows a smooth paste to be prepared. Similarly, liquidised or ground Go-Cat must be made into a holding paste, which can be improved by the addition of a little flour. Or you could use the dry powdered cat foods to bind together a moist tinned meat like tuna or Kit-E-Kat. The possibilities are endless. Listed below are a few combinations which have accounted for many good catches:

> Kit-E-Kat and breadcrumbs
> Pilchards and wholemeal flour
> Tinned Kipper fillets and breadcrumbs
> Liver Sausage and Rusk
> Trout pellets and Whiskas
> Wheat gluten and tinned sardines
> Munchies and tinned pilchards in tomato sauce
> Chappie and ground Go-Dog

Examples of Sodium Caseinate Pastes (add water)

5oz Sodium Caseinate	4oz Sodium Caseinate	4oz Sodium Caseinate
2oz Pym or Yestamin	3oz Herring meal	2oz Layers meal
4oz Milk powder	2oz Soya flour	4oz Trout pellets
4oz Wheat germ		

4oz Sodium Caseinate	5oz Sodium Caseinate	3oz Sodium Caseinate
1oz Farina	2oz Corn meal	1oz W.gluten
5oz ground Munchies	1oz Gluten (or farina)	2oz Bread crumb
	2oz Milk powder	3oz Larvstart
	1oz Codlivine	

4oz Sodium Caseinate	3oz Sodium Caseinate	3oz Sodium Caseinate
2oz Bread crumb or	4oz Cheese powder	3oz Peanut meal
soya isolate/flour	2oz Milk powder	1oz Butter
2oz Milk powder		1oz Corn meal
1oz sugar		
(plain carrier for adding		
liquid flavours)		

4oz Sodium Caseinate	4oz Sodium Caseinate	4oz Sodium Caseinate
1oz Gluten or Farina	4oz ground hemp	1oz sugar
5oz PTX (soft budgie	2oz Milk powder	3oz Equivite milk
food)	1oz sugar	pellets
		2oz Banana Nesquik

There are some rather 'advanced' paste-type baits which may all be used in many different ways. Most substances which have a fairly high protein content are somewhat glutinous by nature or at least possess certain binding or adhesive properties. Fish, for example, is high in protein, hence the use of fish meal and bones in the manufacture of glue. Casein is a milk derived protein of which some types are used as adhesives. Flour contains wheat gluten which makes it sticky; a crude glue may even be made by mixing flour and water together. By mixing ingredients with these protein substances, some new special paste can be produced. Casein, although a beneficial ingredient with a high food value, does not dissolve in water, and will not absorb enough water to make it a good paste bait ingredient. Sodium Caseinate and calcium caseinate (Casilan), are again derived from milk and make excellent binding agents. Texture changes occur when using sodium and calcium caseinates, which give the bait smooth waxy finish.

Wheat gluten is a good binder causing baits to go spongy and rubbery if used in large quantities. A combination of sodium caseinate and gluten gives a better consistency than if they are used individually. Casilan is rather expensive, and as it is really only acting as a binder and carrier it is equally effective and fifty per cent cheaper to use sodium caseinate. Potato starch (Farina) is equally good as another binder and is far cheaper.

Boiled Specials

When looking for a bait which will consistently catch carp with the minimum possible interference from other species, boiled baits are best. Apart from predatory fish there are no other fish with mouths or throat passages the size of a carp's. The only fish that may pick up a large carp bait is a big tench or chub, although even a huge specimen could not easily pass a walnut-sized boiled bait into its 'stomach' or crush it. There are occasions when a hard boiled bait is picked up by a nuisance fish in the lips, despite the fact that it would be an impossible meal. It is therefore reasonable to assume that the largest bait required would be about walnut size. Those anglers who use much larger baits will admittedly receive less attention from nuisance fish, but it may be that such a huge bait will put the carp off! The ideal size for a boiled bait is between half to three-quarters of an inch in diameter.

The general idea is to provide an acceptable bait which, although recognisable to the carp is both practical to use and long lasting once cast out. Carp can be converted into taking baits exclusively, but usually will only rely on anglers' baits when their natural food is not so abundant, or if the water is over-stocked and subsequently a 'hungry' one.

A good boiled bait lasts a long time under water and therefore stands more chance of being found by the carp. This is important, for a wary fish will often inspect a bait many times before eventually deciding to eat it. A boiled special can be made as hard as you like, so the chances are it will eventually be eaten, and by a carp.

Because of these facts and the confidence they instil in the angler, boiled baits undoubtedly remain the most efficient way of presenting a bait. Boiled baits must always be prepared with patience and care and there are one or two ideas which will make this easier. A good boiled bait should have the following:

1) A binding agent (other than the eggs, although occasionally eggs are a sufficient binder)
2) A bulk ingredient
3) A good taste and smell.
N.B. To avoid the expense of eggs, substitutions of ⅓ water may be made in some mixes.

On this basis a good boiled bait can now be produced, for example:

Binding agent: 1 oz Wheat gluten
Bulk ingredient, good taste and smell: 9 oz ground Go-Cat

This is a straightforward boiled special which is easily made and is relatively inexpensive. The combined powders are simply mixed with sufficient eggs to make a stiff paste, then rolled and boiled as usual. Here, the Go-Cat provides a smelly, balanced bulk food with a good consistency, and the wheat gluten helps it to hold together and prevents small problems like 'splitting' when a hook is inserted. A more complete example and another good bait is as follows;

Binding agent:	1oz Wheat gluten or Farina
	1oz Sodium Caseinate
Bulk ingredient:	4oz Linseed meal
Good taste and	3oz milk powder
attractive smell:	1oz yeast powder

There are no hard and fast rules about the preparation of specials other than the need to experiment with the ingredients you intend to use. Some meals for example are rather coarse and will make a bait crumble, while others are oily and soak up the dry ingredients during mixing to make a crumbly inconsistent mixture. Care must also be taken not to mix together

The Ashlea common pictured here after its first-ever capture on a bottom bait. The fish took Spam presented on a hair rig.

too many 'light' ingredients like sodium caseinate or milk powders, daphnia and baby foods, as it can lead to baits almost melting or having a spongy, fluffy effect after boiling. Some mixes will float during boiling. When this happens, it is again likely to be due to too many light, heat affected ingredients. Immediate removal of the baits when they float to the surface will usually ensure that they are 'sinkers' after hardening. If, however, you are having trouble with the lighter ingredients then it may help to introudce an ingredient which is heavy and does not effect the overall mix too drastically. Heavy ingredients include ground rice, ground pasta, semolina, corn meal and maize meal.

Boiled Bait Method

After selecting the blend of 'dry' or 'powder form' ingredients they should all be mixed together first, after careful weighing and listing of ingredients. If the bait is to contain any liquids other than eggs then these should also be prepared in a separate vessel. No matter what ingredients are used the following method should be used on every occasion to achieve the best results.

1) Thoroughly mix all dry ingredients and sieve if necessary.
2) Crack eggs into clean mixing basin, beat eggs and add all other liquid ingredients, then mix together briskly.
3) Now add prepared dry ingredients, a little at a time, mixing thoroughly and keep adding dry ingredients until a 'tacky' paste is obtained. obtained.
4) At this point, depending on the materials used, it is best to add more of the dry ingredients than look to be right. Really thorough kneading and mixing will leave you with a paste stiff enough to roll into balls. If the mix is too soft, the balls of bait will lose their shape before or during boiling (i.e. ◄ instead of ●). A slight flattening may occur while the balls of bait rest on the working surface; this is acceptable.
5) Having already prepared a large saucepan of boiling water, gather about forty baits into your hands and carefully drop them into the boiling water. Begin timing by the second hand of a kitchen clock or watch. As you keep an eye on the time agitate the surface of the boiling water with a spoon to create a whirlpool effect in the water; this avoids sticking. Boiling time varies from 30 seconds to three minutes depending on the hardness required and the type of mix being used, 60 seconds being normal.
6) When the required boiling time is up, pour the water through a fine sieve into an empty saucepan and replace on heat to continue boiling

1. Adding liquid flavouring to eggs.

2. Mixing in the dry powder mix.

3. Rolling baits from paste ball.

4. Tipping baits into boiling water.

5. Laying baits out to dry on kitchen towel.

ready for the next lot. If only one batch is required then simply hold a plate against the saucepan and tip up allowing the water to escape from the saucepan and then empty the baits onto a cloth.

7) Take the pile of steaming baits and scatter on an old blanket or smooth piece of cloth to dry off. They may be left on a fine wire cake tray to dry but a cloth (or similar) lain on the worktop will absorb the moisture which collects on the underside of each bait.

8) The outer skin on most boiled baits can be made harder if the balls are left to stand for five or six hours. One hour's drying and cooling is sufficient, although an overnight dry-off gives them a really tough finish.

9) If a supply is being made for freezing, try to reduce the boiling time and attempt to make a 'moister' bait. Freezing tends to dehydrate baits a little.

List of Typical 'Special' Ingredients

Pet Foods	Meals
Kit-E-Kat	Maize
9 Lives	Corn
Whiskers	Almond
Deli-Cat	Peanut
Purina, Sea Nips	Hazelnut
Go-Cat	Barley
Felix Crunch	Layers
Munchies	Wheat
Go-Dog	Hemp
Minced Morsels	Sago
Tender Morsels	Alfalfa
Hap	Safflour Seed
Lassie	Cotton Seed
Chappie	Coconut
Pedigree Chum	Caplin
Nectablend	White-fish
PTX	Herring
Robin Red	Cod
Sluis	Dried blood powder
Formula One	Soya
Prosecto-insectiverous	Lucern
Frolic dog food	Groundnut
	Linseed

Fish Foods and Animal Feeds

Cow Pellets
Horse Feeds (Equivite, Codlivine)
Pig Pellets
Pig Meal
Chicken Feeds
Pheasant Pellets
Trout Pellets
Salmon foods
Carp Pellets
Larvstart (Carp feed)
Molasine
Nukamel
Tetramin (Fish flakes)
Pond Pride (Fish pellets)
Sepia Fish Food
Dried Daphnia

Flours

Wholemeal
Plain & self raising
Soya
Rice
Corn

Miscellaneous

Dried Rusk
Breadcrumb
Milkfoods (Complan, Casilan, etc)
Milk powder (Cow & Gate baby
  milks, Coffee Mate, 5 pints,
  Marvel, etc.)
Breakfast cereals
Semolina
Tapioca
Dried Yeasts (PYM, Yestamin, etc.)
Cheese powder
Cheeses
Tuna Fish (tins)
Sardine (tins)
Kipper (tins)
Sild (tins)
Pilchards (tins)
Herring (tins)
Salmon (tins)
Pasta
Squid or Octopus (liquidised)
Sodium Caseinate
Wheat Gluten
Liver sausage
Sausage Meat
Farina (Potato starch)
Cal-Pro
Texturised Vegetable Protein (TVP)
Edisol
Offal (liquidised)

Typical Boiled Specials (add eggs)

10oz Munchies	6oz Munchies	8oz Sluis Universal
1oz Sodium Caseinate	3oz W/Germ	8oz Sluis Mynah food
1oz W/Gluten	1oz Sodium Caseinate	2oz Casilan
1oz W/Germ		
7oz Trout Pellets	Liquidised squid & eggs	4oz Dried Daphnia
1oz Sodium Caseinate	stiffened with ground	3oz Go-Cat
1oz Soya flour	pasta or semolina	1oz Sodium caseinate
1oz Codlivine		1oz Semolina

4oz Tetramin	6oz Salmon Fry	6oz Peanut Meal
3oz Soya flour	3oz Milk powder	1oz Gluten
2oz Milk powder	1oz Corn flour	1oz Sodium Caseinate
1oz Ground rice		2oz Nukamel

With some ingredients it is possible to make a boiled bait which does not contain eggs. This type of bait requires no exotic ingredients providing the recipe contains a good proportion of starch-based masterials such as ground pasta, semolina or bean flour. The advantage of these baits is that they can be made quickly and cheaply. Pre-prepared, dry mixes may then be taken to the lakeside, the only additional requirement being lake water! Care should be taken in choosing a recipe; since these baits rarely contain more than two or three ingredients the correct balance of 'binder' will have to be found. Most of the beans and seeds used in carp fishing can be milled down and used as a binding ingredient. Milled chick peas, maple peas, tic beans and black eye beans are all suitable and offer a good change of diet to the carp who may have grown used to protein-based baits.

Typical Boiled Specials (add water)

4oz Soya flour	Liquidized squid stiffened
7oz Semolina	with semolina.
1oz Wheat gluten	

7oz Ground maple peas
4oz Soya flour
1oz Yestamin

Additives

In the earlier parts of this section the inclusion of what is broadly termed, 'additives' was omitted. This is a way of trying to avoid a certain amount of confusion, since additives are really a small proportion of the whole bait which on their own would be too strong or unusable. The inclusion of an additive should make two important changes to the bait:

1) It changes the smell or gives it a new one.
2) It changes the taste or gives it a new one.

An additive can be used when a special bait is losing its effectiveness, although of course, with the multitude of alternatives available it is possible that the original bait my already contain an additive or two.

Additives allow the angler to change the bait quickly and effectively without altering the entire mix too much. It would be a pity to invest in a sack of trout pellets only to find the carp have gone off them in a few weeks. However, by including a spoonful of curry powder or cinnamon powder, a new bait is created.

These ingredients really come into their own when used subtly. It is easy to overdo bait making and end up with a really strong smelling/ tasting bait which can actually put the carp off. It is wrong to say that some of this or that should be added, but it is right to keep notes of exactly what ingredients you have used and then find out for yourself which combination works best. As a general rule it could be said that most of the items listed may be used in the sort of quantity that enables you to detect it once made up (ie, any sensible amount). Those ingredients which will most definitely put the carp off when used in excessive amounts are ones like culinary essences, concentrated flavours, spices, etc. These substances when used in large amounts will certainly make the bait smell, but will also make it taste 'hot, bitter, or sour', which is unacceptable to the fish. There are bound to be exceptions to this rule and quite possibly there are some anglers who have caught fish when using two bottles of clove oil per mix, or neat curry powder and garlic paste! These are quite definitely *exceptions* and on no account will extra helpings of any powerful ingredient make the bait more effective. Carp have highly sensitive smell and taste organs, so the most minute alterations of 'attractor' may be considered as something new. At this point it must be stressed that too slight an alteration for the bait may be insufficient to mask its original smell/taste, so once again it will be down to trial and error.

List of Typical Additives

Sweet

Brown sugar	Horlicks
Lemonade	White sugar
Ovaltine	Treacle
Malted Milk	Black Treacle
Malt extract	Honey
M.C.P. (maple concentrate)	Nectar
Coffee	Saccharin
Chocolate	Glycerin
Glucose	Jelly
Fructose	Marzipan

Sugar Cane
Dextrose
Jam
Marmalade
Maltose

Condensed milk
Evaporated milk
Culinary flavours
Peppermint
Caramelized sugar

Savoury

Peanut Butter
Butter
Culinary flavours
Packet soups
Dripping
Soup cubes
Stock cubes
Beer
Halibut oil
Garlic sauce
Bovril
Clove oil
Sea-food spreads
Curry powder
Tomato puree
Tomato sauce
Monosodium glutamate
Marmite
Wheat Germ Oil
Soy bean oil

Dried soups
Tinned soups
Lard
Peanut oil
Pilchard oil
Corn oil
Cod Liver oil
Fruity sauces
Bisto
Cinnamon oil
Cheese spreads
Oxo
Onion
'Paxo' stuffings
Liver extract
Liver pâté
Mustard
Spices & Peppers
Olive oil
Liver infusion

Flavours and Essences

Nearly all flavours and essences are in some degree concentrated; they are, after all, designed to be added to food products in order to enhance the smell or taste. In carp baits, flavours can be used in many effective ways although great care must always be taken in the amounts used. The flavours most widely known are those used in cake making. Everyone has probably seen vanilla or lemon essence being added to a cake mix, and these flavours are available in any good supermarket at a cost of only a few pence. The drawback is that choice is somewhat limited. Chemists and some continental stores often have unusual flavours tucked away on a shelf, so it's always worth looking around.

There are two types of flavours, natural and synthetic. Natural flavours usually work best and of course they seem more realistic as well as smelling and tasting so. Synthetic flavours are created by chemists known as 'flavourists' whose sole job is to blend various chemicals together to create food flavours. There are many companies which specialise in this field and it is a good idea to write direct to these companies (see list) requesting a list of liquid or powder flavours supplied to the food trade. Care must be taken when using any flavour supplied direct, as these are often very highly concentrated. Solutions vary in strength from as much as 1000-1 to 30-1. It is best to ask your supplier about the concentrations of their flavours. Use an accurate measuring device such as a measuring cup or spoon (supplied by chemists), add powders to powdered bait mixes and liquid flavours to the water or eggs prior to blending in the dry bait mix. The best way to test a flavour is to

'Scaley', the best of three good twenties taken during one hectic afternoon at the School Pool in Kent.

chew a small piece of the finished bait; do not swallow it, and when you are satisfied with its taste spit it out and if necessary rinse out the mouth with water. Many flavours will seem 'hot, bitter or sour' although most will taste bitter. It will be obvious when too much has been used although sweeteners such as glycerin or sugar will counteract some of the bitter taste and render the final bait more acceptable to the carp. Take care when tasting any chemical by mouth as food flavours taste strange because they are concentrated and often give a false impression if smelt or tasted 'neat'. Smelling a flavour straight from the bottle is often appealing but does not always convey an accurate description of the contents. Flavourists use absorbent paper strips which they dip into a liquid and wave under the nose. Powders are often tasted and smelt in solution by dissolving in water.

During the making of a flavoured special the room (and sometimes the whole house!) smells strongly of the flavour. Because you are there all the time you become accustomed to the smell and it doesn't appear quite as strong. Do not let this persuade you to increase the amount of flavour, for when you eventually arrive at the lakeside and open your bait box, the bait flavour may be too strong if too much additive has been included.

Paste baits will disseminate flavour better than boiled baits which tend to seal in some of the flavour, some of which may also have evaporated during the boiling process. It always pays to keep a close record of the amounts used and not to be tempted to add a bit more.

If you have been able to determine the strengths of the flavour you are using then an ideal amount of flavour of say 1/200 strength would be 5-15 ml liquid per 1 lb of bait. When using a flavour at random then a careful tasting and recording of amounts is by far the best method.

If you are dubious about eating bait then even the strongest flavours should not be used at a ratio of more than 10 ml per 10 oz of bait mix.

List of Flavours Known to be Effective (*some of the best)

Raspberry	Cherry	Milk*	Prawn Shrimp*
Strawberry*	Coffee	Cream*	Mushroom
Pear	Almond	Cheese	Crab
Apple	Vanilla	Butter*	Liver
Pineapple	Rum	Creamy toffee	Clove
Rose	Rum butter	Hazelnut*	Cinnamon*
Spearmint*	Maple*	Brandy	(Cassia)
Blackcurrant	Butterscotch*	Nutmeg	Peppermint
Bun spice*	Chocolate	Coconut	Orange

Peach*	Liquorice*	Aniseed	Ginger
Apricot	Malt*	Banana	Lemon
Caramel*	Peanut	Toffee	Sherry
Eucalyptus	Fenugreek	M.C.P.	Creme-de-menthe

Flavour Companies (for addresses see reference guide)

Geoff Kemp (special range available)
Rushside Baits
Dubuis & Rowsell
H. Kohnstamm

Sweeteners

Recent findings concerning the carp's taste responses have shown that while carp are attracted by a flavoured bait their final acceptance is more likely to be governed by its taste. Because so many modern-day carp baits contain chemical-based attractors, which may have an unpleasant after-taste, the use of counteracting taste additives, or taste enhancers, has increased. We know that carp are strongly attracted to sweet, spicy and savoury substances but anglers are only recently finding that catches can be greatly increased by ensuring that the bait has a pleasant or distinctive taste.

Initial research showed that carp found glycerin, saccharin and honey attractive, but more recent experimentation has proved that certain sweet substances will significantly alter the effective life of a bait. Currently there are a number of concentrated sweeteners on the market, nearly all of which are based on a blend of cane sugar and saccharin and each supplier will recommend dosage. It is, however, well worth considering some alternative sweet substances which either singly or mixed will do just as well as the commercial ones. Honey, treacle, fructose, lactose, liquid Hermasetas, Sweetex and caramelized sugar are all worth considering and readily available.

High Nutritive Value and High Protein Baits

The originator of the HP and HNV bait idea was Fred Wilton, who based his theories on the fact that all living creatures require a 'balanced' diet of proteins, carbohydrates, fat, vitamins and minerals if they are to grow well and be healthy. He thought that if correctly balanced baits of this kind could be supplied to the carp, they would instinctively be able to select baits with a high nutritive value, and might even come to prefer these over natural food because of their instinct and the obvious con- venience of finding all the required nutrients in one 'lump', rather than having to use extra energy in searching out the natural foods in the form of different water creatures.

Whether you agree with this idea or not, there was no doubt that Fred Wilton type baits were exceptionally successful, usually outfishing other baits used on the same waters, and the high protein and mineral sub- stances he used for his baits still form the basis for most baits of this type used today. Given the differences between carp in different waters, and the varying chemistry of these waters, it would obviously be quite impossible to provide a 'perfect' carp food, or, indeed, an 'ultimate' carp bait. What is more, low protein baits such as bread, sweet corn, seeds, peas and beans are also very successful, at least for a time, so a high protein level is not necessarily essential, and the palatabiality, taste, and smell of the bait used is often more important than the protein content. While the detailed requirements of a correct carp diet are not known, much research has been done on animal foods, including those for humans, and it is reasonable to assume that a similarly balanced diet to that used for animals will be good for carp. Although it seems that biologists have done little research on carp foods, it is well known that meat, fish and some grains are good foods for carp, and Edward Baker of Sudbury, Suffolk, now produce a carp pellet for feeding which must contain about the right quantity of nutrients as carp fed on these pellets are achieving a very fast growth rate.

Baits, of course, must have other qualities than a good nutritive balance; they must be made to stay on the hook, and must not break down too quickly in water. Although it might be thought that a good HNV bait would be successful in a rich water, this is often not so, and small multiple-size baits are often better. However, HNV or HP baits can be cut into tiny pieces if one has the patience, and these can sometimes be more successful in the richer waters than either larger HP pastes or seed type baits.

Most carp waters today are bombarded with large quantities of all types of bait. If these are 'poor' baits – that is, baits where the nutritive value is low – much of the pre-baiting may be wasted, as the bait may actually not be taken; or, at least, it may be taken as a novelty at first but soon rejected when the carp find they don't like it, or when they sense that it is not doing them good.

After many years of trial and error by carp anglers, there are now known to be a large number of substances from which good baits of this kind can be made, and a list of these substances follows:

Typical Ingredients for HNV Baits

Edible Casein
Cow and Gate Baby Milks
Sodium Caseinate
Complan (Trade name)
Calcium Caseinate or Casilan
   (Trade name)
Lactalbumin
Wheat Gluten
Whey Powder
Wheat Germ
Soya Isolate
Texturised Vegetable Protein
Yestamin (Trade name)
Healthilife (Trade name)

PYM (Phillips Yeast Mixture,
   Trade name)
Codlivine (Trade name)
Equivite (Trade name)
Pure dried blood meal
Peanut gluten
Egg albumen
Edisol (Trade name)
Meal Meal
Soya Flour
Corn Meal
Pure Vitamins
Pure Minerals
Corn Oil/Cooking Oil

Protein Content of Various Foodstuffs

Milk Products	% Protein
Cows' Milk (fresh)	3.5
Cows' Milk (dried)	23
Dried, Skimmed Milk	36
Cheese	15
Casein	90
Sodium Caseinate	90+
Calcium Caseinate	90+
Lactalbumin	80
Whey Powder	45+

Eggs	
Fresh, whole	12
Dried	35
Dried and Defatted	77

Meat and Fish	
Dried Chicken	75
Roast Beef	85
Dried Beef	70
Cured Ham	15
Gelatine	100
Plain Fish Meal	76
Herring Meal	75
Mackerel Meal	70+
Meat Meal	–

A fine leather weighing 33 pounds 5 ounces; part of a fabulous June opening session which included a mirror of 30 pounds 5 ounces plus eight doubles from the Mid-Northants carp fishery.

Seeds and Nuts

Soya Bean	40
Soya Concentrates & Isolates	50+
Lima Bean	20
Lentil	25
Chick Pea	25
Peanut	27
Peanut Concentrate	55
Sunflower Seed	27
Sunflower Seed Concentrate (Defatted)	50
Walnut	19
Cashew	75

Cereals

Wheat Flour	12
Rice	8
Corn	8
Maize	8
Macaroni, Spaghetti (ie pasta)	12
Oatmeal	13
Buckwheat	11
Pearl Barley	11
Wheat Gluten	80

Miscellaneous

Potato	2.5
Tapioca	1.5
Brewers Yeast	40+
Wheat Germ	40
Egg Albumen	80+
Pure Dried Blood Meal	85
Peanut Gluten	60
Soya Flour	40

The food items mentioned in the list will provide a substantial proportion of the protein ingredients. Many of them also contain varying levels of other nutrients. By blending some of these foodstuffs the requirements of an HNV or HP bait can be met. However, the choice of a protein based bait is not determined by nutrient level alone; the ingredients should be selected for two reasons. Firstly, to provide the carp with a good food, and secondly to provide the angler with a practical bait. Fortunately there is some leeway in making these types of bait. By juggling around with small amounts of ingredients a sensible hookbait can easily be made.

By referring to the chart, a quick selection of the ingredients required can be made. Any combination of ingredients is possible depending on the type of bait required. It is advisable not to exceed the maximum percentage amount per bait mix, as this will defeat the purpose of a balanced nutrient bait.

Some examples of high protein bait mixes are:

Example 1	*Example 2*	*Example 3*
5oz Casein	5oz Casein	5oz Casein
1oz Lactalbumin	2oz Soya Concentrate	1oz Lactalbumin
1oz Gluten	1oz Egg Albumen	1oz Calcium
1oz Equivite	1oz Codlivine	Caseinate
2oz Soya Flour	1oz Sugar	1oz Gluten
		1oz Soya Flour
		1oz Complan

If the actual % protein content of a finished bait is required, it may be calculated by multiplying the amount of each ingredient used by its own protein value. These figures are then added and divided by the overall amount of units used, i.e. –

Example 1

5oz Casein	5 x 90	= 450
1oz Lactalbumin	1 x 80	= 80
1oz Gluten	1 x 80	= 80
1oz Equivite	1 x (say) 20	= 20
2oz Soya Flour	2 x 40	= 80
10oz Total	Total	710

Divided by ten for protein content = 70% approximately (prior to adding liquid).

There is no need always to prepare HNV baits in units of ten, although for calculating the protein concent it does make things easier.

Ideas have changed since the term high protein was first used. Modern ideas seem to be leaning towards the preparation of balanced nutritional baits, which may be made with a high, low or medium protein content. Many anglers prefer to make a bait which contains a spread of nutrients.

Some examples of typical HNV baits:

3oz Casein	2oz Casein
2oz Wheat Germ	2oz Casilan (Sodium Caseinate)
2oz Dried Milk Powder	2oz Dried Milk Powder
1oz Healthilife Yeast	2oz Soya Flour
1oz Wheat Gluten	1oz Sugar
1oz Potato Starch	1oz Lactalbumin

TABLE SHOWING THE MAIN 'NUTRIENTS' IN SOME TYPICAL HNV INGREDIENTS

	Proteins	Fats	Minerals	Vitamins	Carbo-hydrates	Suggested max.% per Mix**
Dried Milk	*	*	*	*	*	50
Casein	*					60
Soya Flour	*	*			*	40
Wheat Germ	*			*	*	40
Wheat Gluten	*				*	30
Yeast	*		*	*		30
Sodium Caseinate	*					60
Calcium Caseinate	*					50
Soya Concentrate	*					40
Potato Starch					*	30
Equivite			*	*		10
Codlivine			*	*		20
Egg	*	*		.		N/A
Sugar					*	10
Lactalbumin	*					20
Egg Albumen	*			*		10
Corn Meal				*	*	30
Cooking Oil		*				10
'Complan'	*	*	*	*	*	60

** The percentages in the last column are the suggested maximum amount to be used in the baits.
While this chart shows only the main nutrients found in the ingredients listed small amounts of other nutrients are present in some of these ingredients.

2oz Casilan
3oz Dried Milk Powder
2oz Gluten
2oz Corn Meal
1oz Sugar
2oz Complan

3oz Dried Milk Powder
2oz Sodium or Calcium
  Caseinate
1oz Equivite
1oz Lactalbumin
1oz Egg Albumen
1oz Casein
1oz Sugar

2oz Casilan
2oz Dried Milk Powder
2oz Wheat Germ
2oz Potato Starch (Farina)
2oz Soya Concentrate
1oz Sugar

2oz Potato Starch
2oz Gluten
2oz Dried Milk Powder
2oz Casilan
2oz Corn Meal
2oz Wheat Germ

An Ashlea fish of 27 pounds 2 ounces, taken in September 1977 on a suspended special. This fish, which was nicknamed Scarface, was found dead the following summer and was believed to be one of the original stock fish from 1948.

The most efficient way of introducing a special bait is by first rolling and boiling them. To justify the use of an HNV bait, the same method also applies. Although eggs have proved to be the best ingredients for binding a bait and using them helps to give the bait a rubbery skin, they do alter the nutritional balance. An egg contains:

Egg White	Egg Yolk
88% Water	49% Water
11% Protein	17% Protein
1% Carbohydrate	1% Carbohydrate

Here is a chart to show the types of pure nutrients, in the form of vitamins, minerals and trace elements essential to man.

Vitamins	Minerals	Trace Elements
A	Iron	Cobalt
B_1	Magnesium	Fluorine
B_2 (Riboflavine)	Calcium	Zinc
B_6	Sulphur	Copper
B_{12}	Potassium	Chromium
C	Sodium	Iodine
D	Chlorine	
E	Phosphorus	
K		

We can see little point in going into the 'scientific' arguments for and against these types of bait, especially as proof is impossible, and we recommend readers not to get too obsessed with the science of bait preparation, which is nowhere near as important as angling knowledge and ability. Even if you were to make a detailed study of all the work by biologists on the dietary requirements of carp, you would still not necessarily be able to come up with super-baits. The use of trout pellets is a typical example of this. Since these pellets – and the carp pellets mentioned previously – have been specially formulated for feeding fish, then they must contain a good 'balanced diet'. In fact, as most carp anglers know, excellent baits can be made from them, but eventually the carp will stop taking them because we put hooks in them, and so teach the

The result of tree-top observation – a 32lb 12oz mirror taken at close range
on a single peanut.

fish that there is something unpleasant about them – which is not done when the pellets are used on a fish farm as food. The angler's requirements are not the same as those of the fish farmer; he will need to change his bait mixes, and/or the flavours and attractants in them, once the carp stop taking them. A selection made from the products listed in this chapter will keep anyone supplied with bait recipes for a long time to come, by which time we shall all have discovered, by more trial and error, other substances from which good baits can be made.

Floating 'Specials'

Since floating breadcrust first proved itself as an outstanding carp bait, more exotic floating baits were bound to follow. While breadcrust is still effective, there are many waters where the carp have become suspicious of it and alternatives must be found if any real success is to be achieved. Home-made floaters have the advantage of being more resistant to the attentions of small fry, which is a distinct problem when using breadcrust. Most floaters are more buoyant than breadcrust which is an advantage when using the anchored method. When made correctly, certain floaters have a texture which allows them to be cut into tiny squares and used as a form of multiple bait. This is a method which has proved to be successful on many different waters where the fish respond well to surface baits but carp are shy of anything much larger than thumb nail size. Favourable conditions for successful surface fishing are too rare, or too short, for any substantial degree of preoccupation to be achieved. In addition it can be difficult to put the free offerings where the fish are feeding or basking. It is therefore not really necessary to worry about the protein value of surface baits and more attention should be paid to making a useful, small fry resistant floater. If you refer to previous sections the ingredients already mentioned will serve as an ideal base for a floating special bait, or if you prefer, an HNV floater.

One of the most widely used types of floater is the version which incorporates the same ingredients as a bottom bait but requires double the amount of eggs to make it float. Unless you want to use exactly the same ingredients for a floating bait as you do for a bottom bait then there are some easier recipes and methods which work just as well and are not quite so extravagant. Providing enough eggs are added to a bait-mix before it is put in the oven, almost anything can be made to float in a sponge-cake type form. The chief difficulties arrive when using coarse or 'heavy' ingredients such as pet foods and meals. Consistency can be improved by

Example of fine-textured floater.

grinding the ingredients more finely and adding an extra egg or two to the final mix. When using ground pet foods or fish foods as a bottom bait it is often worthwhile using them in conjunction with a floating bait of the same type. To counteract heavy ingredients a floating bait should contain some light, heat-affected substances. This is achieved in much the same way as when a bottom bait is made. Some light ingredients include sodium and calcium caseinate, milk powders and soya flour. Unfortunately, to make a really buoyant and rubbery floater with, say, ground Munchies or trout pellets as a base, requires a fairly high proportion of light ingredients, which does tend to mask the attracting smell. However, the following recipe will be a good guideline.

'Munchie' Floater

    4oz Pilchard Flavour Munchies
    3oz Sodium Caseinate
    ½ teasp. Baking Powder
    8 eggs

Method

Mix together four ounces of ground Munchies with three ounces of sodium caseinate and the baking powder. In a separate mixing bowl beat together approximately eight eggs. Tip in all the powder and thoroughly mix them together. Having achieved the consistency of thick soup, pour the contents into a well greased baking tin and bake in a medium/hot oven for 20/30 minutes. Do not be frightened to add an extra egg or two as this will make the difference between a 'close or heavy' textured floater.

Examples of Special Floaters

4oz Ground Trout Pellets
2oz Sodium Caseinate
1oz Soya Flour
1oz S/Raising Flour
½ teasp. Baking Powder

1oz Phillips Yeast Mixture
2oz Sodium Caseinate
2oz Soya Flour
2oz Wheat Germ
½ teasp. Baking Powder

4oz Herring Meal
2oz Sodium Caseinate
1oz Wheat Gluten
1oz Soya Flour
½ teasp. Baking Powder

The most efficient floaters may be made by using the various protein ingredients, which, because of their inherent binding qualities, produce some excellently textured baits.

Further Examples of Floaters

(Light & crusty, average)
3oz Casein
3 oz Dried Milk Powder
3oz Soya Flour
1oz Wheat Gluten
1 teasp. Caster Sugar

(Heavy, crusty)
2oz Casein
1oz Sodium Caseinate
3oz Corn Meal
4oz Soya Flour

(Light and soft)
2oz Casein
3oz Sodium Caseinate
3oz Soya Flour
1 teasp. Sugar
1oz Plain Flour

(Good average and consistent, ideal for particle floater)
1oz Wheat Gluten
1oz Sugar
1oz Sodium Caseinate
2oz S/Raising Flour
2oz Casein
3oz Soya Flour
1oz Corn Meal

1. Keep adding eggs until the mix is runny, like thick soup. Each mix makes a lot of floater, so divide by two for a lesser amount.
2. Baking powder may not always be necessary and for this application it is optional.
3. Liquid flavours must be added to eggs prior to mixing. Powder flavours must be added to powdered ingredients.

'Quick & Easy' Floating Bait

If you cannot be bothered to go to the trouble of making a normal floater, then be sure to have in reserve a packet of instant sponge mix which can be bought at most supermarkets. To make a simple and effective floater mix the contents of the packet with eggs; approximately four eggs to an eight ounce mix is ideal. Pour this runny liquid into a shallow baking tray and allow it to cook in a medium oven for 10-15 minutes. If a slightly tougher floater is required add about one ounce of Wheat Gluten to the original mix. Two suitable makes of sponge mix are 'Green's' and 'Tesco's' (own).

Floating Pastes

One floater which will undoubtedly become more widely used in the future is the soft paste type which has several advantages. Once the dry mix is bagged up at home it can be left in the tackle bag indefinitely. Then, when required, it is a quick and simple job to mix it up at the lakeside using lake water. Soft paste floaters allow a good attractor 'leak off' and the unusual presentation can be of further advantage, for three-quarters of the bait's mass lies under the surface making location easier for the carp (and harder for the ducks!). The fact that this presentation is different makes it an almost certain 'winner'.

It is best to mix this bait at the waterside but care should be taken not to knead it too vigorously, as this may dispel most of the trapped air and reduce buoyancy. To increase buoyancy (and to give the bait a more unusual smell), lemonade, Cream Soda or in fact any fizzy drink can be used to moisten the bait instead of water.

'Fizzy' Floater

75% Sodium Caseinate (special light grade from Rushside Baits)
10% Bran
10% Attractor: Yestamin, Larvstart, etc.
5% Sugar
Add Cream Soda or lemonade.

Further Versions of Floating Pastes (add water or 'fizz')

6oz Sodium Caseinate
3oz C & G Baby Milk Plus

6 oz Sodium Caseinate
2oz fine breadcrumbs
1oz Caster sugar

Floating Multiples

On some waters the carp become suspicious of normal size floating baits. The use of a floater which is smaller than the usual sized baits can be just as effective as using a completely new bait. It is even possible to make the most of what are, usually, short surface-feeding spells by introducing a floating multiple bait. This can be achieved by cutting the normal floater cake into very small cubes, or buying a bait which is already in a multiple form. Typical floating multiple baits are trout pellets,

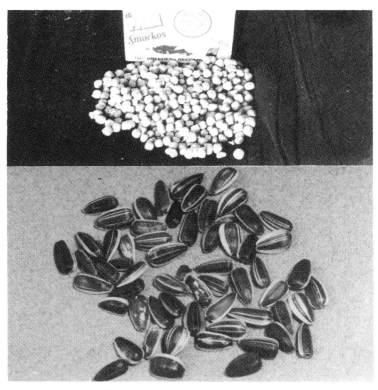

Floating multiples –
Top: Chum Mixer   Centre: Sunflower seeds   Bottom: Purina Sea Nips

or the proprietary brands of cat foods such as Purina Seanips, Go-Cat and Munchies. Breakfast cereals also make good floating baits. Puffed Wheat, Sugar Puffs and Golden Nuggets are good brands to try. Savoury snacks like pop-corn, Watsits and Cheese Savours have all been used to good effect. While there are numerous foodstuffs to choose from it is advisable to test a prospective bait in a bowl of water. Any food particles that soften too quickly will be difficult to use. Try to pick a floater which will keep its shape for a while therefore making it less susceptible to the attentions of other species. Many of these small floaters will sink when put on the hook; for methods of presentation see the Methods and Tactics section.

Multiple Baits

Unlike most other carp baits, multiples, or particles as they are known, are easy to prepare, simple to use and easily obtained. The introduction of small quantities of beans or seeds to a carp water can produce immediate results. Carp may regard multiple baits as something like their natural food simply because of the numbers in which they find them. To obtain the maximum benefit from multiple baits it sometimes pays to introduce them to the water in large quantities to compete with, or even outnumber, the carp's natural food. Depending on the head of carp present in a water it is a good idea to pre-bait with quite a large quantity of prepared beans or seeds, providing it is likely that they will be eaten and not left to rot on the lake bed. Prebaiting programmes undoubtedly help to familiarise carp with the bait but they are not essential. Multiples are no different from any other type of bait. Their efficiency will always be determined by general fishing pressure and individual ability. Complete pre-occupation by all the carp in the lake on multiple baits is rare. In most cases pre-baiting just before the known feeding periods is best, and preferably in those areas where the carp can eat it easily and confidently; gravel bars or gaps in weed beds are likely places. By employing accurate and timely pre-baiting, multiple baits will often account for many carp before they become suspicious. It is even possible to catch several fish in quick succession when the feeding becomes intense. In recent years the most popular have been sweet corn, chick peas, black-eyed beans, tic beans, maple peas, peanuts and sultanas. There are several others which could be included, although those mentioned do fall into the essential category of being easy to use, easily obtained and the carp seem to like them. Individually, certain multiples seem to have special appeal for the carp. Sweet corn, for example, is tasty, strong smelling and easily visible. It may also be used 'as bought', with no soaking or preparation other than opening the tin. Chick peas are cheap and easily visible and again only require a small amount of preparation. The same applies to most other lighter coloured particles.

Although small multiple baits may have some similarity to natural food they can 'blow' quickly especially when they are used on clear waters. For this reason the darker-coloured, smaller multiples are often better for sustaining preoccupation periods. Ideally the best multiple bait should be very small, like wheat, hemp, tares or dari seeds. Although these multiples must be introduced in large quantities to achieve the best results, one is presented with something rather like a needle in the haystack situation when it comes to carp finding the hookbait. In spite of this the smaller particles or 'mass' baits are tremendously effective when used correctly. It could be said that large multiples such as butter beans, broad beans, kidney beans, peeled prawns, etc, are more likely to lose their effectiveness because of their size. Middle sized multiples would include chick peas, haricot beans, maple peas, gunga peas, tic beans and so on. True multiple baits are the small seeds and beans which, when lying on the lake bottom, may look similar to some natural foods.

Multiples do not have the individual attraction of boiled or paste baits and if the hookbait is not lying among a scattering of free samples it is unlikely to be found; this makes accurate casting essential. One common fault is to prebait all round a lake at the maximum range of a catapult, then to fish in the area of the lake where there is no bait.

Dried seeds, beans or cereals may harm the fish. Unsoaked seeds will be taken by carp and then swell up in their gut, causing distress. All dried multiples should be soaked in water for a few hours before use. Some seeds will of course germinate if they are not boiled for a few minutes, so, at some stage in their preparation they should be brought to the boil for three or four minutes. When using seeds or beans which are sprouting then these should be boiled after they have sprouted to avoid harming fish and infesting the bankside with foreign plants! Seeds are sprouted easily by keeping them damp in a closed container for a couple of days. If baits are required quickly a pressure cooker will make seeds ready to use in less than an hour, although some pre-soaking is better. Overcooking in any situation will destroy many of the nutrients in any bean or seed. Short boiling periods are best if the carp are to derive maximum benefit from the bait. When fishing over soft or weedy lake beds then a little extra boiling will make the seeds less dense; they will then not disappear in the silt or weed so easily.

Adzuki
beans

Butter
beans

Kidney
beans

All baits shown are actual

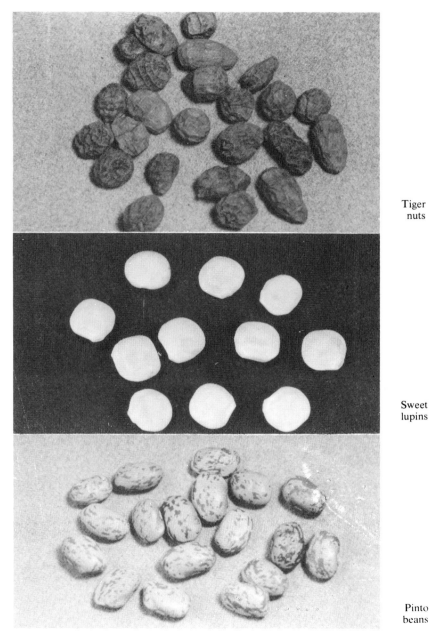

Tiger
nuts

Sweet
lupins

Pinto
beans

size prior to preparation.

If possible try to keep the prepared seeds or beans in the water they were cooked in. Often this juice is dark and strong-smelling and results show that by preparing multiples approximately 24 hours before the trip they will be used just as they begin to smell, a condition which the carp find more appealing.

When storing seeds over a long period they may begin to ferment. First they might smell sour, but if they are kept covered by the original liquid they will not go mouldy. Sometimes, the older they are the more the carp will like them. If the carp begin to be suspicious then the multiples can be flavoured and coloured, and the carp will often start to take them again. In clear waters where fish might be frightened by the sight of the baits, colouring them might be an advantage. Because of the effort involved it is probably more worthwhile changing to a different particle bait rather than attempting to prolong the life of a bait that the carp are already wary of. Flavouring multiples is, however, a far better way to alter the bait. It would be impossible to advise the best flavours for certain particles; chemical and natural flavours both work well. Black eyed, haricot, lima and kidney beans, can all be made 'different' by adding a packet or tin of soup during boiling. Chemical flavours tend to evaporate to a certain extent during boiling and this should be taken into consideration with the amounts used. Natural flavours seem to work best with bean and seed particles; these may be added during the soaking when it is also a good idea to add approximately two tablespoonsful of sugar to each large saucepan of bait. Some of the tried and tested particle/flavour combinations include:

Tic Beans *flavoured with* Paprika
Black Eyed Beans *flavoured with* Maple
Chick Peas *flavoured with* Toffee Flavour
Prawns or Cockles *flavoured with* Kipper Dye
Butter Beans *flavoured with* Oxtail Soup
Haricot Beans *flavoured with* Tomato Soup
Kidney Beans *flavoured with* Curry Sauce

Most of the seed and bean multiple baits can be bought at any health food store or continental grocers. Bulk or wholesale warehouses are by far the most economical places to use. If several anglers can club together and purchase by the sackful, pounds can often be saved and the season's supply of bait secured. Remember to store all grains and cereals in a cool dry place and check sacks regularly for the tell-tale signs of pests or mildew.

Sprouted chick peas (must be cooked before use).

Grain and Seed Bulk Suppliers (for addresses see reference guide)

Haiths   Latymer & Crick
Hurst, Gunsen & Tabor

List of 'Multiple' Baits Known To Have Caught Carp

Almonds	Adzuki Beans	Plain Barley
Pearl Barley	Butter Beans	Brazil Nuts
Broad Beans	Buckwheat	Buck Beans
Blackcurrants	Black Eyed Beans	Cashew Nuts
Coffee Beans	Cockles	Cherries
Chick Peas	Currants	Dry Fowl
Dun Peas	Dari Seeds	Dolly Mixture
Gunga Peas/Beans	Hazel Nuts	Haricot Beans
Hemp	Jelly Babies	Kidney Beans
Lychees	Lima Beans	Lupin Seeds (sweet)
Macaroni	Mung Beans	Maple Peas
Millet	Maize	Oats
Piza Beans	Peeled Prawns	Pine Nuts
Pasta Shapes	Peanuts	Pumpkin Seeds

Pinto Beans	Rape Seeds	Raisins
Sunflower Seeds	Syori Beans	Smarties
Sultanas	Sweet Corn	Soya Beans
Tic Beans	Tares	Tiger Nuts
Winkles	Wheat	

Bait Colouring

Throughout this chapter we have referred to the benefits of colouring various baits. There can be no rules for this although in clear water where carp may be wary of light coloured baits it may help to make them darker in colour. In waters which are slightly coloured overall visibility is greatly reduced and in depths which exceed approximately four feet bait colouration is usually of little or no benefit. When using suspended or surface baits, carp approaching from directly below the bait will probably only see it as a dark coloured shape against a light background. Although carp may become more easily suspicious of large, light coloured baits rather than dark ones, the chances of attracting the attention of cruising fish are often improved by using a light coloured bait which may be more easily visible to the fish. Some may still be put off by the light colour but these may well be outnumbered by those which show interest because the bait was easily seen.

It is worth remembering that the bait colour may not be the reason for carp refusing to take the baits. The true reason may be poor presentation or some other mistake of the angler's. If the carp in a water are used to seeing large baits, either light or dark in colour, smaller baits, well presented, might succeed. Carp are often curious and may be tempted to pick up light coloured baits, so they are well worth trying. While the light coloured bait may initially attract the attention of the carp because they can see them easily, on close investigation they may discover that the bait has an attractive smell, and may take it immediately, or swim away and return a number of times, sometimes taking, and at other times refusing the bait in the end. Darker baits may make it harder for the carp to find the bait again, although it is more likely that they will be able almost automatically to return to the bait, whatever its colour. Baits containing light coloured ingredients such as milk powders, even after the bait has been dyed, tend to go lightish in colour after some time in the water. Even black and dark brown dyes soon begin to 'leak' from the baits, which then revert to a light colour. If you want a bait to stay dark in colour, select ingredients, such as yeast, which are naturally dark, and cut down on the white or light coloured substances.

Powder and liquid bait colourings can be obtained from:

Rushside Baits
Dubuis & Rowsell
Bait '78
Geoff Kemp

Amino Acids

Definition: Amino acids form the basic construction of proteins which can contain many hundreds of different types. It is the various combinations of just twenty principal amino acids which give each protein its character and property.

Lysine	Valine	Tryptophan
Phenylalanine	Isoleucine	Methionine
Leucine	Threonine	Histidine
Cystine	Tyrosine	Cysteine
Arginine	Glycine	Glutamic Acid
Alanine	Proline	Serine
Aspartic Acid	Asparagine	

In the early seventies a great deal of work was being carried out with proteins and nutritious foodstuffs and their uses for carp baits. It was about this time that anglers considered adding certain amino acids to their bait in the belief that these highly complex chemicals would in some way attract the carp. Initially the ideas were gleaned by reading scientific research papers which listed detailed experiments on various species of fish. It was found that increasing research was being done into using amino acid solutions to create feeding responses in cod, whiting, trout and later carp. Because of man's increasing food requirement, carp farming is now becoming big business and it therefore follows that technology will be constantly striving to improve growth rates and increase farming efficiency.

Assuming an ideal amino acid blend could be found to affect sufficiently the carp's metabolism, theory would suggest an almost permanent state of hunger, or food searching activity, could be created. Because all living things contain proteins in some form, it follows that they must also contain groups of amino acids. Ideally we must try to recreate chains of amino acids and stimulate a food source for the carp to home in on. The difficulty is finding a correct grouping of acids and then applying it to a bait which will also allow those acids to reach the carp in the most natural way possible. Further difficulties arise when calculating the exact amount of amino acid to use at a given water temperature, or pH level. Certain blends of A.A.s may even attract other species more than carp; you could end up catching nothing but roach or bream.

In spite of this there are still many first class anglers who swear by their use. It is again up to the individual to consider whether the cost and effort involved in using these chemicals is worthwhile.

Numerous experiments with amino acids on carp have taken place over the last few years in several different countries. If you consider it worthwhile studying the reports of these experiments, as we have done, it will be noticeable just how conflicting the results are. Some of the amino acids that have stimulated feeding responses in carp in one part of the world have been found to have no response whatsoever elsewhere. It is also noticeable that different strains of carp respond to different amino acids. If we consider these variations and all the other factors which affect the attractiveness of the A.A.s it will be appreciated just how many problems the angler needs to overcome if he is to use A.A.s to his advantage throughout the season and on a variety of waters.

To prove to ourselves that carp could at least be seen to react favourably on coming into contact with amino acids, some tests were carried out in a large 150 gallon indoor tank. The fish involved in the tests

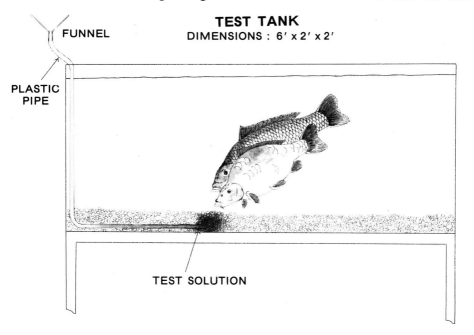

FUNNEL

TEST TANK
DIMENSIONS : 6' x 2' x 2'

PLASTIC
PIPE

TEST SOLUTION

were two commons of three and four and a half pounds and a mirror of one and a half pounds. What follows is a brief description of the methods we used to introduce the amino acid solutions into the tank and the observations which were made.

Experience from testing other liquids suggested that the best way to introduce the amino acids was by impregnating a small area of the gravel bottom. This was done via a funnel and plastic pipe set up as shown in the diagram.

The funnel was fixed in position above the water level of the tank so that any solution poured into the funnel would flow down the pipe until a common level in both the tank and pipe occurred. By means of trial and error in previous tests using dyed water, an accurate measure of water was poured into the funnel after the amino acid solution had found its level. This measure of 'back-up' water had the effect of pushing the A.A. solution down the pipe, and then into the gravel immediately surrounding the end of the pipe. Again, the water found its own level in the pipe. The object was, in fact, to impregnate a small area of gravel and cause a slow 'leak off' of A.A. solution rather than quickly dispensing the solution into the open water. This was the best way we could find to watch any response the carp made to the outlet area.

While these tests were not carried out under laboratory conditions, great care was taken to maintain continuity in each experiment. The fish in the tank were rested for several days after each individual acid combination was introduced, the water was changed regularly and each test was carried out at the same temperature levels and approximately the same time of day. The position of the outlet was frequently altered to avoid familiarising the carp to one area of gravel. One conclusive finding was that those acids which were best on their own, proved to be ineffective when used in combination. A considerable number of other combinations were tested but have not been included in the results as there was no response.

Conclusion: After having spent a whole season using the best of the single or combinations of acids indicated by the tank tests our results were still inconclusive. In order finally to convince ourselves that amino acids were worth using in a boiled bait, a final controlled experiment was undertaken.

Experiment: For the first four months of the 1978/79 season a standard carp bait, made from dried cat food, was used on two different waters using two rods. At all times the baits used on one rod were plain and the other contained the combination No. 35, Phenylalanine, Lysine

	TEST TANK RESULTS		
Very Good Reaction	**Fair Reaction**	**Poor Reaction**	**No Reaction**
Immediate response by fish on introduction of acid solution, fish rolling on gravel and against side of tank. Fish also mouthing gravel and digging into area of outlet. Continuing high activity even clearing gravel around pipe outlet. Fish attempting to eat everything in tank and around them.	Fish responding to acid solution several minutes after introduction. General increased activity around outlet area, occasional rolling and turning over gravel, definite feeding reaction.	Fish seemed stimulated in some way and reacted slowly after acid solution had been introduced. Occasionally mouthing gravel but no turning or rolling and no homing into outlet area.	No apparent response to any solutions introduced.
Valine Lysine Combination No. 35: Phenylanine/Lysine/ Cystine	Phenylalanine Histidine Glycine Isoleucine Asparagine	Alanine Proline Cystine Combination No. 31: Asparagine/Isoleucine/ Glycine/Histidine/ Phenylalanine Combination No. 37: Tyrosine/Lysine/ Phenylalanine	Methionine. DL Argenine Glutamine Threonine Leucine Serine* Phenylalanine. DL Tyrosine Aspartic Acid Glutamic Acid Methionine

*This acid had an adverse effect on the carp which showed signs of respiratory difficulties, eyes rolling, and obvious distress. Its use is therefore not advised.

N.B. All acids tested were 'L' versions unless indicated otherwise.

and Cystine. Despite swapping rods, changing venues and recording every bite on each bait, results were identical. No evidence was found to indicate that amino acids improved the attraction of a boiled bait and for this reason they were no longer used.

Because there are many other substances which definitely do produce good feeding reactions and have proved themselves when used in a bait, it was decided to concentrate on these rather than continue using amino acids. After the experiments and trials we formed the conclusion that amino acids in baits may be used successfully as attractants, but that they had no advantages – and possibly some disadvantages – compared with other types of attractants, and we do not intend to use amino acids in baits in the future. It is a fact that some amino acids used in quantity, or in certain combinations, can be poisonous, and in our opinion should not be used in carp baits except by those with a considerable degree of knowledge on this subject. However, none of our experiments involved the use of soft paste baits and we feel we are not qualified to discuss the use of A.A.s in this type of bait. To provide some information on A.A.s in soft pastes we were able to gain some useful tips from Duncan Kay who has done more practical work on the subject than most other anglers. Duncan recommends that one gramme of amino acid powder (in total) can be detected in one pound of bait, it being unwise to exceed two grammes to the pound. He suggests that any acids should be handled with great care and kept locked away. Having added the acids to a bait the best results are obtained if it is used within 12 hours, and kept cool. Two good acid combinations advised by Duncan for soft paste use are:

Glycine, Methionine, Arginine, Cystine   ¼ gramme of each acid to one pound of dry bait.

Phenylalanine, Cystine, Lysine (HCL)   ⅓ gramme of each acid to one pound of dry bait.

Amino acid suppliers: (for addresses see reference guide)

    Rushside Baits
    Aldrich Chemical Company

Unusual Baits

In the constant search for originality and the longing to find a unique and irresistible bait there are some which come under the heading of unusual. Some of these are described in the following pages; all have caught carp and are at least worth considering, or improving on!

Solidifying or Setting Baits

To avoid the tedium of rolling and boiling a bait and to offer the fish something different, a 'jelly mould' or solidifying bait can be useful. Favourable setting agents include alginates, agars and gelatine although the latter is by far the cheapest and easiest to use. Theoretically it should be possible to make a bait which will set rock-hard. This can be achieved with certain gums used in the confectionery trade although applying these to a useful carp bait can be very difficult. One of the best ingredients for making a fairly hard setting bait which will last for eight or more hours in water without breaking down is gelatine. By using three or four ounces of gelatine to one pint of water almost any type of powder can be made to set in a block. Other more moist ingredients such as tinned fish and pet foods can also be made to set by reducing the amount of water. Before preparing any gelatine-based bait, it is advisable to include a small amount of dilute glycerol or glycerin, or one of the sweeteners mentioned earlier. These sweet liquids help to counteract the slightly repellent effect of the gels and assist in the overall consistency of the finished bait, as well as enhancing their taste.

Typical setting bait recipe

1 pint water	6oz ground trout pellets or dried cat food
3-4oz gelatine	25ml dilute glycerol or glycerin

Method

Dissolve the gelatine by adding it to the pint of cold water and slowly warming on a very low heat. When the gelatine crystals are gone and the liquid is hot and runny add the 25ml of glycerin or dilute glycerol (one part glycerol/5 parts water). Always stir continuously. At this stage the 6 ounces of prepared and finely sieved powder may be added; do this

A rare fish indeed – a 23¾ fully-scaled mirror caught in 1982 on a cream boilie.

A 'setting' bait in its tray.

quickly and mix it all in at once, stirring well. Wait until the mix begins to simmer then pour the contents into a shallow tin tray or similar. Allow 30 minute to cool in the tin on a flat surface them cut into cubes as desired. This mix will keep indefinitely in the freezer with no apparent loss of quality.

Transparent Bait

By using gelatine in the previous method mentioned but omitting any powder or opaque additive, a transparent bait may be made. Gelatine, even in large amounts, together with glycerin or dilute glycerol, will make a good, clear, bait although because of its softness the use of this will be limited to margin fishing and stalking. Small quantities of colourless flavour may be added for the carp to home in on. This can be deadly on hard fished, bait shy waters where the carp are frightened by baits cast in their path. If they cannot associate colour or even tone with the bait then only touch and smell will guide the fish; clear waters are a likely place to try them. Some agars may be used in much the same way as gelatine. Ion agar is one which will solidify on its own, although this material is extremely expensive.

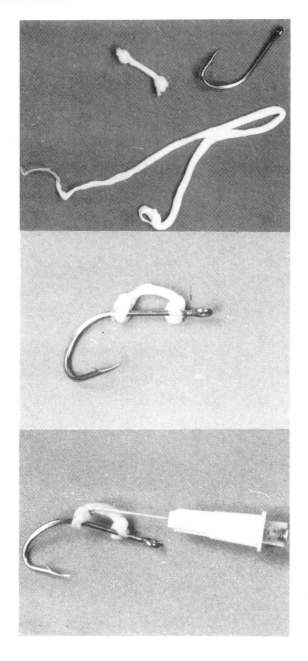

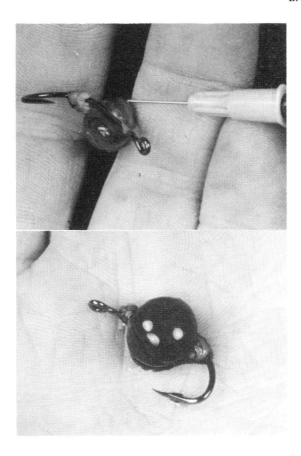

Liquid bait

1. A section of pig gut sausage skin knotted and ready for mounting on hook.

2. Mounted on hook.

3. Inserting needle.

4. Introducing solution.

5. The finished bait.

Liquid Baits

Liquid baits would seem to be impossible to use, but in fact we have used them to catch carp up to 23 pounds, after overcoming numerous problems in their development. Because carp respond so well to solutions of confectionery flavours in baits some experiments were first carried out on tank fish by using various other attractive substances to see what responses could be observed. By far the most successful solutions introduced through the tank's feed pipe were liquidised bloodworm and liquidised lobworm. As the liquid passed down the pipe and filtered into the gravel it did not take long for the carp to show great interest in the outlet area. They soon maintained sufficient interest in the filter pipe and its contents to set us thinking of ways to present the carp with a similar solution, and hopefully lead to a capture. After a number of ideas, a sausage skin was eventually used as a reservoir for the bloodworm or lobworm solution. Pig gut type of sausage skin was found to be best. Having tied either end of a small section of skin, the solution was introduced by means of a hypodermic syringe. After attaching the bait to the hook (see photo), the tiny hole made by the needle and the porous sausage skin allows sufficient attractor to filter through the water to interest the carp. This method is of course open to improvement, especially in view of the various attracting ingredients now favoured by the carp angler, such as amino acid solutions and flavours.

Colours and Shapes

On those waters where visibility is good and the carp respond to daytime fishing, colour and shape can play a vital role in bait appreciation. Sometimes it is worthwhile altering the shape of paste or boiled carp baits or even the way you cut up luncheon meat, especially if a pre-baiting scheme is envisaged. Carp soon become used to picking up baits of the same smell and shape so it follows they will also become used to being caught on them. Try to vary the size and shape of any bait whether it is the hookbait or free samples. Do not be tempted to prepare a nice uniform box of 'boilies' just because you always get an exact number from your mix. Cylinders and pyramids are a good shape to use although sometimes it would be impracticable to prebait with this idea in mind; hookbait variation is usually sufficient.

Colours for carp baits seem to follow fashions, but there are really no rules for colouring baits. Carp can detect colours on the red side of the spectrum (red, yellow and orange) better than those on the blue side of the spectrum, according to scientific research. This of course does not mean that baits of these colours will be more successful. They may be more noticeable (depending on the colour of the lake bottom) to the carp, but could also frighten the fish more easily. It is often the case that different coloured baits are effective simply because they carry different smells or tastes. Regular success with bait colourisation usually coincides with the presentation of baits against contrasting lake bottoms; light coloured baits on dark brown lakebeds may 'stand out' more and be taken by cruising fish. Brighter, sandy gravel will provide a more contrasting background to a dark brown or black bait. Really the use of coloured baits is only worth considering if the water is clear or partially clear. There has never been any benefit in using red or green baits at night! The most effective colours seem to be red, yellow, dark brown or black.

Mystic

Most well-stocked tackle shops carry a range of 'Mystic' pastes, which have an attractive smell and are highly sticky. Mystic paste originated in France for use in match fishing. There are several varieties which are all suitable for carp. Some useful applications for the product include moulding pieces of it on the hook and then dipping it into a bag of seeds to simulate a larva case or for fishing among a bed of multiples. As Mystic is slightly adhesive it can be used to attach a wide variety of objects to a hook. Alternatively a squeeze of Mystic paste onto the hook bait may give it that final touch which will tempt the more wary carp.

Exotic Live Baits

There are some occasions when the carp may be taking interest in surface or midwater fish but cannot be caught on conventional baits. For those who have the stomach to use them, crickets, locusts, moths, tadpoles and leeches will all take carp. Other delicacies may include pea mussels, swan mussels, wasp grubs, mealworms, slugs, large fresh water shrimps, bloodworm, jokers, freshwater fleas or whatever creeps, crawls or hops!

*

In this chapter we have attempted, perhaps for the first time, to give carp anglers a comprehensive guide to modern bait making and bait materials. We can guarantee that all the materials and baits listed have been used successfully to catch carp, but what we cannot guarantee is that the reader will find immediate success by using these baits. There are many other factors which affect catches apart from bait, such as correct presentation, the use of the baits at the right time and in the right waters, and the angler's individual ability, so if you don't succeed at first with baits made from listed materials in this book, continue to experiment, vary your methods and tactics, and you should eventually find the right combination of bait and method for the water you fish.

A 30½ that took over an hour to land, after picking up a single peanut.

A freshly spawned female weighing 32¼ pounds, from a Surrey gravel pit, August 1981.

6 Lake Cassien

Discovery of Cassien

In February 1984 Brenda and I went down to Kent to stay with Paul and Kerry Regent for a few days. Over dinner one evening, we discussed the possibility of running coach trips for anglers to carp and catfish waters on the Continent as Paul was looking for ways to combine his coach business with pleasure. Spain, France, Czechoslovakia and Holland were all considered.

We decided to contact various people we knew of in these countries and one of these, whose address we got through the Carp Anglers' Association, was David Stockton, who lives in France. David wrote to Paul a long letter suggesting various venues, one of which was Lake Cassien. This sounded ideal, as it was 750 miles away in the South of France – too far away to become spoilt by rule-breaking English anglers, or so we thought. This sounded much better than anything we heard about in Spain; Cassien was in a very hot area, ideal for holidays, and Dave told us that carp had been caught to 55 lbs. One problem was that no night fishing was allowed anywhere in France, so we should have to stay in hotels. Dave also sent us pictures of big carp – all dead, of course – which had been published in French newspapers.

We decided that Paul and I would go over for a few days, find an hotel, and try to see what the water was like; we were going to go to Santiliana in Spain as well. Later we gave up this idea but passed on all the information to someone else who later claimed to 'discover' the water!

We drove down overnight in September '84, and arrived at the bottom end of the South Arm, where we slept in the car park. We soon saw just how big the lake was, and then looked for a tackle shop and found Chez Pierre's Cafe which has now become well known. Here we were shown pictures of big carp by Pascal, who spoke good English, and also informed us that the Cassien record was now 72 lbs. This was even better – with fish of that size being caught there must be a good chance of 30's, 40's and even 50's.

We decided to fish and picked a spot close to Chez Pierre's where some boats were anchored. We baited up in the morning with a 6 lb tin of sweetcorn – one of six which we had taken. We continued to explore the lake by road and track and returned to the swim at mid-day for our first taste of French carp fishing.

The tackle we decided to use was typical of what we used in England, much to the amazement of the local French anglers: 2-2¼lb TC carbon rods, ABU Cardinal 55 reels, 8lb Sylcast main line including hook link, small Partridge Hilton hooks and running leads. We decided to use hair rigs, about 3″ long, because we felt that bite-offs could occur, plus the fact that most of the carp had not been landed before – all were usually killed and eaten.

We had action from bream and tench on the corn and hair rigs, and at 3pm Paul soon had a good take to the butt at only 20 feet from the bank. The fish took 90 yards of line in the first rush – he had never had a fish fight so hard and it seemed obvious that this carp had never felt a hook before. We were soon surrounded by Frenchmen who were amazed at our light tackle – they kept playing with the buzzers while Paul was playing the fish! Some of the spectators were topless women! The fish, a beautiful mirror, was landed after a terrific 40 minute fight but weighed only 23lbs. We were very interested to see how the rigs were working and on inspecting the hook-hold we discovered that our set-ups had been the right choice as the hook was at least 3″ inside the mouth.

We had to pack up at 8.15 pm, or we should have been in trouble with the Rangers, but at 7.45 Paul lost a fish after the hook pulled out on the initial run. We were rather concerned that the hook had pulled out indicating that perhaps the rig was not right! Paul decided to shorten the hair to about 1″ before re-casting. Just at packing-up time he had another good take – a short fat fish of 20½lbs hooked nicely in the lips: not a bad start!

The next day we had nothing at first, though we spent a lot of time looking round. Later in the evening, after Paul had lost a fish earlier due to a tangle around the indicator, he had a 35 pounder, and by now we realised we had really discovered something special. I continued to fish on the right hand side of Paul but only had action from other species. On the third day Paul had a small common and I managed two but they were all about seven pounds. On departure, we spoke to Pascal in Chez Pierre's and he was surprised to hear of the small commons we had caught as these had never been either seen or caught before.

We returned home as planned, very pleased with the trip, and Paul arranged a coach trip for January 1985. We believed that this would be a good time, as English fishing would be at its worst and weather conditions at Cassien would still be plenty warm enough to catch fish. As it happened, the region suffered its worst winter for 90 years and although the water temperature was around 50°F, this was obviously the coldest the Cassien fish had ever experienced. Nothing was caught, though a few fish were lost.

Other English anglers who had heard from us about Cassien started to go, both on Paul's coach trips and independently – and the rest is history.

About Lake Cassien

The *Lac de St Cassien* is in the South of France, about 10 miles from the Mediterranean. It is about 800 miles from England. It was constructed as a reservoir and a hydro-electric station in the late fifties/early sixties by building a dam across the end of the natural valley.

It was stocked with carp in about 1964, and more fish of a good size are put in each year. The lake is at least 15 miles round and the acreage is about 1,500. Massive alterations in the level of the water are frequent; the water level often goes up or down by six feet in a week.

As it is a flooded valley there is much natural food, especially crayfish and mussels, and with the high average annual temperature the fish can grow all the year round; it is not surprising that the fish reach such massive sizes. It still amazes me that often when carp are caught their mouths and gills are full of crayfish in great quantities.

Since the lake was 'discovered' by Paul Regent and myself it has become very popular with English anglers, most of whom go there in an attempt to catch a personal best fish. Fifties, sixties and seventies have been caught by inexperienced anglers who have never even caught a '20' in England, so it's worth remembering that one or two huge fish from Cassien does not make one a top carp angler. Each year the fish are getting bigger, and it seems possible that a fish from the water might eventually reach 100lbs, so Lake Cassien is almost certainly the best carp lake in the world.

French rules are very strict. Night fishing is not allowed and frequent checks are made by armed Rangers. There is a good reason for this rule as there are French professional anglers who, it is felt, could empty the waters of fish by the use of set lines.

At first English anglers breaking the rules had their gear confiscated for 24 hours; later they had to spend a night in a cell, but now, with continued rule breaking, all their gear is permanently confiscated. No fires or camping are allowed, and now you cannot spend a night on the water. Fishing is from half an hour before sunrise to half an hour after sunset.

WEST
ARM

NORTH
ARM

SOUTH
ARM

Lake Cassien.

Enormous amounts of litter are left by English litter louts. There has been much bad behaviour by some English anglers, who are almost as notorious there as some English football 'fans' are elsewhere on the Continent! All those who go to fish at Lake Cassien should remember that they are in a foreign country whose rules and laws should be strictly adhered to.

Permits are obtainable from restaurants on the bank and cost £16 a year, and this allows the use of three rods. There is no close season.

The lake and its surroundings are a French holiday resort and as soon as the sun comes up the place is invaded by hundreds of holiday makers, who don't affect the fish but who certainly obstruct the anglers. There is sailing and boating, trolling, swimming and wind surfing, often by topless women and naked bottoms of both sexes!

The scenery around the lake, and everything else about, is totally un-English, and it seems that you either love or hate the place. Some English anglers go once and would never return. For me Cassien has a certain fascination; the thought that at any time a 70lb carp might pick up your bait, although there are things I hate about it also.

The other side of Cassien – English carp anglers have continually broken the rules and abused the place. English litter, shown here, is strewn all around the lake among the bushes. Filthy louts who leave huge amounts of litter behind deserve the stiff penalties now being enforced by French armed Rangers.

Fishing Lake Cassien

Before offering advice I should like to say that I am not a Lake Cassien expert – others have spent much more time there than I have, and been more successful, but I feel I have been there enough and caught enough to offer some advice to those interested in fishing the water.

Because of the huge size of this lake, and the comparatively low density of carp per acre, location is even more vitally important than on English waters. It is best to start by trying to find visible fish, and fishing in the area. Apart from some rough tracks there is only a road on one side of the south arm, so a boat is almost essential. Boats can be hired from any of the restaurants, and the pedalos are best. Apart from being very stable a pedalo is big enough to carry all your fishing gear, you can watch the water in front of you, unlike a boat, and you can pedal them for miles while long distance rowing is much harder. Normally these boats are hired out at £4 an hour (in 1987), which means a price per week of £80 at a reduced rate for a longer period.

What I call resident fish can often be seen in ones, or two's, but these are harder to catch, so it is best to look for a number of travelling fish which are usually seen to be rolling on the surface. Once four or five fish are spotted in this way, then you should start fishing in the area. These Cassien fish behave quite differently from English fish; they are never

A pedalo, although expensive to hire, is a must if you want to explore the lake searching for fish. They are very stable and large enough to carry 2-4 anglers and their gear. In this picture Dave Powell is scanning the water for moving fish using binoculars while we are fishing directly off the boat using the KM Rod Units. This was in the South Arm and the pedalo is grounded on to what is often an island at low water level.

Returning a '30' – the result of only two hours fishing but eight hours looking! It was here that Dave Powell and I hooked four carp but unfortunately Dave lost his three.

View across the South Arm, most of which is fishable with regard to depths.

seen basking in hot weather and in spite of the clear water they are not seen swimming close in. Most of the fish caught are taken in this way – by people who have spotted groups of fish before they started.

Normally I prefer to fish in water of from 15 to 25 feet deep, but I have no qualms at fishing in depths of up to 40 feet, and other anglers have undoubtedly caught fish at depths of up to 60 feet. In the South Arm there are depths of about 60 feet in the north end and so most of this arm is fishable. The east end of the West Arm is about 80 feet deep in the middle, but the remainder is reasonably shallow and is almost all fishable. Much of the North Arm, which is least fished, is up to 180 feet deep, but there are some good marginal areas so don't ignore it.

If you are going to fish Cassien only once or twice, you would do best to fish known fish-holding areas or to try to find out from people when you arrive where the fish are being caught. Make sure that it is from where they are *being* caught and not from where they *have been* caught as the productive spots can alter quite quickly. If you intend to stay long, or go often, the use of depth-finding equipment is desirable, but there is little point in using expensive and sophisticated fish-finding equipment. Go for a standard depth-finder, or echo sounder. Even when we have been able to locate actual fish on good quality equipment, this has never helped us to catch them, but knowing the depths has made a difference. Depths can also be found by practice casting especially in very deep water.

Weed beds, like this one at the end of the West Arm, very rarely hold any carp at all.

Since the lake is a flooded valley, an indication of the contours of the marginal areas can be obtained by taking note of the landscape adjacent to the area. For example, if the bank enters the water steeply the depth drops off quite quickly, whereas if the bank is fairly level, you can assume that shallow water will extend well out into the lake.

Unlike English carp, the fish in Cassien do not appear to be attracted by weed beds or areas of warm shallow water. Very hot sunny days can be really good for bottom fishing in most depths of water. The use of good binoculars is recommended and the features of the points or peninsulas that venture out into the water are good fishing areas, especially if you don't fish too far out. Fish patrolling near-in cross these extended shallow areas, so if you cast too far you are often casting beyond the fish. If fish are seen to be rolling at long distance it is sometimes worth taking a boat out and leaving polystyrene markers. Use a fairly heavy stone but very light line of 1-2lbs BS, as this will avoid the problem of losing fish on your own markers, which has happened often; this is a good opportunity to bait up, of course.

Tactics

Standard carp tackle is all that is needed. Heavy lines, preferably Sylcast as this line is particularly abrasion resistant, are needed, and 11-15lb BS is recommended.

Cassien has a very irregular bottom, and when the lake was made hundreds of cut-off tree trunks about 18 inches high were left. There are also many large rocks and boulders and about half of all fish hooked are lost.

Standard hair-rig set-ups work well – highly sophisticated rigs are not necessary at present, although as time goes on, and more fish are hooked, lost and returned by English anglers, more advanced rigs may be needed. Leads must be detachable because of the number of times snags are encountered, and the easy way is to attach the lead by means of a weak link or the lead can be put on the link with a leger stop lightly fixed so that it can slip in snags. This is absolutely essential, as in some swims you will never get your tackle back as the snags are so bad. Take plenty of leads, swivels, hooks and beads with you.

In these really bad swims, the following method is worth trying. A fixed lead is used with a hair rig in the normal way. Sliding on the line above the lead is a small pilot float about ¾ inch in diameter. This is stopped about 15 feet up the line by means of a stop knot of the type which will cast through the rod rings (see diagram). There are two distinct

TYPICAL DEPTH-FINDER READINGS

Depth shown in feet

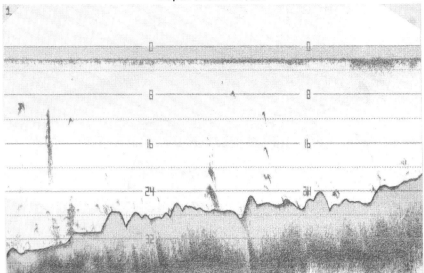

A rocky, but fairly level, bottom showing some fish of various sizes in the area.
The pilot float rig described is most suited to this type of swim.

This very steep drop-off in the margins (shown on the left) would put most
anglers off but the area thereafter is an ideal depth.

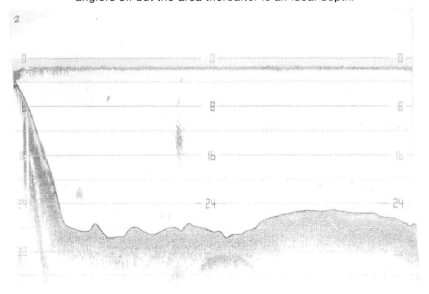

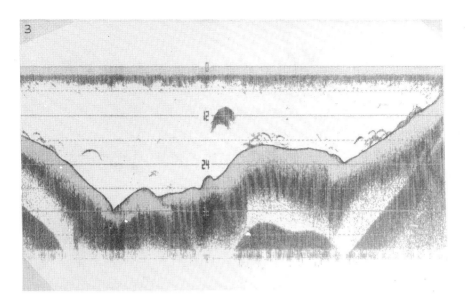

So varied is the bottom on the above print-out that a cast anywhere into the swim could produce fish, yet pick another spot, such as that shown below, and a cast could either put you in 'No man's land' or 'A pot of gold'.

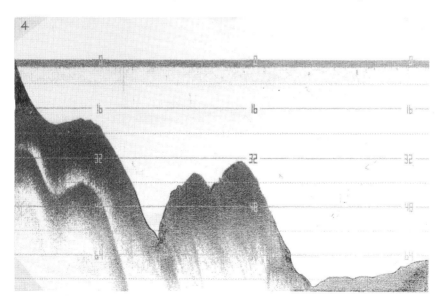

DROP-OFF FIXED LEADS

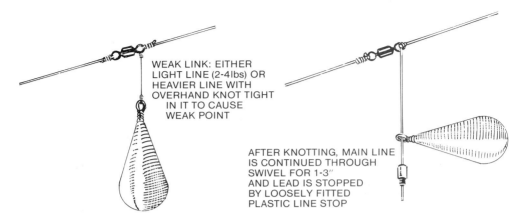

WEAK LINK: EITHER
LIGHT LINE (2-4lbs) OR
HEAVIER LINE WITH
OVERHAND KNOT TIGHT
IN IT TO CAUSE
WEAK POINT

AFTER KNOTTING, MAIN LINE
IS CONTINUED THROUGH
SWIVEL FOR 1-3″
AND LEAD IS STOPPED
BY LOOSELY FITTED
PLASTIC LINE STOP

advantages of fishing in this way. A lot less tackle is lost and the line comes straight up from the bottom and so the fish cannot see it so easily. It is becoming increasingly obvious that Cassien carp are becoming line shy, so this method will help.

Initially it paid off to do an enormous amount of pre-baiting – people often put in several thousand baits – but now I think this is less successful, and it would be better just to put a small number of baits around the hookbait if the fish are rolling. If they are not, it would be worth putting in several hundred. It is not worth mixing your own boilies. I have used, and seen used, very high quality home-made baits and these are no more successful than the proprietary baits. I always use my 'Maestro' packet baits and would use about 1,000 baits a day. Peanuts, chick peas and tiger nuts also do well. Sometimes an enormous number of crayfish are present, and it pays to re-cast often when the crayfish are at the bait, otherwise you could be sitting there for many hours with no bait on the hook!

Weather conditions seem to make no difference at Cassien. Because of the three separate arms, winds are often blowing in different directions in different areas. Don't be put off by the excessive heat; the fish are used to it.

Don't be put off if you are catching other species, and don't move if this is happening. I regard this as a good sign. In a lake of this size there must be areas where fish never feed, so if you are catching tench and bream, you are in a good feeding area, and carp are often caught among

These two pictures were taken after the water level had dropped eight feet in one week. The numerous tree stumps and rocks, which result in at least 50% of the carp being lost, can be seen quite easily.

CASSIEN SET-UP

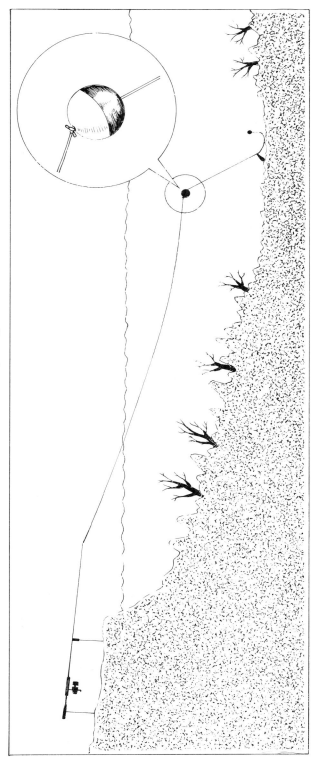

By using a pilot float the line is kept off the bottom clear of boulders and tree stumps and this also scares the fish less than the normal position of the line. When casting, the pilot float rests against the rig and after casting is stopped about 15 feet up the line by means of a nylon stop knot tied to the main line.

the other species. Most people play the fish from a boat, and I would certainly advise this. I would have a boat ready with a landing net on board. Cassien fish make long runs and fight very hard – they can empty the spool quite quickly. Also the fish can get into snags at long range when the boat is needed. It takes longer to play the fish from a boat, but you are much more likely to land them. If possible, get someone to reel in your other rods if you intend to play a fish from a boat – I once lost a good one because it got tangled with one of my other lines. Always use a reel with a large spool and much more line than you would use in England.

I have spoken to many people who have been to Lake Cassien and disliked it, sometimes so much that they have driven the 800 miles back to England several days before the end of their holiday. In most cases their disappointment has been due to bad planning, poor organisation, independent travel and a lack of knowledge of the lake and its fishing. All of these, and much more, anyone can obtain at no more than the cost of independent travel by booking with Regent Coaches. I have been both independently and with Regent Coaches, and I would never consider going in any other way but on an organised coach trip.

Paul Regent was the 'discoverer' of Lake Cassien, and I doubt if anyone has more knowledge of the water, and how and where to fish it, than Paul. All of this information is freely given to those who travel on his coach trips. He has spent many hours on the lake studying the lake bed with sonar equipment, so you will be able to get off to a good start instead of having to depend on local stories and incorrect information on how to find the best swims.

Travel is by luxury hi-line coach with reclining seats, video, coffee machine, cold drinks and a toilet with washing facilities, and the coach will take you to and from the lake each day, even dropping you at a convenient spot near your selected swim or boat.

You will stay in a beautiful two star hotel only two miles from the lake – and so avoid the temptation to break French law, as many other English anglers have done, by fishing at night and getting into trouble. Breakfast and the evening meal are timed so that you can spend the maximum permitted hours fishing the lake. Packed lunches are available and during the day the coach visits nearby towns and the Mediterranean sea, and those not wishing to fish can go along at no extra charge; an ideal chance to combine carp fishing with visits to places of local interest.

All rooms in the hotel have a private bath or shower, and there is a freezer in which bait can be kept. Travel with Regent Coaches and you will have many advantages over those who go independently; you are

Ordinary rod rests are useless in rocky swims like this. Pictured here is the KM Rod Unit which can be picked up and dropped down literally anywhere in a couple of seconds.

View across the east end of the West Arm. The main road bridge on the far bank signifies the start of the huge North Arm.

much more likely to succeed and to enjoy your holiday at the same time. Families can go too, and there are reduced prices for children under 14 sharing a room with their parents. The hotel has a new outdoor swimming pool.

I strongly recommend a Lake Cassien holiday with Regent Coaches, and with Paul Regent himself, who is a successful and well-known carp angler as well as a professional tour operator. For further details contact Regent Coaches at 64 Harbour Street, Whitstable, Kent CT5 1AG.

The 13 Hour Fight

At the end of June 1985 Dave Stockton and Paul Regent went to visit Lake Cassien, for two reasons. Firstly to fish the lake, and secondly to test the locals' reaction to the recent bad publicity about rule breaking by English anglers who had now swarmed to the water. The second reason was important to Paul as he had two coachloads of anglers going to the water to fish in the autumn and didn't want to involve them in any possible trouble. The trip started badly with Paul having his car broken into on the first day in broad daylight, and worse still, having to suffer two days with no action. On the Wednesday they changed swims and started to bait up round the islands in the South Arm with chick peas.

They started to fish in the late morning, watched by their wives in bikinis on the island. The temperature was about 90°F. Baits were cast out about 20 yards into 25 feet of water. Fish were jumping and rolling regularly, and they were soon getting twitches. At exactly 1.50 pm Dave had a take, struck, and hooked the fish, which at first he thought was not very big.

The fish went straight into a snag, so they loaded the net into the boat and went out to free the fish, which turned out to be buried in some weed. The fish then took off and the line pulled out of the snag. The line appeared to be frayed and so the fish would have to be played carefully – and for a long time as it turned out! Dave's immortal words at this stage were 'Sorry to say this, mate, but I don't think it's very big'. The fish, now clear of the snag, had decided to swim down the South Arm towards the small bridge. After about 20 minutes they were out of sight of the island, and were trying to calculate how much the fish might weigh, compared with a 70 pounder which had taken two hours to land. The fish just swam slowly about the lake going where it pleased.

After two hours of the fight they were attracting some attention, various boats and pedalos came out to see what was happening, though the best interest came from a topless woman who came out to wave to

Commons are quite rare in Cassien and this 29¾ pounder is one of the biggest landed so far.

Dave Stockton with a French fish of 27 pounds caught near his home.

This 33½ pounder was caught just two rod-len\
out from the east end of the West A\
on the first day of a Regent coach \

Kent carp angler Ken Bishop – now a driver for Regent Coaches, with a terrific 47 pounder from the West Arm.

Another big fish to Maestro Cream RM30 boilies;
a huge 57 pounder for John Pooler
caught on a Regent coach trip.

Ken Bishop with a 'hard earned' leather of 32½ pounds caught in relatively deep water in the South Arm.

An historic fish – the first Cassien carp to be caught by an English angler – a 23 pounder to Paul Regent.

Carp are not the only fish to grow big in the warm French waters; this 79 pound
river catfish measured six feet in length!

After making his own way to Cassien, and being unsuccessful, Dave Thorpe decided to try
a coach trip and caught this magnificent 46 pounder from the North Arm

Initially, a boat was needed to free the snagged line with this fish in 'American Bay', but after about 30 minutes in the boat making no impression, it was necessary to finish the fight from the bank.

Not all Cassien carp are huge; this 4¾ pounder was my fifth carp from the water, three of which were under 10 pounds!

Carp angler Dave Stockton, now living in France, with a Cassien fish of 34 pounds.

Coach tour operator and top Kent carp angler Paul Regent with a 35 pounder from Chez Pierre's

them every time they passed by, which was about six times. Each time they got the fish anywhere near it just went off again, and they simply couldn't stop it on the 11lb BS Sylcast.

The fish stayed in deep water for the first few hours, but occasionally it swam into shallow bays, when the fish would turn at right angles and swim out again into deeper water. It got hotter and hotter, and Dave and Paul had only one shirt between them, which they had to wear in relays.

After about four hours a boat full of Frenchmen started spinning right next to them, and they were afraid that the spinner would foul the line. At last their frantic shouts were understood and the boat moved away. By now they were discussing the possibility of a world record carp, and joking about the money they could make out of it by testing the tackle they used, the make of watch they wore, the bait and everything they had with them and which they were wearing. They were still in high spirits, and had been up to Seagull Point several times.

They had one try at playing the fish from the bank, but once the fish started to run they couldn't hold it, and had to get back into the boat. The fish then ran for an incredible 400 yards down the centre of the lake, literally towing the boat – and this was after it had been on for 6 hours! By now it was 8 pm, and the fish had returned to where it was hooked, and got back into the same snag, and at about this time they were 'buzzed' by a chap in a light plane who was doing aerobatics just over their boat. They thought he was some sort of nutter. They still had no idea of what they had hooked – after 6 hours! It was still hot but the sun was at last going down.

As it was snagged only a few yards from their wives on the island, they decided to leave it snagged, put the rod in rod rests, have a cup of coffee and row their wives back to the mainland so they could drive back to the hote¹. It was three-quarters of an hour before they tightened up on the fish again only to find the line had now caught around a small twig about 10 feet from the bank in three feet of water. No amount of tugging and fiddling with the rod would free it so Dave at this stage waded up to his waist and freed it by hand. Success! They now got into the boat again and tried to detach the fish from the snag. They spent 20 minutes trying to get the fish out, while all the time strands of weed were floating to the top; when it did come out, off it went again. Now they thought they would get the fish, and they really bent into it as they now knew after the battle to get the fish from the last snag that the line was a lot stronger than it looked. The sun was setting and everyone was now leaving the lake, and it was getting colder. They seemed to be getting the fish nearer to the surface, but during the next two hours they made little more progress.

They were cold and wet after 9 hours, and they decided to land once more on the bank. Paul went back to the island to get some food and clothing but looking back saw that the fish was off again, the spool was emptying and the boat was needed once more. The fish now headed towards Chez Pierre's, in complete darkness except that the centre of the lake was illuminated by the moon with the edges of the lake in darkness. The fish went in and out of the light and darkness until it all seemed very eerie. By midnight the fish seemed to tire, and stopped near the boat, spinning it round when it moved. By now Dave's arm was swollen to twice its normal size and his back was rubbed raw and bleeding after 10 hours of fighting the fish; he was totally exhausted. He asked Paul to continue the fight for him, handed the rod to Paul, and off they went again. Paul gave it all the stick he could, while Dave recovered, and they decided to try once more to play the fish from the bank. The fish followed as they rowed towards Chez Pierre's, and they decided to play it out from a pontoon. With the rod bent double, Paul could just hold the fish. They were freezing, starving, and Dave was suffering from possible sunstroke. Dave paddled off in the boat to the island to try and find some food and more clothes, and Paul was left alone on the pontoon, keeping the fish on 30 yards of line, and trying not to panic it into a long run. Dave picked up the gear although it took him about 1½ hours because he got lost in the darkness and Paul kept playing the fish, which had now been on for 12 hours; it was 2 am.

Paul kept expecting a guard to come down, cut his line and throw him off for illegal night fishing but at last, still alone, Paul walked back too far; he felt a grating on the line and realised that he had pulled the fish under the pontoon and the line was touching something. The problem was that the rod was bent well past its test curve and it was almost impossible to tell where the fish was by the feel of the rod alone – at one stage during the fight Dave thought the fish was at least 10-15 feet from him when it was actually at his feet swirling just under the surface. He eventually heaved the fish from under the platform and back into open water, and wondered where Dave was. How would he net this monster on his own? Paul thought the fish was now beaten; it was within 15-20 feet of him, swirling in the surface, but he could still only see huge white flanks in the moonlight. Once more the fish broke the surface and again Paul found that it was under the pontoon. Again there was a jarring on the line – but now, after 13 hours, the rod straightened, the line went slack, the lead shot out of the water – and the fish was gone; the line had broken about an inch from the hook. Looking into the water, Paul saw that the line had caught on a chain in the water. He felt sick – it was 3 am, and they had played the fish since 2 pm the previous day – and he had lost it for Dave. What could he say to him – the fish of a lifetime, lost after a 13 hour fight!

Ten minutes later Dave returned and realised the fish was gone; he was not surprised. Sadly, they returned wearily to their hotel, completely exhausted and beaten by a fish!

What was it? We shall never know, but they both felt it couldn't have been a carp, however big. At the time it was not known that there were catfish in Cassien, but later the accidental capture of a *Silurus glanis* estimated at 150-200 pounds made them realise that a huge catfish was almost certainly what they had played and lost.

In retrospect, this fish must have been even bigger than they had imagined at the time. Had it been a carp, however big, even foul hooked it in the tail, it could never have fought for so long. Even if it was a big catfish, fish of between 100lbs and 200lbs have been landed on fairly light tackle in Czechoslovakia and Germany in little more than an hour – what could fight for 13 hours?

In Russia, catfish have been recorded weighing up to 650lbs and 18 feet long. There is no reason why catfish couldn't grow to this size, or even bigger, in Lake Cassien, especially as there are so few of them there and so much food.

This means that the huge fish played by Paul and Dave on that day could have weighed six or seven hundred pounds; possibly the biggest freshwater fish ever hooked and played by rod and line anywhere in the world. It is unlikely that we shall ever know the truth unless someone catches it and finds Dave's hook and short piece of line in its mouth!

Kent angler Paul Regent with a School Pool fish of a little over 20 pounds.

7 Mission Impossible

It was April 1980 and with the season fast approaching I began to make my final decisions on where I was to fish. In previous seasons I had enjoyed setting targets and achieving them but with all the targets I have ever set myself, once achieved they always seemed to be an anti-climax and I then said to myself:'never again'; until the following close season that is! Most anglers say it is a bad thing to set yourself a target and that you should enjoy what comes along. I would agree that with many people this may be best but with me it is different; I am not so easily satisfied. Perhaps I am just peculiar but one thing I am sure of is that I have thoroughly enjoyed my carp fishing and that we should all enjoy it in our own way; and my way is to set myself targets - and to achieve them!

Assessing the potential of the big carp waters that were available to me presented the first problem. What could I try for this season?. It was no good aiming to beat the record as this has always been an impossible target for me. I was almost certain that the waters at my disposal, and in fact all of those I had fished in the past, did not contain fish over 44 pounds.

Ashlea Pool was one of the lakes which could possibly produce a fish over the magical 40 pounds mark. Although I had not seen any of the shy monsters that supposedly lived there, several of the syndicate members were convinced there might be one very big fish in the water. This fish was thought to be approaching 50 pounds and had been called Sandy for many years. However, I felt that unless I saw this fish myself I could not go on fishing for it – after all, the known fish were hard enough to catch, let alone the unknown ones!

In the past three seasons at Ashlea I had caught several carp over twenty pounds, the best being a mirror of 33 pounds two ounces; in fact I had landed all the known fish except for the one which just happened to be the biggest. This fish was a female for we had witnessed her laying eggs in June 1979 and she was a healthy fish with a growing potential for the future. I agreed with fellow syndicate members, Geoff Booth and Alan Downie that she would be approaching 40 pounds by the start of the 1980 season. Thinking about the great fish I realised that the first part of my target had now been set. I had caught every other known Ashlea fish so I must now stand a good chance of catching the biggest – and if I succeeded, it would be a personal best for me, and a worthy 1980 'target' fish.

A plan – ambitious but just possible – was now forming in my mind, and throughout April and May I often paused in what I was doing to think about it. Shortly before the season started I obtained membership of Savay Lake, a huge, 70 acre water which was said to contain some very big carp, and although I was unable to find out much about them, thirties had been mentioned – and now my half-formed plan for coming season seemed to be coming nearer to reality.

I like to fish two 'new' waters each season, as this keeps my interest going and helps me to learn about different aspects of carp fishing, so the '70 acre' could be one of these, and the other, which I had been considering for some time, was the School Pool, in Kent. I had been in constant touch with fellow BCSG members who fished this 20 acre day ticket water, which contained several big fish that appeared easy to catch by all but those who fished there. Publicity had given people the impression that the beautiful grandaddy of the pool, a huge mirror, in the mid-thirties, was easy to catch but the facts were different, as usual. Most of the good anglers at the pool caught less than six carp in a season, and had spent many unsuccessful years trying to catch the big one. The largest number caught was by BCSG member Bill Phillips, who landed 20 in one season. The water presented many problems to the carp angler, one of which was just getting a swim to fish from, let alone a good one! This is a very popular water, especially in the school holidays.

The plan which finally evolved was to concentrate early season efforts at Ashlea, for the huge leather that had eluded me for so long and also at the big Middlesex water, with the intention of fishing the Kent water in the autumn when the school holidays had finished. The target then, was now set; three thirties, each one from a different water.

Since I didn't want to start the season on a day ticket water, and the other two waters were on a rota system, I decided to start at Duncan's, where I have always enjoyed the opening days. The atmosphere is always very pleasant, the fishing good and who could forget such an explosive start to the season? And I mean explosive – literally; at the stroke of midnight the previous season Duncan had set off a bomb to signal the start. We all wondered what was in store for us this year. Duncan kept assuring us that our slightly fast watches would not be necessary. 'You'll know when it's time', he kept muttering. Anyone who known Duncan will be able to imagine him saying that; nodding his head and chuckling at the same time. He is a truly remarkable character, as well as being an accomplished all round angler.

The start was certainly an interesting one as we all sat in our pitches itching to cast out. The night was overcast without a breath of wind, the traffic on the nearby road had ceased and all was very quiet. I kept looking around wishing that Duncan would hurry up and it was well and truly midnight. It was then that I noticed something on the other side of the lake, something which glowed bright red. Then there was a terrific 'woosh', immediately followed by another one as two huge rockets sped their way up into the night sky. As they reached their peak they exploded into hundreds of green and red stars that came fluttering down onto the water. A few seconds later some 40 baits dropped into the four and a half acre water, thus ending the three months wait. Duncan certainly has that knack of breaking the seriousness of many carp anglers with a little bit of fun, and without upsetting anybody or spoiling the fishing. On behalf of the whole syndicate I would like to thank Duncan for being such a decent bloke and for running the water in such a sensible manner. It was an enjoyable start to the season in more ways than one; in the three day session I had 13 carp, all of which were doubles.

By early July the season was well under way and after four visits to the Middlesex water for observation, I decided to take on the massive task of learning about the water. My first trip was for a four day session. My friend Len Middleton, who had also never fished the water, agreed it was about time he had a go too, for some good fish had already been caught. On arrival, Len and I spent about six hours looking around and we eventually decided where to fish. Just before dark Len fancied an area where we had seen some fish bubbling and I picked a swim at the other end of the fishery, about half a mile away, where one or two fish were rolling. Early the following morning I had a run on the long distance rod and after a terrific heart pounding fight I landed my first fish from the water; one of the best feelings in carp fishing. It was a long, lean mirror weighing 23 pounds. I called Len up on the walkie-talkie and he was pleased to hear the news. The following day and night remained quiet in my swim with no further signs of fish. Len buzzed me just after dawn on the second day with the following unforgettable message: 'I've just had a 28, a 26 and a 19 and the fish are bubbling like mad. Get your gear and get round here'.

The threequarters of a mile walk seemed more like ten miles with the huge amount I had to carry but an hour later I was settled into a swim to the left of Len. Unfortunately, the fish had stopped feeding shortly after he had called me. We had no action throughout the day, and so we waited in anticipation for a possible feeding spell during the next night which was quiet, apart from one isolated run just after midnight resulting in a short, fat mirror which was just over 20 pounds.

Despite having caught two twenties I was not at all happy in my new swim; something kept telling me I ought to be somewhere else. I then spent the following day looking for signs of fish, trying to make a decision on where to spend the last night.

A little before dark I made a decision to fish from a point overlooking the largest expanse of water. As the light faded odd fish began to roll about 100 yards out so I quickly changed the spools for ones with shock leaders, stepped up to two and a quarter ounce leads and just managed to reach the fish on the best of my casts. Throughout the night I felt confident but the only action was a lot of twitches from bream. I struck many of these short bites and landed two six pound bream. As dawn broke, the bream departed and once again the occasional carp began to roll over my baits. At five a.m. I had a steady lift and struck into a powerful fish. For the first minute the fish just stripped line from the spool making its way further and further down the lake and as it slowed down I felt a grating on the line and all went solid. The next hour was spent carefully nursing the

Bob Baldock with a near '20' from Linear Fisheries at Milton Keynes. Full information about this excellent complex of lakes, which has produced carp to over 30 pounds, is available from: Linear House, 2 Northcroft, Shenley Lodge, Milton Keynes, Bucks.

fish out of snags as it uncannily found new ones. The whole area appeared to be a mass of gravel bars and rocks but with careful playing the 11 pound BS shock leader withstood the non-stop grating until I eventually got the fish into clearer water. Just before netting I caught a glimpse of it as it broke surface. It looked a big one but I was worried when I saw the last few yards of line which were very badly frayed. However the Sylcast line held out and I eventually netted the fish exactly an hour after hooking it. The fish proved to be well worth the care; it weighed 30¾ pounds. Len kindly walked the half mile to take some photographs and after returning the mirror I packed up and happily made tracks for home. One third of my season's target had been achieved.

In late July I visited the water again for a two day session and took two nice fish weighing 19½ pounds and 22½ pounds from another area of the lake. This was followed by another visit the following week which resulted in a blank.

It was now mid-August and I had arranged to meet Peter Mohan at the Mid-Northants fishery for a 24 hour session after an invitation from Duncan. I arrived at 4 a.m. and eventually settled into a swim we call the 'small beach', situated in the SW corner of the bay. It was overcast and very hot, with a light southerly breeze and as the morning passed it became obvious that I could not expect to catch using bottom baits in these conditions; some stalking was called for.

Walking round the bay I catapulted about a quarter of a box of Felix Meaty Crunch onto the surface where I had seen some carp cruising and basking. Whilst setting up a stalking rod back at the swim, I could see the fish responding well to the free offerings. Huge backs broke surface as the baits were being taken – the conditions were perfect. It didn't take me long to get into position in the bay with the light wind behind me. The carp were feeding in and around the weedbeds at a range of about twenty yards. I quickly 'superglued' a single F.M.C. to the back of the hook shank and cast to the fish. With this presentation, the hook hangs under the water and the carp usually prick themselves as soon as they touch the bait; a small piece of weighted peacock quill served as indication and casting weight. Although they were taking free floaters confidently I only had two takes in the next hour. Both fish were landed, and both were doubles.

As the evening approached I wound in and sat back to watch the fish for a while. I soon noticed one very large fish swimming amongst the others; it was a leather which looked to be about 30 pounds. I was quite surprised at this for I had never seen a fish of these proportions taking floaters on this water before. I sat for a while working out a way to catch the fish. I could not get my tackle to drift the 40 or so yards to where the fish were now feeding due to the surface weed. My thoughts were interrupted by the arrival of Peter's car at the top of the field. We quickly got talking about the fish and I showed him where they were feeding. However, by the time he had sorted his gear out, the clouds had thickened, the temperature dropped and the fish had moved off.

Peter settled into a pitch opposite me and just before dark it started to rain heavily. Anticipating a wet night, I carefully positioned my baits in a clear gravel area 40 yards out as my intention was to leave them in the same spots until daylight for accurate recasting during darkness would be difficult. After scattering some thirty hookbaits in the area I settled under my brolly and brewed a cup of tea.

A little later the clouds darkened to an ominous grey and it began to rain very heavily. The distant thunder became louder and the heavy rain which had started around 8 pm became an intensive downpour, the like of which I had never seen before. Rain lashed the surface of the lake and vivid streaks of lightning were followed by massive claps of thunder. I could clearly see Peter on the other side of the lake holding onto his umbrella for dear life.

It was 12.30 am when my buzzer first sounded. Although confident of some action I had forgotten about my rods as I had been employed full time in attempting to keep dry. As soon as I saw the bobbin move I struck hard and was into a fish. At first I was a little surprised. For a start I didn't want to come out from under my brolly and secondly, I just couldn't understand why a fish should feed with the ground shaking from continuous violent thunder and non-stop lightning flashes. Anyway, the first part of the fight was no problem as the fish gradually worked its way in and out of the weed beds coming towards me. I sunk the other rod tip so as not to pick up the line, but the rain was so intense I could hardly open my eyes, and was completely soaked to the skin within two minutes. The water was running down my neck, past the more vital areas (urgh!) and ending up in my boots and it eventually actually began to come out over the top of them. The fish moved to the left so I squelched my way to the side of the swim. About a minute later I heard a faint voice to my right. It was Peter on the other side of my brolly. He was almost shouting and it was only after three increasingly louder replies that brought him to my side. The noise of the rain pounding the water was absolutely incredible and the loud conversation went something like this:

'Oh, here you are, I wondered where you'd gone. I couldn't see you from behind your brolly. Hell of a storm isn't it?' said Peter.

'Yeah, it's fantastic.'

'I can't stand it any more round there, the wind's blowing it right into my face and I'm drowned. I've packed my gear, I thought I might as well as nothing's happening.'

'Yeah', I said again, trying to pay attention to the feel of the rod.

'Had any action?'

'Not a lot, just the one take.'

'Oh, you had a take did you – no good?'

'Yeah, it feels reasonable, moving quite slowly.'

'What! Have you got a fish on?'

'You should know', I said, 'you're standing right next to me.'

'Crikey, I couldn't see – the rain's so heavy, I suppose I might as well wait to see it. How long have you had it on?'

'About five minutes.'

The fish moved further to my left and started to take line from the clutch much to Peter's amazement, for he doesn't allow such things! A minute or so later he said:

'Don't you play your fish for a long time! Do you know, the longest I've ever played a carp for is 12 minutes?'

'Yeah, but how many thirties have you played', I said jokingly, not having the slightest idea of how big the fish was. I couldn't even tell how much pressure I was putting on it! Another couple of minutes passed and Peter, who by now was also like a drowned rat, assured me of an execution if it wasn't a thirty. After a very dogged fight in the margins I netted the fish and hauled it onto the bank. Sure enough it was a very big leather. We weighed it by torchlight together and agreed on a figure of 30 pounds 14 ounces, although I said I would weigh the fish again in the morning because of the rough conditions. Peter swore at the weather and departed.

I recast and by about 3 am the rain stopped. I was wet and very tired and now all was quiet I decided to jump in my sleeping bag until light. The wind dropped and I quickly went off to sleep dreaming of all the things carp anglers do – naked women and huge carp! However I was just getting into my first dream when a terrific clap of thunder made me leap up. This time the wind had changed completely and the storm was returning! After repositioning my gear I somehow managed to drop off again and the next thing I knew about was a wet feeling all along my underside in the morning. I opened my eyes and could hardly believe it; the lake had risen THREE FEET during the night. Originally my gear was well away from the water's edge, but I was now completely surrounded in water which was up to the underside of my bedchair despite its extended legs. The first thing I looked for was my boots which I leave standing up next to my bedchair. I couldn't see either of them so I felt around under the water and located one. It was pinned against the underside of my bed chair! I just didn't know what to do as I sat on my bed chair with a wet posterior. I knew I was going to have to step into a foot of water. I then looked across the lake and burst out laughing – there was my other boot, floating out in the middle of the lake! It was all quite extraordinary and as I looked at the swim around me I could see my food box, gas stove, one piece suit, tackle bag and everything else was either completely under water or floating around. Carp were even swimming around in the adjoining fields.

After retrieving my gear from the lake, I weighed the fish again and just as I had expected the fish had lost a quarter of a pound after four hours in the sack. I settled for a weight of 30-10, took two photographs and returned the fish before organising a rescue operation which lasted all day. I shall never forget that 'thunderstorm thirty'.

Although I had now had two thirties, the Mid-Northants fish was one which I had not planned to catch, and which I should never have had if I had not agreed to do the trip with Peter, so I made up my mind to keep to the original plan. I wanted 30s from both of the other waters – so the

A few hours earlier the front rod rests were on dry land!

altered target was now four thirties in the season, from four different waters! I had been concentrating my efforts at Ashlea every other week since the start of the season and although I'd caught a carp each visit, the biggest was only a 16¾ pound mirror, so at this stae I decided to switch my efforts from the Middlesex water and start to fish the School Pool. It was late August and even though the school children were still on holiday I arrived at the Kent water at dawn for a mid-week session. There were already about 40 anglers on the 20 acre lake but I managed to get a swim just within casting range of where I had seen some carp rolling during the first hour of light. By mid-day there were about 100 anglers on the water; every swim was taken and the gaps between the close swims were also filled. Despite teaching a 12 year old boy in my swim how to float fish for tench (and to keep them away from my lines), I did manage to catch six good doubles, the best two being just under 20 pounds. The locals told me that a catch of six fish in one sitting was very unusual and so I looked forward to my next trip.

My next visit to the Kent water was in mid-September. The conditions were perfect – a strong south westerly and overcast. Fishing into the teeth of the wind I had a lot of action, landing three twenties, their weights being 25-12, 24-10 and 20-4, plus four other doubles. Paul Regent and Bill Phillips, both local carp anglers assured me tha if I continued to catch fish at this rate it wouldn't be long before I'd catch the big one; in fact they were surprised I hadn't already caught it. Things were going so well for me now that a big thirty was on the cards from at least one of the waters.

At Ashlea, three quarters of the syndicate had given up after catching nothing and none of the big fish had been caught. I was catching at least one fish per visit and I was still very confident. I spoke to Alan Downie about the situation and we both agreed that we would probably catch one of the big ones if we kept working hard at it. Alan was visiting the pool at weekends following my mid-week visit every fortnight and we noticed an unusual pattern forming which we had never witnessed before. In early September they started to respond to heavy baiting and would stop at the baited areas, clearing up all the baits, instead of their normal procedure of completely ignoring them. Not knowing the full reason for this certainly didn't deter us from taking full advantage of this new behaviour.

On the 15th of September I arrived at Ashlea Pool for a three day session, a session I was never to forget. The one and a quarter acre pool was looking its best, the water was gin clear and the lilies were just beginning to weaken, for in a month's time they would all be dead. A breeze was blowing towards the deeper end of the pool, making it

A torpedo-like mid-twenty from a Faversham A.C. Water.

impossible to spot the fish properly, so I climbed a tall sycamore tree overlooking the spot where I thought the fish might be and soon spotted several large carp, two of them clearly over thirty pounds; one of them was the big fish I wanted. They seemed to be swimming in a clear patch amongst a mass of dense weeds, and every so often they would sink out of sight below the mid-water lily leaves and bubble profusely. I put some floating baits in the swim up wind of them but as the baits drifted over their heads they showed no interest. So, by about noon, I set up two rods in the swim nearest to where I had seen the fish. My plan was to fish one into the clear hole and the other right in the thickest part of the dense patch of cabbages.

The bait was a special concoction which I had used with remarkable success on several waters since the previous winter. It consisted of: three ounces of Casilan, three ounces of Complan, one ounce Lactalbumin, two onces of C & G baby milk, once ounce of wheatgerm and one ounce of castor sugar. To this was added three eggs plus 15ml. of cream/butter flavouring obtained from Geoff Kemp Bait Ingredients. Each bait was rolled into quarter of an inch balls and dropped into boiling water for one minute and then left to harden for a full 24 hours.

I cast a bait into the small clear area without problems but the other bait needed to be presented on the bottom under the cabbage leaves if I was to stand any real chance of success, for this is where the carp were obviously feeding. I had put a lot of thought into this problem and was already prepared for such a situation. Firstly I fixed a two ounce Arlesey bomb to the line via a link swivel, stopped by a small Berkley swivel tied in the line. The baited hook and six inch tail was tied to the bomb using PVA strips. The hook point, which I always leave bare, was masked by a PVA pad formed by continual folding of the PVA. This bolt rig then had the effect of blasting its way through the thick leaves, coming to rest on the clear bottom under the cabbages. Although I was initially worried about the line rising vertically through the cabbages I decided that once a fish did pick up the bait the bolt rig would make it run and disregard any possible line resistance.

Once my rods were set up I baited the area heavily and sat back and waited. Around 2pm that afternoon I had a line bite which I struck at and spooked the fish concerned. The rest of the carp immediately followed and from then right round until the following afternoon nothing happened.

That afternoon I carried on stalking as was given the first opportunity in four years to have a definite chance of catching the fish I was after. I had spotted the big leather while up a tree and decided to have a go for it. I climbed down the tree but lost sight of the fish because of the 'chop' and glare on the surface of the pool. However, I was determined to catch this fish, so, leaving my stalking net at the bottom of the tree I took my rod and some bait back up the tree with me. I immediately saw the big leather again and quickly dropped a small free offering of bread-flake in front of the fish. As the flake sank slowly the fish moved forward and took it. I couldn't believe my eyes. I gently lowered a second piece of flake, this time with my hook on it, some 15 feet to the fish. As it sank the fish followed it down, looked at it for a while, circled it, touched it with its lips and then decided it wouldn't have it.

I don't really know what would have happened if I had actually hooked the fish. On reflection I intended to throw my rod into the water, after hooking the fish, and immediately jump out of the tree into the same spot. I then proposed to get hold of the rod, hoping the fish was still on and continue to play it standing in four feet of water – a dubious proposition!

By evening all the fish had returned to my original swim and were feeding like mad on the baits I carefully introduced. I had tied each free offering to a stone using PVA to give it a better chance of reaching the bottom. I settled down for the second night confident that something was going to happen. I rebaited the swim and set up a third rod to cast out to another spot where bubbles were continually rising.

After dark it rained heavily and I immediately lost confidence but when it finally stopped around midnight, the wind dropped and it got very cold. The signs started to look right and I knew I was going to get some action. Around 2 am I had a six-inch lift on my left hand rod, but nothing else happened. An hour later I had a couple of four inch twitches on my 'extra' rod. This didn't develop into anything immediately but 30 minutes later I had a jerky lift on the bobbin. I struck straight away and met with solid resistance. It was pitch dark and I had no idea what was happening. I couldn't feel any movement or see the rod tip and so I thought I was weeded. I kept the pressure on, feeling fairly confident that the fish would move, and a few seconds later the bobbin on my left hand rod started to rise. It then dawned on me that the fish had kited across in front of me,

The tree swim at Ashlea Pool overlooking the less densely weeded area of the deep end.

maintaining an uncannily even pressure. The swim was very confined and I knew that the fish was near the sunken branches of the sycamore to my left so I lowered the rod tip into the water and pumped the fish back. Within 30 seconds it was on top and ready to net. The gap in the front of the swim was only three feet so it was necessary to net the fish over the top of the other lines. I lowered the other rods off their rests and picked up my landing net, but as I pushed the net forward over the top of my rods the mesh became entangled. Not being able to see what I was doing as it was so dark, I struggled to disentangle the mesh from the rods whilst keeping the fish on top using the other hand. This went on for about half a minute and I decided that I would never do it unless I could pull the mesh and rods back away from the water into my pitch which would be impossible with one hand, so I then released the bail arm, dropped the rod onto the ground and nipped round the back of the swim to get my stalking net. Under the circumstances, it turned out to be the best thing to do and luckily, when I got back the fish was still on. Because the net was only 30 inches wide I had to kneel down, peer into the darkness and wait until the fish's nose touched the spreader block of the net. When I was sure the fish was over the net I lifted the surprisingly heavy fish out and put it on the ground at the back of the swim. I kept looking at the fish trying to decide how big it was and I just simply had no idea as it was so dark. I got my small pocked torch from my kit bag and switched it on – only to have it fail immediately. The battery must had got wet from the rain. For a few seconds I didn't know what to do as I was keen to know what fish it was before sacking it. I couldn't even weigh it without the torch. I thought it must be a thirty. After picking it up again with my heart pounding I very gingerly felt round the lower bone of the tail to see if it was only half length, as the 33 pound mirror I caught two seasons previously had an old tell-tale scar. As my fingers felt round the lower bone a wave of excitement flowed through me – it wasn't the mirror so it could well be the big leather I'd been hoping for for so long.

I decided to carry the fish in the weighing sling back down the lane to where my car was parked with the intention of weighing it using the headlights. As I walked down the lane I kept saying to myself 'I've got you at last, you bugger', and wondering if it might go 40 pounds.

I lowered the fish onto the ground in front of the car, switched the headlights on and pulled the weighing sling back. It was the big leather. The scales registered just under 39 pounds and after deducting the weight of the sling the true weight was 38¼ pounds, my biggest carp ever. I then sacked the fish until first light when it was witnessed and photographed before being returned to its weedy home.

Got you at last – the 38¼ pound Ashlea leather.

The four years of hard work had been fully rewarded. That afternoon was a sad one for me as I knew when I glanced back at the pool on departing that I might never fish the water again. My plan was to move onto new waters, although I might well regret this, and at the end of the season I left the Ashlea syndicate.

It was late September and with the school holidays over I decided to concentrate on the Kent water in an attempt to catch the big mirror there. My intention was to fish the water every week until I either caught the fish, or the season ended. On the week following the capture of my Ashlea fish I had another successful trip to the Kent water taking three twenty pounders and one other double. Filled with confidence, I was back again the following week, but things were not going quite so well this time. I had only one take the first day which resulted in the fish being lost after playing it in and out of snags for 30 minutes – a great problem on this extremely snaggy water, making it essential to use 'snag leaders'. The second day was also quiet, producing one bite which resulted in an 11¾ pound common. The problem was that the fish were feeding like mad – but at a range of about 90 yards out and opposite the swim next to me. There were no swims vacant on my side of the lake and the carp angler who had the fish in front of him could see them jumping like mad but couldn't reach them. His best casts were dropping about 15 yards short of the fish and he was getting no action at all. The two fish I had hooked were actually 'stolen' from his area as I was casting my right hand rod a little towards the area at the edge of the feeding fish. After a lot of thought I decided to move round to the other side of the lake to a swim directly opposite and although the lake is some 200 yards wide at this point I planned to fish as far out as I could in order to reach the active fish.

I settled into the swim just before dark and managed to put my baits a good distance out. I wasn't expecting much action through the night but I was hopeful for the next day. The night was quiet and I cast some fresh baits out just before dawn. About 7 am, Paul Regent, who had dropped into a nearby swim for the night, came along for a chat. I was very pleased to see Paul as we had become good friends during my visits to the lake so I put the kettle on for a cuppa. We both talked about the bites we didn't have during the night and we soon got onto the subject of the big mirror. Paul kept saying, 'I can't understand why you haven't caught it so far, but you will'. I made the tea and we sat back enjoying the early morning sun. A few sips of tea later my buzzer sounded and I was into a fish. Ten minutes later I had the fish in the margins and the fight became dogged with huge boils and swirls coming up from the bottom – a good sign that often means a big fish. Paul stood alongside with the net assuring me that this was the big one. He had no doubt in his mind. After nearly ten minutes fight in the margins we netted one of the most beautiful looking carp I had ever seen. A long, well built fish with a pretty cluster of scales towards the back end of its body, it was gold in colour and in absolutely immaculate condition. Yes, you've guessed it – it was the big mirror all right and it looked huge. Paul patted me on the back and we admired the fish as other anglers and passers-by gathered round. We weighed the fish on my scales. It went 35 pounds exactly which was later verified on the official club scales. My twentieth fish from the water in four visits, and I was delighted. The plan had worked, and the target had been achieved. I had caught four thirties from waters in four different counties.

I now decided to take it a bit easy. After a break and a week or two of catching up on some odd jobs, I arranged a swop with my friend John

One of the nicest big mirrors I've ever seen – an immaculate 35-pounder from a day ticket water.

Baker. John offered to take me to one of his waters for a two day session and in return I'd take him to one of mine.

The two sessions turned out to be very enjoyable ones. The first trip was to a private water which I used to fish in my earlier days of carp fishing and as I hadn't fished the water for four years, I was really looking forward to it. The temperatures dropped suddenly, as it was late October now, and with two heavy frosts I thought we would struggle to catch fish in this shallow lake. John proved me wrong however, by landing a fabulous, fully scaled mirror of 13¾ pounds at mid-day on the second day. Assuming that the fish must be feeding I spent some time looking around and found several commons under the trees at one end of the lake. Two of these looked about twenty pounds, the others being doubles. Two hours after settling down in the new swim, one of these commons must have taken a fancy to my chick pea bait for after a spectacular fight in the darkness I landed a lovely common of 20½ pounds. It was as if the lake owed me that fish, for I had fished there for seven years, catching only three twenties and then ironically in my first visit after four years away my only fish of the session turned out to be a 20.

The following week John and I made tracks for another water and as usual when we get together we wound each other up until we were confident that we were going to catch lots of fish. As it happened we both caught some good fish but one in particular highlighted the trip. At 2.30 pm, after sitting by my rods for seven hours with no action I had a slow run. On hooking the fish it kited at a tremendous speed to my left, heading into an area of thick weed beds. It was all I could do to keep a tight line as I'd hooked the fish at about 60 yards and as well as kiting, it was heading towards my bank. As the fish neared the bank I really gave it some stick to try and cut down the distance between us. Just as I was gaining some line the fish buried itself in a huge weed bed and everything went solid. John must have seen what was going on and he soon arrived at my pitch. After some derisive comments like 'What are you playing at, Maddocks, hurry up and land this silly little bream and let me get back to my swim', I managed to free the fish and got it into the margins in front of me and all went solid again as the fish explored another weed bed. This time I couldn't move the fish at all no matter what I tried. After five minutes or so John decided it wasn't a bream and said,'I think you're going to lose this one, Kev'. I was inclined to agree with him but was still hopeful. The water was about nine feet deep where the fish was and it was just a huge mass of weeds from the bottom to the surface. We had given up trying to think of ways in which we could land the fish when I noticed an old coil

The weedbed 29¼ pounder.

of wire with a rope attached to it, lying on the bank. Apparently it had been used for weed clearing as there was some old dried up weed around it. Being the sort of chap who will try anything, I gave John the rod and decided to test out the weed clearer further up the bank; after throwing it out into the centre of a large patch of weed, I found it worked perfectly – it hauled the whole weed bed out in one go! I carried the weed clearer back to my swim and whilst John held the rod I threw the bunch of wire right into the centre of the weedbed which my line was entering, not really knowing the fish was still there or not. The wire mass sank into the weedbed and I slowly pulled the whole lot into the margins. Parting the weed as it came in I discovered to my surprise a very big fish lying quietly amongst it and I remember saying to John, 'Crikey, I think it's a thirty, give me the landing net quickly'. John got the net to me within seconds – which I laid at the side of the weedbed. This time I parted the weed properly and got both hands under the fish, which fortunately remained motionless; I rolled it out and over the top of the weed into the landing net. We were both really surprised at how smoothly the whole operation went and the fish turned out to be a long lightly scaled mirror weighing 29¼ pounds; well worth the effort after all.

That was to be my last summer fish, for during and after that session the November frosts set in for several consecutive nights. Throughout November and December I fished a Kent water with another good friend of mine, Ron Middleton, where I had had considerable success in previous winters and hence I caught 20 nice doubles including two over the 20 pound mark. But by the beginning of January, Ron and I got fed up with fishing the same old places during the winter so we picked two 'new' venues which were rarely winter fished by anyone. These were waters accepted as being very difficult in the winter. Our change of venue turned out to be a good decision for the winter fishing. Ron and I went on to spend a very enjoyable ten weeks, catching plenty of carp including some big ones, up to 28¾ pounds. It was the final session that really capped the

A nice end to the season with mirrors of 23 pounds 4 ounces and 20 pounds 8 ounces, plus seven doubles.

season for me and it was one which I shall always remember. On March 11th John Baker and myself loaded up the car for a final end of the season fling, arriving at the lake during the small hours. Our hopes were high for it was very mild with a gentle southerly wind blowing across the lake. Ron Middleton joined us later in the morning although he had to pack up early and leave for home suffering from a bout of flu. I often wonder what our combined catch would have been if Ron hadn't gone home, for in the next three days John and I landed 13 good doubles between us. The last day brought the real bonanza when I landed two twenties, 23¼ and 20½ pounds and, one hour before we were due to pack up John caught a fat leather of exactly 28 pounds. We had fished hard and were very tired, but the whole season seemed to have ended just right.

My 'target' system had worked again, providing the incentive for me to have my best season ever – but where do I go from here?

31, 34½ and 25 pounds!

REFERENCE GUIDE

British Carp Study Group	BCSG Headquarters, Heywood House, Pill, Bristol BS20 0AE.
Carp Anglers' Association	CAA Headquarters, Heywood House, Pill, Bristol BS20 0AE. (Open to all; no application form required, send £9 to Membership Secretary, Castle Cary Press, High Street, Castle Cary, Somerset.)
Kevin Maddocks (KM) Carp Rods	Simpsons of Turnford, Nunsbury Drive, Turnford, Herts. Tel: Hoddesdon 468799 (exclusive).
Mitchell 410	Manufactured by Leeda Tackle, Cannon Street, Southampton, SO9 2RB.
Cardinal 55	Manufactured by Abu Ltd, Clydebank Industrial Estate, Dunbartonshire, G81 4HA.
Shimano Baitrunner	Manufactured by Shimano Ltd., Cross Buildings, 49 Gower Road, Sketty Cross, Swansea SA2 9BH.
Panatone Pen	Manufactured by Letraset, available from art shops.
Pike Strand	The Tackle Shop, Bridge Street, Gainsborough, Lincs. (exclusive).
PVA Strip & String	Poly Vinyl Alcohol (water soluble) available from specialist angling shops.
KM Mobile Bedchair System	KM Tackle Developments, Withy Pool, Bedford Road, Henlow, Beds. SG16 6EA
KM Safety Sack & Sling	KM Tackle Developments, Withy Pool, Bedford Road, Henlow, Beds. SG16 6EA
Gardner Tackle	2 Pepper Box Lane, Palmers Cross, Bramley, Surrey, GU5 0LL.
British Record Fish Committee (N.A.C.)	Daytime 0733 54084 Evening 0733 252428

Bait ingredients which are exclusive or difficult to locate

Farina	Rushside Baits, Unit 27, Trojan Centre, Stewarts Road, Finedown Industrial Estate, Wellingborough, Northants. Tel: 0933 228226.
Soya Isolate	Rushside Baits, and Geoff Kemp.
Larvstart	Rushside Baits.
P.T.X.	Soft Budgie food. John E. Haith, Park Street, Cleethorpes, South Humberside, DN35 7NF.
Nectablend	John E. Haith (as above).
Robin Red	John E. Haith.
Sluis	Bird food, available from most pet shops.
Formula One	Red bird food, available from some pet shops.
Prosecto Insectiverous	John E. Haith.
Codlivine	Rushside Baits and Geoff Kemp.
Nukamel	Rushside Baits.
Cal-Pro	Rushside Baits.
Carp Pellets	E. Baker & Co, Cornard Mills, Great Cornard, Sudbury, Suffolk.
Texturised Vegetable Protein (TVP)	Available from most health shops.
Edisol	Rushside Baits.
Egg Albumen	Geoff Kemp.
MCP (High Maple Concentrate)	Rushside Baits.
Lactalbumin	Geoff Kemp and Rushside Baits.
Casein	Geoff Kemp and Rushside Baits.
'Floater' Caseinate	Rushside Baits.
KM Maestro Boilies & Floaters	Available from all good tackle shops or direct from KM Tackle Developments, Withy Pool, Bedford Road, Henlow, Beds. SG16 6EA.
KM Rod Unit	Available from KM Tackle Developments (as above).

Flavour Suppliers

Dubuis and Rowsell Ltd
    Duroma Works
    Elmwood Road
    Croydon, Surrey

H. Kohnstamm & Co (UK) Ltd
    76 Glentham Road
    London SW13

Geoff Kemp Bait Ingredients
    Pilgrims Court,
    Days Lane
    Pilgrims Hatch
    Brentwood, Essex

Rushside Baits
    Unit 27
    Stewarts Road
    Finedown Industrial Estate,
    Wellingborough, Northants.

Bulk Grain and Seed Suppliers

Hurst, Gunsen, Cooper, Taber Ltd
    Avenue Road
    Witham
    Essex CM8 2OX

Latimer & Crick Ltd
    2/4 Cattle Market Road
    Northampton NN1 1HL

John E. Haith
    Park Street
    Cleethorpes
    South Humberside DN35 7NF

Index

That's all folks . . . . .